BIBLE, BORDERS, BELONGING(S)

SBL

Society of Biblical Literature

Semeia Studies

Gerald O. West, General Editor

Editorial Board:
Pablo Andiñach
Fiona Black
Denise K. Buell
Gay L. Byron
Jione Havea
Jennifer L. Koosed
Jeremy Punt
Yak-Hwee Tan

BIBLE, BORDERS, BELONGING(S)

ENGAGING READINGS FROM OCEANIA

Edited by
Jione Havea, David J. Neville, and Elaine M. Wainwright

Society of Biblical Literature
Atlanta

Copyright © 2014 by the Society of Biblical Literature

All rights reserved. No part of this work may be reproduced or transmitted in any form or by any means, electronic or mechanical, including photocopying and recording, or by means of any information storage or retrieval system, except as may be expressly permitted by the 1976 Copyright Act or in writing from the publisher. Requests for permission should be addressed in writing to the Rights and Permissions Office, Society of Biblical Literature, 825 Houston Mill Road, Atlanta, GA 30329 USA.

Library of Congress Cataloging-in-Publication Data

Bible, borders, belonging(s) : engaging readings from Oceania / edited by Jione Havea, David J. Neville, Elaine M. Wainwright, Society of Biblical Literature.
    p. cm. — (Society of Biblical Literature. Semeia studies ; Number 75)
Includes bibliographical references and index.
ISBN 978-1-58983-955-7 (paper binding : alk. paper) — ISBN 978-1-58983-957-1 (electronic format) — ISBN 978-1-58983-956-4 (hardcover binding : alk. paper)
1. Bible—Criticism, interpretation, etc.—Oceania. 2. Oceania—Social conditions. 3. Oceania—Environmental conditions. 4. Christianity—oceania. 5. Christian life—Oceania. I. Havea, Jione, 1965– editor of compilation.
 BS511.3.B523 2014
 220.60995—dc23   2014002890

Printed on acid-free, recycled paper conforming to
ANSI/NISO Z39.48-1992 (R1997) and ISO 9706:1994
standards for paper permanence.

Contents

Abbreviations vii
Preface ix

Engaging Readings

Engaging Scriptures from Oceania
    Jione Havea 3

"Save Us! We Are Perishing!": Reading Matthew 8:23–27 in the
Face of Devastating Floods
    Elaine M. Wainwright 21

Calamity and the Biblical God—Borderline or Line of Belonging?
Intratextual Tension in Luke 13
    David J. Neville 39

On the Crossroads between Life and Death: Reading Birth
Imagery in John in the Earthquake-Changed Regions of
Otautahi Christchurch
    Kathleen P. Rushton 57

The Prologue of John: Bridge into a New World
    John Painter 73

Jewish Readings of the Fourth Gospel: Beyond the Pale?
    Ruth Sheridan 93

Mapping the Boundaries of Belonging: Another Look at
Jacob's Story
    Merilyn Clark 109

Slipping across Borders and Bordering on Conquest:
A Contrapuntal Reading of Numbers 13
    Judith E. McKinlay 125

Border Crossing/Body Whoring: Rereading Rahab of Jericho with Native Women
Nāsili Vakaʻuta 143

Deuteronomy 30: Faithfulness in the Refugee Camps of Moab, Babylonia, and Beyond
Jeanette Mathews...157

Reading Rizpah across Borders, Cultures, Belongings … to India and Back
Monica Jyotsna Melanchthon..171

Borderless Discipleship: The Syrophoenician Woman as a Christ-Follower in Mark 7:24–30
Jeffrey W. Aernie..191

Bare Feet Welcome: Redeemer Xs Moses @ Enaim
Jione Havea..209

The Sign of Jonah: Reading Jonah on the Boundaries and from the Boundaries
Gregory C. Jenks..223

Engaging Responses

Gospel Maps: Intersections of Life
Michele A. Connolly..241

Breaking Bible Boundaries
David M. Gunn..249

Bordering on Redemption
Mark G. Brett..259

Contributors..269

Index of Primary Texts 273

Index of Modern Authors..281

Index of Subjects..287

Abbreviations

Ag. Ap.	Josephus, *Against Apion*
Ant.	Josephus, *Jewish Antiquities*
BDAG	Bauer, W., F. W. Danker, W. F. Arndt, and F. W. Gingrich. *Greek-English Lexicon of the New Testament and Other Early Christian Literature*. 3d ed. Chicago: University of Chicago Press, 1999.
BDB	Brown, F., S. R. Driver, and C. A. Briggs. *A Hebrew and English Lexicon of the Old Testament*. Oxford: Oxford University Press, 1907.
BDF	Blass, F., A. Debrunner, and R. W. Funk. *A Greek Grammar of the New Testament and Other Early Christian Literature*. Chicago: University of Chicago Press, 1961.
Comm. Jo.	Origen, *Commentary on John*
Embassy	Philo, *On the Embassy to Gaius*
FIR	First Information Report
Haer.	Irenaeus, *Adversus haereses* (*Against Heresies*)
JB	Jerusalem Bible
J.W.	Josephus, *Jewish War*
KNLA	Karen National Liberation Army
LXX	Septuagint
MT	Masoretic Text
NJPS	*Tanakh: The Holy Scriptures: The New JPS Translation according to the Traditional Hebrew Text*
NRSV	New Revised Standard Version
NSW	New South Wales
Ps.-Clem. Hom.	Pseudo-Clement, *Homilies*
RSV	Revised Standard Version

Preface

Biblical studies are not conducted in a vacuum and are necessarily influenced by sociocultural contexts and concerns. The studies in this collection focus on various interpretive issues relating to current big-picture concerns in Oceania. The contributors are located around the edges of the Tasman Sea, but the issues, views, arguments, blind spots, and concerns that they address extend over the currents of Oceania onto the shores of Asia, and further. The chapters reflect the competencies and concerns of their respective authors—biblical scholars of diverse backgrounds who currently read, live, play, work, and worship in Aotearoa New Zealand and Australia—but the collection as a whole illustrates the potential contribution of the Bible and biblical studies to public discourse on matters of general concern.

The collection came together as follows: Ten of the thirteen contributors met over three days (April 19–21, 2012), thanks in part to a grant from the Public and Contextual Theology Research Centre of Charles Sturt University, to present and discuss some "drafty drafts" of our thoughts, with two contributors presenting by video conference. This seminar was at United Theological College, North Parramatta (NSW, Australia), and though we did not consult the traditional custodians of the land, we each learned what the others were doing, and we helped one another sharpen and deepen our thoughts on our texts, topics, and concerns. The three respondents did not participate in the seminar, but they have been invited to respond because of their rootedness in Oceania and expertise on the subjects of *Bible*, *borders*, and *belongings*.

Each of the contributors engages biblical text(s) and/or character(s) that crop up in the intersection of the *Bible* with *borders* and *belongings*. The *Bible* is of course vast, complex and slippery, and the meanings of *borders* and *belongings* are fluid: from *belonging* in a place (home, land), a group (identity, nation), or a movement (disciples, cultures), to *belongings* as material and cultural possessions (property); and from the *borders* of a text, discipline, or thought to the edges of a nation, community, or body. As a collection, this book pokes at conversations on location, context, and identity, nudging those toward *belongings*. The senses of *belongings* in this collection are rooted, reciprocal, and homely rather than individualistic and segregating. *Belongings* call attention to *borders*, which *are* (borders) when they are crossed. The *Bible* sits uneasily at this juncture, for there are times when the Bible roots and protects *belongings*, and times when the Bible *borders* (bars, prevents) *belongings*.

The contributors and respondents write from positions where different borders cross: the crossing of textual limits, race and ethnic lines, disciplinary and theological barriers, and religious and cultural strings, as well as the crossing of traditional views about biblical texts and characters. In their crossing of *borders*, with *Bible* in hand, the chapters of this book point back to the various shades of *belongings*.

Several events in our region—such as earthquakes, tsunamis, floods, shipwrecks and oil spills, movement of political and ecological refugees, resettlement of displaced peoples, and the changing political structures—challenge us to reflect on the practices of biblical interpretation and how consequently to read biblical texts. Loss of homelands and the withering of resources due to climate change make attention to *Bible, borders,* and *belongings* urgent. This collection does not represent all that our region offers, but herein is the start of a routing for *engaging readings from Oceania*. The chapters of this book are engaging, and they invite readers from the region and beyond to be more engaging.

ENGAGING READINGS

Engaging Scriptures from Oceania

Jione Havea

                        Scriptures travel
                            borders rise
                              bodies flow
                                homes drift
                           belongings part

          The Hebrew-Christian Bible was brought to Oceania, a region whose physical borders (especially the sea, which Polynesians call *moana*) are deep, fluid, and fiery (the Pacific Rim's Ring of Fire), on a fleet of boats that also carried geographers, explorers, botanists, missionaries, convicts, and teachers; traders of goods, tools, and in some cases bodies (Blackbirds); and more.* Back then, the Bible was *fresh off the boat*[1]—tall boats with piercing masts and shadowing sails that crossed the southern seas for various reasons, introducing new ways and fabrics, and adding more languages to an already polylingual and diversely cultured Oceania. The Bible came as a "talking book" (cf. Callahan 2006) said to contain sacred (*tapu*), respected, and traditioned words, but the lore-and-story-cultured people of Oceania did not know how to make it talk. So, at first, the locals depended on the bearers of the Bible to give it voice. They also assumed that the bearers were all biblical.

          Nowadays, the Bible has been given the slurs of some of the local languages,[2] almost like Jacob's speaking as if he were Esau (Gen 27:18–19),

---

    * I am grateful to Nāsili Vakaʻuta and David J. Neville for their careful reading and helpful comments on earlier drafts of this chapter.

    1. Islanders and Asians are often called FOBs, whether they migrated by boat or by plane.

    2. The Bible has been translated into the majority language in polylingual lands, and people from minor language groups are expected to use the language, which

and kept fresh by interpreters who use imported practices with smirches of local images and metaphors. The interpreters are now local and primarily Christians, but their purposes for interpreting the Bible still uphold those of the first bearers: to save, to teach, to heal, to civilize, to convert, to control, et cetera, the local people. Some local readers hold the ways and teachings of European missionaries as still authoritative (Palu 2012), without pondering who taught the foreigners local languages and practices (Fakasiʻiʻeiki 2010). To twist a popular feminist charge: the Bible and the ways of reading it are still the master's tools (Lorde 1984, 110–14), but the master these days is local or localized. Then and now, there is a strong tendency to read the Bible as if it "talks" only in the language and interests of the missionary drive.

Looking ahead, how might readers from Oceania refresh the Bible? My question is loaded and unapologetic for i[3] am charging that the Bible is going stale in Oceania, that the freshness of the Bible depends on readers,[4] and that some of us in Oceania, for better and for worse, dare to keep the Bible fresh and/or ignore the staleness of the Bible. Since there is a connection between the Bible and its interpretations, the freshness (or lack thereof) of one is bound to the freshness of the other. A popular joke between islanders indicates that readings are going stale: we *poke* local preachers who pull sermons (based on biblical texts) from "the fridge" (something already delivered or, more recently, downloaded from the internet) but do not warm (i.e., freshen and locate) those up before they mount the pulpit. To refresh the Bible therefore requires that readers and preachers too freshen up, for it is still true that identity (read: their staleness) influences how/what one reads (see also the essay by Sheridan in this volume).

In Oceania, where refreshments are always crosscultural,[5] to refresh readers and their modes of reading requires crossing cultural and linguis-

---

influences culture, of the dominant (majority) group. This is the case in language-rich lands like Papua Niu Guinea, Vanuatu, and Solomon Islands.

3. I use lowercase "i" because i use the lowercase with "you," "she," "they," and "others." I do not see the point in capitalizing the first person when s/he *is* in relation to everyone/everything else.

4. I have outlined some options on what the future of biblical studies might be for Pasifika islanders in "Drifting Homes" (Havea 2012), and i offer a wider reflection in this chapter over the region, attending to Aotearoa New Zealand and Australia as well.

5. We joke about how a "traditional" Tongan feast now includes items like KFC chicken (rather than *moa tunu*, coal-roasted chicken) and cordial drinks (instead of

tic borders and engaging with migrants and with natives. This is not to say that migrants can't be natives also. We have internal and external migrants in Oceania, from other islands (Solomon Islanders to Samoa) and from over the seas (French to New Caledonia). Many natives are descendants of voyagers, people whose roots trace back to other places. Migration, therefore, the event that takes peoples and their *belongings*[6] across *borders*, ripples in the tides of Oceania. Migration brings people to engage with borders and belongings, and this is one of the undercurrents of this collection of essays. Migration also makes any attempt to clearly and rigidly define borders troublesome; with regard to this collection of essays, Oceania overflows into and out of Asia (see also the essays by Mathews and Melanchthon in this volume), and beyond.

My question is also naïve and potentially insulting, for i assume that the Bible is worth keeping fresh in Oceania, a region that was colonized with the help of missionaries and their Bible. So i apologize in advance, *faa molemole* (in Samoan), to people who will be insulted by my naïveté, especially locals who have courageously named the Christian mission as responsible for bringing darkness to the region (see also the essay by Vaka'uta in this volume). This would include Siniva, the village fool in Sia Figiel's novel *Where We Once Belonged*, who commits suicide out of a combination of frustration and courage. Her friend Alofa words Siniva's reasons for taking her life in a critical way:

> "We are *not* living in Lightness," she [Siniva] would say. "We are not. Lightness is dead. Lightness died that first day in 1830 when the breakers of the sky [*papālagi*, a reference to white people] entered these shores, forcing us all to forget … to forget … to bury our gods … to kill our gods … to re-define everything, recording history in reverse. (Figiel 1996, 236)

Figiel makes Siniva blame Western missionaries and colonialists for bringing darkness, rather than light, to Samoa. Siniva and her companions would be insulted by my proposing to keep the Bible fresh in Oceania. I have my reasons, to which i will come later, when i argue that there are

---

coconuts), and a Samoan feast offers canned corned beef (with brand names *Pacific* and *Palm*). In other words, without imported items, our feasts are untraditional!

6. "Belongings" here applies to migrants' feeling of place (that they belong somewhere) as well as to their material possessions (which root them in their contexts, or link them to their home cultures).

more to the "scriptures *from* Oceania" than the Bible of the Christian mission.

Bordering Oceania

The edges of Oceania are difficult to map, and so are the borders that intersect within. Borders, some visible and some unseen, somewhat timeless and somewhat spacious, fasten and portion Oceania, as well as extend Oceania into neighboring regions.

"Oceania" here refers to the expanse commonly known as the Pacific, which extends from the edges of Asia at the northwest to the west coasts of North America, and down to South America and across to Australia at the southwest. This is an area dominated by water, with dots of lands stretched over what Spivak calls the "absent" part of the Asia-Pacific region. Oceania/Pacific is the part of the region that people prefer to fly over (Spivak 2008, 9–10, 248) and that people from the outside consider useless. The latter is evident in the comment by analyst Zhixing Zhang, who is reported to say concerning Hilary Clinton's visit to Australia and New Zealand in 2010:

> This is the bit that I don't understand, why does anyone want to counter Australian and New Zealand dominance of Polynesia/anything east of the Australian/NZ coast? It doesn't have population, its resources are tiny ... and its position is not very strategic in nature. Australia and NZ are the jewel of Australasia, the islands are hardly anything at all and all you'd take Australia for is resources and to deny other nations from using it as an FOB [forward operating base]/surveillance point with which to push up from the south. And even then all you have to do is hold Indonesia/Melanesia and you've blocked that route anyway. I just don't get why anyone gives a shit about Polynesia. (Hubbard and Hager 2012).

The contributors to this book, to the contrary, are committed to Aotearoa New Zealand and Australia, as well as to the sea of islands in the Pacific Ocean, which are always more than Melanesia and Polynesia. We may not be precise about where the borders of Oceania run, but we "give a shit" about Micronesia also, where islands continue to be suppressed by Western colonization (by esp. the USA) and made vulnerable by climate change.

There is something about borders that draws attention to the exercise of power and the obsession with (border) security. The powers that be establish and enforce borders in order to exclude foreign bodies and/or to push subjects to the margins through processes of minoritization. Borders exclude and set apart, separate and divide, but not in the interests of the small, the weak, or the ugly. Borders also get shifted, so that new patrons are brought under the security of the mighty. Now and then, voices from the margins speak up (Sugirtharajah 2006) and the minoritized take a stand (Bailey, Liew, and Segovia 2009), but the borders that marginalize and minoritize remain. Borders are, nonetheless, in fact necessary. Borders maintain order and condition people. To break through borders does not necessarily dissolve order, or break people up, but transforms and redefines who people are (see also the essays by Aernie and Jenks in this volume). Notwithstanding, whose order do borders maintain? Whose people do borders safeguard?

In Oceania, borders are many and different. There are solid, fluid, and fiery borders, from the depths of the southern seas to the hidden fiery vaults of the Pacific Rim, and from the diverse customs between nation groups to the polylingual tongues in settlements and communities. 'Epeli Hau'ofa (1993) once described Oceania as a "sea of islands," but it is appropriate also to speak of Oceania as a "sea of borders." Our contexts are fluid, as our cultures are oral, but this does not mean that our borders are all comforting. Awareness of and attitudes toward borders vary also. There are differences in the modes of thinking between smaller islanders and larger-land(-locked) peoples, between coastal dwellers and highlanders, between saltwater and freshwater peoples, and between peoples of the backwaters and of the hinterlands (cf. Manoa 2010). Islanders come from smaller and narrower lands, but they are not therefore small or simple minded. In fact, islanders too think big! Islanders deserve more than the "shit" of the West.[7]

Though varied, harboring contradictions and tensions, borders are homes, places where people feel that they belong. This is true of the Bible also: it is not always comforting, but people feel that the Bible makes them belong wherever they are, on the one hand, and that they belong in the Bible, on the other hand. There is another sense: the Bible makes some people *not* belong also (where they are, as well as in the Bible itself).

---

7. While i was working on this chapter, Hilary Clinton was visiting the Pacific Island Forum (PIF) at the Cook Islands, even though the United States is not a member of PIF. This visit was publicized as the United States' response to China's involvement in the region, so Oceania continues to be the wrestling (shitting?) ground for major powers.

The Bible invites and welcomes, opens and bridges (see also the essay by Painter in this volume), but it also excludes and repels.

Without the commas, the title for this collection of essays is playful: *Bible borders belonging(s)* suggests that the Bible protects (harbors) and/or bars (prevents) belongings (identities, valuables). The dual sense of the title is similar to what Job experienced. On the one hand, he was protected by God's blessings:

> Ha-Satan answered Yhwh, "Does Job fear God for nothing? Have you not *put a fence* around him and his house and all that he has, on every side? You have blessed the work of his hands, and his possessions have increased in the land." (Job 1:9–10)

For Ha-Satan, Yhwh's fence protects and enriches. But for Job, on the other hand, God's fence is limiting:

> Why is light given to one who cannot see the way, whom God has *fenced* in? (Job 2:23)

Borders in Oceania, and beyond, like the fences in the story of Job, have double effects: they protect, and they prevent. Borders have more than one face, more than one impact.

Unfinished Business of Reading …

The twines of Anglo North American and Western European modes of reading hold fast also in Oceania, with some variations, as one would expect. For the sake of sampling those, i offer observations on attempts by biblical scholars in four general, open, and intersecting, areas: (1) mainline modes of reading, (2) contextual readings, (3) ecological readings, (4) critical theory and postcolonial readings. This sampling intends to be inviting rather than comprehensive, and i apologize in advance to the many scholars of the region whom i will not name as well as to the few whom i categorize in ways that they may not appreciate.

The first area, mainline modes of reading that come from Europe and the United States, is the most crowded of the four areas. Following or imitating what comes from abroad is not limited to this area, but i focus here on the dominant modes of reading, by which i have in mind those who find shelter under historical and literary criticisms. Of special interest to me are scholars in Oceania who give mainline modes of reading a different twist. I have in mind, for example, the reconsideration of the documentary hypothesis by Anthony Campbell and Mark O'Brien (2005), inviting the thrust of source criticism to shift from seeking to find the origin of biblical texts toward embracing the voices in the text. They see the assumed literary sources of the Pentateuch not as products that signal the literary origins of texts but as "voices" that invite ongoing pondering and retelling. Sometimes the voices complement each other, but sometimes they are at tension (see also the essay by Neville in this volume). It is not clear whether the Australian situatedness of Campbell and O'Brien influences their views, but this is the case for M. E. Andrew (1999), who is open about reading the Bible in and for the context of Aotearoa New Zealand. In Andrew's case, it is possible for one to read the Bible under the direction of mainline modes of interpretation and at the same time be attentive to one's location.

There continues to be general dis-ease among mainline biblical critics with locating themselves geographically and culturally, in part because of the privileging of "unbiased" readings in the (mainline) academy. On the other hand, the contributors to this collection of essays, which includes some mainline biblical scholars from our region, are in general not troubled with being rooted and belonging somewhere, whether in terms of method, theology, ideology, and/or culture. No one reads outside some kind of border, with no sense of belonging, from no place, outside of time. To read requires one to be located, and in Oceania attention to location (on land, in the ocean, or along the edges) has stirred interested interpretations.

The second general area leads from the first: scholars who take contexts seriously, even if they do not see themselves as contextual critics. Owing to the solidarity in resistance of liberation hermeneutics (cf. Havea 2009), earlier on, and the affirmative subversive acts of postcolonial hermeneutics (cf. Havea 2005), more recently (see fourth area discussed below), contextual reading is usually expected from minority cultures and subalterned races and classes (cf. Brett 1996; Vaka'uta 2011). Context is, however, more than people and their ways, a point that is made strongly by ecological critics (see third area discussed below), and the rich understandings of *borders* and *belongings* in this collection of essays give evidence to the variety of understandings of context and affirm that no critic is context-free.

One cannot get a sense of what *borders* do without also understanding the context that those borders encircle and/or exclude, and along that line, *belongings* make sense within context. Context is, like borders and belongings, sometimes stable and visible but at other times unseen and fluid, yet they—context, borders, belongings—all in some way *frame* (cf. McKinlay 2004). In this regard, whether or not one prefers to be so known, all readers, and their readings, are already *contexted*. However, not all contexts receive the attention of biblical scholars. One of the contributions of this collection of essays is its intentional drawing of attention to Oceania, Spivak's "absent" part of Asia-Pacific, but there is of course much more to our region than the contributors re-present herein.

Any attention to context will also hint at those things that do not belong, some more obvious than others. Each of the contributions to this collection does both, engaging with what it means to be contexted as well as calling attention to those things that are out of place, in different ways, some more obvious than others.

Ecological hermeneutics is a third reading mode that has been shaped to a significant extent by contributors from Oceania. The five volumes of *The Earth Bible* (Habel 2001–2) rise out of Oceania, from Australia, drawing biblical critics from the region and beyond to read with care for Earth (standing for land, sea, and sky), guided by six ecojustice principles:

1. **The principle of intrinsic worth:** Earth and all its components have intrinsic worth/value.
2. **The principle of interconnectedness:** Earth is a community of interconnected living things that are mutually dependent on each other for life and survival.
3. **The principle of voice:** Earth is a subject capable of raising its voice in celebration and against injustice.
4. **The principle of purpose:** Earth and all its components are part of a dynamic cosmic design within which each piece has a place in the overall goal of that design.
5. **The principle of mutual custodianship:** Earth is a balanced and diverse domain where responsible custodians can function as partners with, rather than rulers over, Earth to sustain its balance and a diverse Earth community.
6. **The principle of resistance:** Earth and its components not only suffer from human injustices but actively resist them in the struggle for justice.

The ecojustice principles invite suspicion, identification, and retrieval when reading texts for and in the interests of Earth. There have been other developments from other parts of the world (Davis 2009; Horrell et al.

2010), and at different spheres of biblical criticism, but the Earth Bible project has made a mark on the terrains of ecological hermeneutics (Habel and Trudinger 2008), and on the horizon is a commentary series from Phoenix Press (Sheffield). The ecological agenda is also favored in the leaves of this collection, with special attention to the intersection between calamities and the notions of God (see esp. the essays by Wainwright, Neville, and Rushton in this volume).

Fourth is the expanding area in which critics knock at the doors of critical theory (Boer 2008; Carden 2004) and postcolonial hermeneutics (Brett 2009; Leota, forthcoming) and spread out (feminist) mats for healing and inclusion (McKinlay 2004; Wainwright 2006; Kelso 2007). This area is the home for a seminar and e-journal that bear the same name, *Bible and Critical Theory*, beaconing welcome signals to scholars, students, and laypeople from disciplines that are nontraditional, and who may not feel that they (want to) belong among mainline critics. While the majority of these critics march to beats from outside the region, the legacies of colonialism across Oceania necessitate (even if unconsciously) engaging critical theories and postcolonial imaginations.

What lacks still is the *browning* of this complex area. Native and indigenous voices are pushed to the contextual corner (e.g., Havea 2004, 2006), implying that the wisdoms and traditions behind those are not "critical," "postcolonial," or "theory" enough. In other words, "critical + theory" seems to be a formula still reserved for White critics only. I beg to differ, as i show below, in a *blackfella* way.

The foregoing sampling does not suggest that Oceania is unique and separate from the rest of the world. In fact, Anglo North American and Western European values flow strong in the bloodlines of Oceania. We cannot speak now of indigenous or native modes as if those are free of the influences by outside cultures. While many in Oceania are village people, we are not cut off from the rest of the world. And we can no longer speak of indigenous and native peoples as if we live in isolated settlements or as if our precontact ancestors were savages. The people of Oceania and our ways do not exist in isolation.

… Color In …

The fact that some people from outside do not "give a shit" about us does not mean that we are useless in the eyes of everyone. What is more painful is when some of our own people do not "give a shit" about our ways and things, or about local subjects, especially those who are of a different gender, class, orientation, or ethnicity. These markers of difference have received fair (though not sufficient) attention by biblical critics in Oceania, but color has not received the attention it deserves (and this neglect is especially obvious given that Oceania is rich in colors). It makes sense that any attempt to refresh reading in Oceania engages with the difference color makes in one's preferences and perspectives, and what zhe (for "she/he") privileges, ignores, and/or undermines. The difference that color makes was clear in the media coverage of recent shootings in the United States. On July 10, 2012, a gunman entered a theater at Aurora, Colorado, and fatally shot twelve people. Major national and international networks broke from their scheduled programs to cover this sad event. Two weeks later, on August 5, another gunman fatally shot seven people at a Sikh Gurudwara temple in Wisconsin, but the media did not seem to care. Only one major network broke from its scheduled program to give coverage to the later shooting, and Riddhi Shah (2012) asks a critical question, "Consider, for a minute, a situation in which the skin colors of the victims and attacker were reversed."

Most people think of color as the outward manifestation of race, and it becomes a matter of concern because of the abuse of darker-skin-color people by domineering authorities. Color in this regard is about White (rulers) versus Black (dispossessed), with the colonial legacy as the spark that brings color to the surface (cf. Pattel-Gray 1998; Maddison 2011). Without watering down the *tears* of Blacks, questions remain. Would color be a concern if authorities performed their responsibilities justly and carefully? Is color an issue only in relation to the use of power? Would color be an issue of interest even if there were no abuse? And should attention to color be the burden of nonwhites (like Riddhi Shah) only and not an obligation for White people also?

Color is something everyone sees but only a few notice. Ironically, colorblind people are more conscious of color. Color is most clear when something is out of place: "That does not suit (because it is too bright or too dull)" or "Those colors do not match." Color is high on the scale of reasons for judging whether something belongs or does not belong, and in the realm of relations and politics, one's *likes* and tolerance of colors influences how zhe uses power.

In Oceania, color has to do with (lack of) privileges. White people have more privileges, and there is something about whiteness that makes nonwhite people feel inferior. I might have wisdom and experiences equal to or more than that of a white colleague, but zher color makes me feel unimportant. Zhe is not always conscious of the difference zher color makes, but i get labeled a racist when i raise this kind of observation. So continues the (dis)privileging effect of color.

There are more colors in Oceania than Black and White. Australia and Aotearoa New Zealand provide the majority of the White population, and we have around fifty shades of black and brown. Fairer-skin people imagine that they are better and more privileged than darker-skin ones. There are many reasons for this. Fair skin is closer to white and further from black, which is associated with dirt and dirtiness; fair skin indicates one who is shaded and protected from the burning sun, which darkens the skin of workers, fishers, and laborers of the land; fair skin suggests zhe who is watched, kept, and groomed, rather than a homeless wanderer; and so forth. So while Caribbean and African people on the shores of the Atlantic speak with pride of being Black, blackness is stigmatized among the people of Oceania. In attending to color, in Oceania, Whites and Browns think that Black/blackness is defiled. Black/blackness, however, is defiled not in itself but in the eyes of Whites and Browns.

When it comes to belonging and not belonging, and to who enjoys the privileges from crossing borders, color makes a difference. One of the unfinished businesses for readers in Oceania is to see color in scriptures, which should be not the burden of nonwhites only but an obligation for all readers—in other words, to hear the blood of their siblings crying from under the ground of blackness (Gen 4:10). How might Brown and Black/blackness become the default colors "seen" by readers in Oceania?

... Oceania's Scriptures

I have a broad and (non)traditional understanding of what pass as scriptures, so a working definition would aid: scriptures are texts honored by members of a community because those reveal something that helps them/others understand what the community is about and how it may endure and thrive. It is in this sense that the Hebrew Bible, Apocrypha, New Testament, Qur'ān, and Bhagavad Gita are scriptures.

But there are more forms of scriptures than literary documents and written sutras. Texts that were painted, drawn, woven, strung, performed, engraved, lashed, and/or storied (oral) could also be scriptures, and the community that scripturalizes those may be a religious or cultural institution, but it could also be a political, ideological, or spiritual movement. The community decides its scriptures, which they might borrow from another community, across time and space. Of course, the scriptures of one community may not be honored by other communities. My interest herein is with the scriptures of smaller communities, which do not always get the attention and respect of mainline communities.

When Lucky Dube refers in his 1993 song "Victims" to Bob Marley—"Bob Marley said, 'How long shall they kill our prophets / while we stand aside and look'"[8]—it is obvious that Marley's "Redemption Song" (1980) has reached scriptural (or canonical) status in the Rasta world (see also Havea, "Bare Feet Welcome," below). Marley's text is honored in Dube's community, in a way similar to how the composition "Hala kuo papa" by Kuini Salote of Tonga is respected by contemporary Tongans (Māhina 2012; Vete 2012).[9] The songs by Bob Marley and Kuini Salote are examples of Brown and Black "texts" reaching scriptural status.

Dube respected Marley, but this does not mean that Marley's text was unproblematic and so he had the final say. Dube sings on to correct Marley with these critical lines: "But little did he [Marley] know / that eventually the enemy will stand aside and look / while we slash and kill our own brothers / knowing that already they are the victims of the situation." Marley's text is scripture, but it still needs to be corrected. The situation has changed, and Marley does not have unchecked license in the Rastafari world. The corrective by Dube is evidence of the workings of cross-scriptures, for Dube's "Victims" does not replace but rather supplements Marley's "Redemption Song."

Supplementing takes place at a different level with regard to Kuini Salote's "Hala kuo papa." In this case, corrective takes place at the level of interpretation. Māhina (a scholar in Western standards) claims that "Hala kuo papa" celebrates the landing of the United States Marines in Tonga during World War II (Māhina 2012), but Vete (an ordinary Tongan composer) argues that the composition celebrates an event at which Kalaniuvalu (Semisi) handed over the place of honor ('olovaha) at the head of Kava ceremonies in his land to Kuini Salote (Vete 2012).[10] Two Tongan kings before Kuini Salote were not honored at Kalaniuvalu's land until the significant event that "Hala kuo papa" scripturalizes.

---

8. Cited by Abel 2010.

9. The song is available at http://www.youtube.com/watch?v=8w1TUk9qG8M.

10. Vete's wife is from Kalaniuvalu's household, and his argument is based on the "storied text" of his father-in-law. My father participated at the event that Vete references, and i prefer his interpretation.

These two examples show that scriptures are not exempt from being out of date or from being supplemented, and the same applies to scholars and their interpretations. Ironically, it seems more acceptable when one supplements scriptures belonging to local, nondomineering communities than when one supplements the scriptures of globalizing religions.

Turning back to Oceania's scriptures, i make two appeals to close this chapter, one about other scriptured texts in Oceania and the other about scriptural interpretations in Oceania. The two appeals overlap.

First, there are native scriptures throughout Oceania, from days of old and from recent times, but we have had to deal with texts that serve the interests and scriptures of the Anglo North American and Western European communities. Two examples will hopefully suffice: There is an overwhelming expectation that speakers or writers from Tuvalu and Kiribati will address something related to climate change, as if they do not have other cultural gifts to offer those of us from outside. The politics of climate change (cf. Havea 2010) squeeze these two island nations into the interests of ecological scholarship, driven by economic interests, where they are assumed to be of one soul and body. But Tuvalu and Kiribati are very culturally different from one another.

The other example relates to the dominant assumption that the theology of Australia's Aboriginal People will have something to do with Sorry and Reconciliation, without examining the upshots of these catchwords. Sorry and Reconciliation constantly remind Aboriginal People of their victimization, that they are a broken people, in need of apology and reconciliation, which they cannot give or receive without the blessings of White Australia. Sorry and Reconciliation are the default expectations, but Aboriginal People would be perceived differently if indigenous theology is about, for instance, hospitality, welcome, adoption, covenanting, and so forth. This is why, i argue, readers need to engage with Oceania's local and colorful (Brown and Black) scriptures.

Allow me to muse. Imagine three natives, a Tuvaluan, an I-Kiribati, and an indigenous Australian from Arnhem Land, sitting under a breadfruit tree. Imagine also that they are there to dream of how to read scriptures and do theology for their diverse communities. It will not be long before they talk about land and trees, hunting and fishing, gathering and sharing, and the survival of their peoples.

The Tuvaluan might talk about the Tongans and Samoans who came to steal from their islands, and those who came to settle and take over. They were the pirates of the southern seas. The Tuvaluan might also talk about those islanders from Vaitupu who were moved to Kioa (Fiji) in 1946 because of environmental strains. Ecological change is not new.

I imagine the I-Kiribati adding something about the people from Banaba being moved to Rabi (where the Indian indentured laborers to Fiji were first placed in 1879) in 1945 because their home island was bought and mined for phosphate, then destroyed in the American-Japanese war. Colonization relates to the wealth in native lands.

At this point, the indigenous Australian might echo the lines in the Yothu Yindi song titled "Gone Is the Land" (from the album *Garma*, released in 2000): "This land is not 40,000 dollars or more, but 40,000 years of cultures here." What is important in land is not its monetary value but the cultures it homes.

Time would move under another tree, as these imaginary natives get to what—legends, myths, songs, dances, practices—in their different cultures give value to land. When this happens, they are engaging some of Oceania's scriptures. If i joined this trinity of natives, i would share the reflections of a Yolngu (indigenous) woman, Gamiritj Gurruwiwi, that i received under a frangipani tree at Nungalinya (September 20, 2012; cited with her permission):

> **Land**
> Land important to me and people. It is
> A motherland
> Every part is divided and belongs to someone
> Land holds safety
> Land provides us with something ... seeds
> Land holds ceremony ... the songlines of the land
> Land is precious
> **Seeds**
> Seeds are a gift from land
> If right, seeds will grow
> If wrong, seeds will not grow
> Worlds like seeds ... if take back to wrong climate, they will not grow
> Land and seeds know each other.

When Oceania's scriptures like these ones are brought to bear on reading of biblical texts—whether it be the stories of gardens (Gen 2–3, 1 Kgs 21), of trespassing (Num 22–24), or of invading lands (Josh 2) (see also the essays by Clark and McKinlay in this volume)—my second appeal comes to shape. Oceania's scriptures are worthy not only as illustrations for but as supplements to biblical texts. Whether one calls this an appeal for contrapuntal, crosscultural, or border-crossing reading does not matter. What matters is that readers of the Bible engage the (other, minor) scriptures from Oceania. Only then, i argue, will readers see the richness of *engaging with scriptures from Oceania*. We (from Oceania) engage scriptures from other places; we (from other places) engage scriptures from Oceania; and we (from wherever) realize that scriptures from Oceania are engaging.

Scriptures from Oceania come in many shades and shapes, and in many tongues, and it is in the interest of these (local) scriptures that i wish readers and readings of the Bible in Oceania to freshen up. The Bible, affirmed as Scripture over time and across lands, can aid in the engaging of the scriptures from Oceania and, in the process, come to belong in Oceania.

Works Consulted

Abel, Lee. 2010. Respect to Lucky Dube. *United Reggae*, June 7. Online: http://unitedreggae.com/articles/n374/060710/respect-to-lucky-dube.

Andrew, M. E. 1999. *The Old Testament in Aotearoa New Zealand*. Wellington, N.Z.: DEFT.

Bailey, Randall, Tat-Siong Benny Liew, and Fernando F. Segovia, eds. 2009. *They Were All Together in One Place? Toward Minority Biblical Criticism*. Atlanta: Society of Biblical Literature.

Boer, Roland. 2008. *Last Stop before Antarctica: The Bible and Postcolonialism in Australia*. 2d ed. Atlanta: Society of Biblical Literature; Leiden: Brill.

Brett, Mark G., ed. 1996. *Ethnicity and the Bible*. Leiden: Brill.

———. 2009. *Decolonizing God*. The Bible in the Modern World. Sheffield: Phoenix.

Callahan, Allen Dwight. 2006. *The Talking Book: African Americans and the Bible*. New Haven: Yale University Press.

Campbell, Anthony F., and Mark A. O'Brien. 2005. *Rethinking the Pentateuch: Prolegomena to the Theology of Ancient Israel*. Louisville: Westminster John Knox.

Carden, Michael. 2004. *Sodomy: A History of a Christian Biblical Myth*. London: Equinox.

Davis, Ellen F. 2009. *Scripture, Culture, and Agriculture: An Agrarian Reading of the Bible*. New York: Cambridge.

Fakasiʻiʻeiki, ʻIkani. 2010. ʻIkai taʻofi he maka, ko e ʻoneʻone ʻe lava (Rocks Can't, but Sand Can). Paper presented at the Oceania Biblical Studies Association. Trinity Theological College, Auckland, New Zealand. July 9.

Figiel, Sia. 1996. *Where We Once Belonged*. Auckland: Pasifika.

Habel, Norman C., ed. 2001–2. *The Earth Bible*. 5 vols. Sheffield: Sheffield Academic.

Habel, Norman C., and Peter Trudinger, eds. 2008. *Exploring Ecological Hermeneutics*. Atlanta: Society of Biblical Literature.

Hauʻofa, ʻEpeli. 1993. Our Sea of Islands. Pages 2–16 in *A New Oceania: Rediscovering Our Sea of Islands*. Edited by E. Waddell, V. Naidu, and E. Hauʻofa. Suva: University of the South Pacific Press.

Havea, Jione. 2004. Numbers. Pages 43–51 in *Global Bible Commentary*. Edited by Daniel Patte et al. Nashville: Abingdon.

———. 2005. Stor[y]ing Deuteronomy 22:13–19 in Missionary Positions. *The Bible and Critical Theory* 1 (2). doi:10.2104/bc050003.

———. 2006. Whoring Dinah: Poly-nesian-Reading Genesis 34. Pages 172–84 in *Voyages in Uncharted Waters: Essays on the Theory and Practice of Biblical Interpretation in Honor of David Jobling*. Edited by Wesley J. Bergen and Armin Siedlecki. Sheffield: Sheffield Phoenix.

———. 2009. Releasing the Story of Esau from the Words of Obadiah. Pages 87–104 in *The Bible and the Hermeneutics of Liberation*. Edited by Alejandro F. Botta and Pablo R. Andiñach. Semeia Studies 59. Atlanta: Society of Biblical Literature.

———. 2010. The Politics of Climate Change, a Talanoa from Oceania. *International Journal of Public Theology* 4:345–55.

———. 2012. Drifting Homes. Pages 196–206 in *The Future of the Biblical Past*. Edited by Roland Boer and Fernando Segovia. Semeia Studies 66. Atlanta: Society of Biblical Literature.

Horrell, David G., Cherryl Hunt, Christopher Southgate, and Francesca Stavrakopoulou, eds. 2010. *Ecological Hermeneutics: Biblical, Historical and Theological Perspectives*. New York: T&T Clark.

Hubbard, Anthony, and Nicky Hager. 2012. WikiLeaks Proves Brutal US Diplomacy. Stuff.co.nz, April 4. Online: http://www.stuff.co.nz/national/politics/6519429/WikiLeaks-proves-brutal-US-diplomacy.

Kelso, Julie. 2007. *O Mother, Where Art Thou? An Irigarayan Reading of the Book of Chronicle*. London: Equinox.

Leota, Peniamina. Forthcoming. *Ethnic Tensions in Yehud and Samoa: A Postcolonial Reading.* International Voices in Biblical Studies. Atlanta: Society of Biblical Literature.

Lorde, Audre. 1984. *Sister Outsider.* Berkeley: Crossing.

Maddison, Sarah. 2011. *Beyond White Guilt: The Real Challenge for Black-White Relations in Australia.* Sydney: Allen & Unwin.

Māhina, 'Okusitino. 2012. Scripture and Literature: Fakatātā and Heliaki as Scriptural and Literary Devices. Paper presented at the Pacific Hermeneutics Seminar. University of the South Pacific, Tonga. August 28.

Manoa, Pio. 2010. Redeeming Hinterland. *Pacific Journal of Theology* 2 (43):65–86.

McKinlay, Judith E. 2004. *Reframing Her: Biblical Women in Postcolonial Focus.* Sheffield: Phoenix.

Palu, Ma'afu. 2012. Ta'anga ko e Folofola 'a e 'Otua: Ko hono ngaue'aki 'o e lea 'ta'anga' 'ia Nomipa 23–24. Paper presented at the Pacific Hermeneutics Seminar. University of the South Pacific, Tonga. August 29.

Pattel-Gray, Anne. 1998. *The Great White Flood: Racism in Australia Critically Appraised from an Aboriginal Historico-theological Viewpoint.* Atlanta: Scholars.

Shah, Riddhi. 2012. "Sikh Temple Shooting: Why Do the Media Care Less about This Attack?" *Huffington Post*, August 7. Online: http://www.huffingtonpost.com/riddhi-shah/sikh-temple-shooting_b_1749866.html.

Spivak, Gayatri Chakravorty. 2008. *Other Asias.* Oxford: Blackwell.

Sugirtharajah, R.S., ed. 2006. *Voices from the Margin: Interpreting the Bible in the Third World.* 3d ed. Maryknoll: Orbis.

Vaka'uta, Nāsili. 2011. *Reading Ezra 9–10 Tu'a-wise: Rethinking Biblical Interpretation in Oceania.* Atlanta: Society of Biblical Literature.

Vete, Henelī. 2012. Felāve'i e maama e folofola mo e fatu ta'anga. Paper presented at the Pacific Hermeneutics Seminar. University of the South Pacific, Tonga. August 28.

Wainwright, Elaine M. 2006. *Women Healing/Healing Women: The Genderization of Healing in Early Christianity.* London: Equinox.

"Save Us! We Are Perishing!":
Reading Matthew 8:23–27 in the Face of Devastating Floods

Elaine M. Wainwright[1]

The theme of this collection of essays, "Bible, Borders, Belonging(s)," is evocative, placing together elements that seem quite disparate at first sight. One needs to move around in the space created by the combination of borders and belongings: to what extent do borders render belonging possible or impossible, and, if not impossible, then extremely difficult? And are these borders material as much as social, economic, and political? "Belongings" too conjures up the material elements secure within borders or carried across them as well as sociopolitical and relational belongings. All of these play out not only in the biblical narrative but in our reading of it, especially from contemporary perspectives and places.

Laying Out Borders and Belongings

One border that rises up in my consciousness as I engage with this project is material, that of the Tasman Sea (in Māori, *Te Tai-o-Rehua*), a large body of water, 2000 kilometers across and 2,800 kilometers in length, that separates the Australian mainland from the islands of Aotearoa New Zealand. I cross it regularly by air as I move between two places of belonging: my native Australia, whose lands and peoples I love and with whose story mine is intimately linked; and Aotearoa New Zealand, the land which has been "home" to me for ten years now and in whose stories I am newly

---

1. I wish to acknowledge the critical insights and editorial eye of Drs. Anne Elvey and Veronica Lawson, both of whom read an almost-final draft of this essay very thoroughly.

and much more tentatively inserted. It also links both countries into the region of Oceania, stretching off to the right. It is in and from this nexus that I engage with the biblical story aware that, for the sake of this project, the place of belonging from which I read is that of one side of the Tasman, namely the Australian. The issues that I engage, however, are not only national and regional but also global. The biblical story that I will read is appropriate to my evoking of the Tasman Sea, namely, Matt 8:23–27, the story entitled "The Calming of the Storm."[2]

In early January 2011 I was exploring this story from an ecological perspective, safely ensconced in the bowels of the library of the Ecole Biblique in Jerusalem. All my senses, however, were strained elsewhere, to the devastating floods that were wreaking havoc in my home state of Queensland, Australia. Walls of water were taking before them crops and trees, roads/bridges and houses, livestock and other animals small and large, together with human lives. No more-than-human constituent (no-body, no-thing, no ecosystem) was safe before the power of water, wind, and storm swamping the state in the latter half of December and early half of January 2010/2011. Boundaries were breached, borders were crossed within the entire Earth community.[3]

Before engaging the Bible with such breaching of boundaries and crossing of borders, it is important to give more detailed attention to the devastating floods. Through the month of December 2010, the Queensland people watched daily as town after town was evacuated because of rising floodwaters: Theodore, Emerald, Chinchilla, and Dalby to name but four. The materiality and sociality of the more-than-human community was in tension. One might metaphorically hear echoing from the inhabitants of these towns the biblical cry: "Save us! We are perishing!" (Matt 8:25).

The rain continued to fall as December gave way to January, and a saturated earth could not contain the rain that fell in volumes not remembered during the previous years of searing drought. On January 10, 2011, the city of Toowoomba, the place of my birth and the location of many of my family members, received 160 millimeters (6.3 inches) of rain during

---

2. This is the heading used with the RSV text (2d ed.) in the *Greek-English New Testament* (8th ed.; Stuttgart: Deutsche Bibelgesellschaft, 1994).

3. I use the term "Earth community" to signify the human and the other-than-human constituents of any time and place in the unfolding of planet Earth. Together they make up what I call the more-than-human community or the Earth community with all its ecosystems.

the hours of the morning, water that the sodden earth could not absorb, so that it ran down the two natural waterways that meet in the city center as a raging torrent, taking before it cars, cemented rubbish bins, and anything that could not resist its force. Four human lives were lost, material objects in the city such as shops and their contents (people's belongings) were swept away, and other-than-human lives were destroyed. The effects on entire ecosystems, both negative and positive, are as yet unknown. One might again hear the cry go up: "Save us! We are perishing!" And within that cry one hears echo the voice of a thirteen-year-old boy, Jordan Rice—"Save my young brother!"—which rescuers did, but which left them unable to save him and his mother as their car was washed away (Saulwick 2011).

This, however, was but a prelude to further devastation. Another wall of water, the result of the torrential rain, raced down the Toowoomba range through Withcott (described by locals as if it had been hit by a cyclone), Murphy's Creek, Helidon, and then Grantham, making Grantham its most devastated victim. Here houses, vehicles, indeed anything that could not resist was taken in the wake of the raging torrent. Here, too, many people were caught unprepared for the force of the water; nine lost their lives, and others are among the people still missing, while the bodies of some residents were found 70–80 kilometers away. Again the cry: "Save us! We are perishing!"

The next day, January 11, the Brisbane River broke its banks, and so began a flooding of the state's capital city, Brisbane, equal to that of 1974. Over twenty thousand homes were inundated, thousands of people were evacuated, and so many lost not only most of their possessions but their dwelling place and for some their very lives. Once again, the entire Earth community felt the effects of the combination of weeks of rain, at times of deluge proportion, which combined with a tropical cyclone and a La Niña event, the latter being a weather pattern that brings heavy rainfall to the river catchments of the eastern states of Australia.[4]

Later in January 2011, many towns of southern New South Wales and Victoria would be likewise inundated. One could add to this the devastating floods of early 2012 that struck southwestern Queensland and northern New South Wales. How are we to understand what seem like the breaking of the boundaries within Earth's ecosystems and the breaching of

---

4. For a more extensive account of the flooding, see "2010–2011 Queensland Floods," *Wikipedia*, http://en.wikipedia.org/wiki/2010-2011_Queensland_floods.

areas of belonging, so that rain and the waters of the Earth seem to unleash their power against anything or anyone who would seek to contain them—human and other-than-human communities and interrelationships?

What might it mean to read Matt 8:23–27, the story so often called the "Stilling of the Storm," in the face of two years of such devastating floods? And as this question reverberates, it catches up others as we cross borders into the region of Oceania. The Matthean text is interrogated by the wild storms that have threatened the small islands of Oceania in recent years.[5] Questions rise up from the splitting open of Earth in Christchurch, New Zealand, February 22, 2011, in which 185 human lives were lost and ongoing aftershocks impacted and continue to impact Earth itself and all its constituents. The resulting liquefaction as earth and water rise up from large cracks reminds us yet again of the power of water and the ongoing movement of Earth, which we generally regard as stable.[6] The most devastating recent experience in the region of the Pacific was the earthquake in Japan on March 11, 2011, which resulted in a tsunami in which sixteen thousand people died and damage to nuclear reactors threatened and still threatens all Earth's more-than-human beings as the Earth community's sociality was disrupted.[7]

The cry "Save us! We are perishing" rises up across borders in the region, and with it come questions. Climate and earth scientists such as David Karoly (Smith 2011) and Kevin Trenberth (Fogarty 2011), for instance, interrogate the relationship between extreme weather events such as the Queensland flooding and global warming, careful not to isolate single events but to examine patterns and trends. A key question arises: is the human community ethically responsible for such climate change, and what seem like its effects? Others will raise a more specific religious question—is, or how is, G-d[8] embroiled/involved in such disasters (Fretheim 2010; Edwards 2010)? The question raised in this paper is, how might one

---

5. See "Pacific Storms Climatology Products (PSCP)," http://www.pacificstormsclimatology.org; and Roach 2006.

6. See "2011 Christchurch Earthquake," *Wikipedia*, http://en.wikipedia.org/wiki/2011_Christchurch_earthquake.

7. See "2011 Tōhoku Earthquake and Tsunami," *Wikipedia*, http://en.wikipedia.org/wiki/2011_Tōhoku_earthquake_and_tsunami.

8. I use the designation "G-d" for the divine one in order to invite a thinking anew of the ways in which the biblical text and the ongoing Christian tradition have imaged the divine as male and as having absolute power and control over the Earth community.

read a Gospel story of a dangerous storm at sea out of and into engagement with Earth and its movements and moments within and beyond our borders and our belongings, even our belonging in relationship with the divine one whom our tradition names as G-d?

Approach

In order to facilitate such a task, I will undertake a sociorhetorical reading of Matt 8:23–27 from an ecological perspective. Such a hermeneutic, named as "ecological," is no longer new to biblical studies, with the Earth Bible project[9] and the Exeter group (Horrell et al. 2010) both developing reading approaches that take account of the ecological crises confronting planet Earth and all its constituents. My own approach draws on aspects of these, especially that of the Earth Bible project, but it is informed organically by the work of Lorraine Code, who calls for a profound shift to *ecological thinking* (Code 2006). She envisages this as a new social imaginary that is in process of shifting from the prevailing social imaginary of mastery, a paradigm analyzed extensively by Val Plumwood (1993; 2002). It is, therefore, a critical hermeneutic bringing to the text a hermeneutic of suspicion in relation to any form of mastery—human, other-than-human, and even divine—as these are encoded in the text. This functions interactively with a rereading or reconfiguring that will be attentive to not only the human within the text but also the entire more-than-human constituency and relationship with divinity.

The way of reading that is shaped by my ecological hermeneutic is a modification of the sociorhetorical approach developed by Vernon Robbins (1996). New analytic categories can be brought to bear when exploring the *inner texture* and *intertexture*, especially the category of *habitat*, which can be understood physically as well as socially (Code 2006, 25). I shift Robbins's third textual approach, which he names as *social and cultural*, to an analysis of what I call the *ecological texture*. This expands what he names as the social and cultural textures to include the material and the dynamics of all Earth interrelationships. With such tools, I turn now to a reading of Matt 8:23–27.[10]

---

9. See http://www.webofcreation.org/earth-bible.
10. For a fuller exposition of this approach, see the theoretical segments of some of my more recent publications: Wainwright 2010, 159–61; 2011, 375–78; 2012a, 125–29; and, in particular, 2012b.

Reading Matthew 8:23–27

In the Gospel of Matthew the story of the calming of the great *seismos* at sea is included in a collection of healing stories (Matt 8–9) by way of a logic that is not easily apparent to the anthropocentric reader. Suffice to suggest here at the outset that it is human corporeality and other-than-human materiality that intertwine in all the healing stories and that demand the attention of an ecological reader, Matt 8:23–27 being no exception.

Following Jesus's descent from the mountain of proclamation in 8:1, there are three groups of three healing stories (8:1–15; 8:23–9:8; and 9:18–34), or four in the third grouping if one reads the intercalation of the healing of the woman with a hemorrhage into the raising of the ruler's daughter as two stories. The whole section is framed by a reference to the crowds (8:1 and 9:35–36) and intercalated with two narrative sections that John Meier calls buffer pericopes (Wainwright 1991, 81). Except for 8:23–27, all the other stories are concerned with the healing of human bodies by touch or by a word, and just prior to Jesus and his disciples getting into a boat in verses 16–17 there is a summary passage referring to his casting out of spirits from those possessed with demons and curing all who are sick.

In 8:23–27, however, it is not bodies that touch or that speak/hear healing, but it is Earth that speaks in a language that is loud and, some might say, abrasive. The story opens in the human/material nexus. Jesus gets into a boat (*ploion*), and his disciples (*hoi mathētai*) follow him (*ēkolouthēsan*). The language situates this story firmly within the unfolding Matthean narrative. *Ploion* recalls the fishing boat that James and John left (4:21, 22) to follow Jesus (*ēkolouthēsan*)—echoes of this boat's very materiality still linger in the Matthean text for those readers who have either seen or touched the Galilee boat excavated at Kibbutz Ginosaur (Wachsmann 1988). Anne Elvey (2011, 86) asks, in relation to what she suggests is the disciples' "rejection of a market economy," if "we can also infer a shift from a use-based approach to the lake."

James and John (together with Peter and Andrew, who are likewise called from their engagement in the fishing industry) are not called *mathētai*, or disciples, at that point. Immediately after their call, however, the reader meets a group called *mathētai*, who come to Jesus on the mountain (5:1), although this group is undefined. Out of the crowds in 8:21, just prior to our focal story, another "disciple" engages with Jesus in relation to conditions for following him. The reader, therefore, is unclear about the composition of the *mathētai* of 8:23, but the verb (*ēkolouthēsan*) carries all the connotations of an emerging group of new fictive kin becoming more intimately connected with Jesus's *basileia* ministry (see 4:17). Discipleship carries, therefore, connotations of belonging, and references to such discipleship both precede and open this small narrative. This human kinship group is located in the material context of the boat. The reference in 8:18 to Jesus commanding that they go over to the other side of the sea evokes the border constituted by the sea between Galilee and the Decapolis with all the religio-political differences and antagonisms it signifies.

The text gives no clear indication as to why Jesus wants to make this crossing, especially given that the time setting evoked at the beginning of 8:16 is late afternoon into evening (BDAG, 746). Following that designation, he undertakes multiple healings and exorcisms. It is only after this activity that 8:17 links Jesus's command to go over to the other side with his seeing the crowds around him. Hence, it is night, a time when danger might lurk, and the command is to negotiate a border, in this instance a sea, which in ancient times was always considered treacherous. It is difficult to determine the impetus for such a crossing, but the mention of the crowds reminds readers of the reference in Matt 4:25 to such crowds, who were said to be following Jesus, some of whom were from the Decapolis. Perhaps, in narrative terms, it is this memory that is triggered for Jesus by the Galilean crowds around him, and he is seemingly impelled to undertake a crossing of the sea so that he might engage the Decapolis crowds in their own context. He sets out to negotiate the border without fear of danger from sea or land. Eric Stewart in his study of spatial practice in Mark reminds us that "people who reside in borderlands frequently have more in common with other people in that borderland than they do with people in distant administrative centers" (Stewart 2009, 144). He goes on to suggest that in antiquity borders were as much points of access as boundary markers. Jesus's desire to cross to the other side of the sea can be seen in such light, namely, giving access to his ministry of healing to the people of the Decapolis.

The Matthean exclamation *kai idou* ("behold"), which demands the attention of the reader at the beginning of 8:24, turns the reader toward Earth, Earth that speaks in the *seismos megas* that occurs on the sea—a "moment of revelation," Elvey suggests, "both theophany and geophany" (Elvey 2011, 87). The Matthean narrative contains hyperbolic language here. *Seismos* generally indicates an earthquake (see 24:7, 54; 28:2) or a storm of earthquake proportions at sea (perhaps what we have come to know as a tsunami in these days of global warming and our recognition and experience of violent movements of Earth recalled earlier in this essay). *Seismos megas* (i.e., the addition of the adjective *megas*) brings to greater awareness the power of such a movement of Earth. It also draws into the ecological texture of the text the meteorological conditions around the Sea of Galilee, where, during the summer months at least, Mediterranean breezes coming from the west increase or almost double their speed over the lake due to the "rift relief," leading to regular and at times violent storms (Volohonsky et al. 1983, 141–53; Nun 1989, 3, 20). Earth's processes and movements of tectonic plates are both ancient, within the almost four billion years of Earth's unfolding, and ongoing into our own time and region. The other-than-human Earth has different borders from those that the human community constructs, and yet together we constitute Earth.

In the Matthean text, readers are told that the *seismos megas* is swamping the boat with its waves. The human community of disciples and their material context (the boat) are no match for the power of Earth's processes of wind and water, an insight that resonates with contemporary readers' experience of the power of water in the floods discussed earlier and the movement of Earth's plates in earthquakes and tsunamis. It reminds us as readers that the borders that we have constructed in our thinking about our built environment and about our belonging within the Earth community, with all its ongoing movement toward its becoming, are indeed profoundly anthropocentric. The small boat caught in the force of the *seismos megas* with its crew of a small group of human persons brings to the fore very powerfully borders and belongings that are those of the entire Earth community and its unfolding.

Intertextually, only three Septuagintal occurrences of the phrase *seismos megas* echo in the Matthean text (*seismos* alone occurs many more times): Jer 10:22 and Ezek 3:12 and 38:19. The Matthean reader hears, in the echo of Jer 10, a prophet theologizing, within the three-tiered worldview of his day, that G-d commands the unfolding of Earth (10:11–13) as well as what befalls the people, in this instance, the coming of the Babylonians, who will take the people of Israel into exile. Their coming is envisaged as a *seismos megas* from the north (Jer 10:22). The *seismos megas* of Ezek 38:19 carries connotations of a manifestation of G-d's judgment. In both theologies, Earth with its possibility of a *seismos megas* can be used by G-d to punish in order to renew. In the Jeremian intertext however, the *seismos megas* brings a recognition that "the way of human beings is not in their control" (10:23), while in the Ezek 38:18–23 intertexture, one finds a strong example of the *seismos megas* bringing judgment on the enemies of both G-d and Israel. Such intertexts appear more strongly and function more metaphorically in the developing apocalyptic literature.

For Matthean readers, this *seismos megas* carries this cosmic and metaphoric significance intertextually. It can also draw readers into the ecological texture of the text that encodes the violent storms on the lake, which first-century residents of the lake's waterfront and its fishing industry had come to expect and to relate to in their habitat (Nun 1989, 3).[11] Inter-con/textually and metaphorically, the *seismos megas* could also evoke the political, social, and economic storms that first-century readers faced in the context of the Roman Empire (Carter 2000, 210). In this reading, however, I want to give primary attention to the materiality of the *seismos megas* and the engagement with meaning making in relation to this aspect within the various textures without neglecting the sociopolitical.

Later in Matthew's Gospel, *seismos* has an eschatological and apocalyptic import reminiscent of Ezekiel (Matt 24:7, 54; 28:2). In that context, it characterizes the end times in a future imaginary that belongs to G-d, if Malina's understanding of how time functioned for the Gospel writers is correct (1989). In the Matthean Gospel that future imaginary circles back into the present of Matthean ethics. The response to those eschatological phenomena, which include earthquakes, is to endure to the end so that the good news of the *basileia* will be proclaimed (24:13–14), implying the ongoing activity of disciples to preach that good news. The ecological, ethical, and political intersect in this Matthean narrative as they do in contemporary contexts. There are contexts in which the effects of global warming, which in some instances are the result of sociopolitical and economic nexuses, are threatening entire ecosystems, causing violent storms of earthquake proportions. There are also, as we have seen, movements of earth and water that are an integral part of the incredible story of Earth's complex unfolding. All this is evoked in the Gospel in vivid material terminology: the boat is being covered or swamped by the waves (8:24), reminding me of the wall of water meters high that raced through the streets of Toowoomba or down the Toowoomba range, or through the city of Brisbane during the 2011 flooding, taking cars, furniture, and people, indeed all in its path.

---

11. Nun suggests that the occurrence of sudden storms on the Sea of Galilee led to the constructions of "protected mooring place[s] for their boats" because of the lack of natural inlets. This demonstrates the complex interrelationships within the materiality and sociality of the more-than-human.

In the face of this seismic storm at sea, the text makes the simple statement about Jesus, whose presence we have almost forgotten: he was sleeping (*autos de ekatheuden*). While recognizing the materiality of the cosmic forces evoked in this text, one is also conscious of the metaphorical layer of the text, especially by way of its intertextuality. The simple statement of Jesus's sleeping oblivious to the *seismos megas* evokes Jonah's sleep in the face of a mighty storm (Jonah 1:4–5). In the book of Jonah, however, it is G-d who casts a great wind on the sea, giving rise to the storm, whereas the Matthean text gives no such cause. The *seismos megas* simply appears on the sea.

Bernard F. Batto has drawn attention to further intertextuality, namely, the sleep of the deity in Israel's Scriptures (1987a, 153–77; 1987b, 16–23).[12] He recognizes a twofold theme of G-d resting. The first is as a divine prerogative after the work of creation (and, he says, possibly struggling with chaos). This is akin to the activity of the divine one that Denis Edwards speaks about as

> acting in a way that lovingly respects and accepts the limits of finite processes and entities.... God waits upon, empowers, and enables the 3.7 billion-year history of life on Earth with modern human beings appearing only in the last 200,000 years.... All of this suggests that the God of creation is a God who loves to create through processes that involve emergence and increasing complexity and who is a God of immense patience. (Edwards 2010, 51)

As well as a divine prerogative, Batto recognizes the rest of G-d as symbolic of divine power in a way that seems to be akin to Edwards's theologizing. The call to awake addressed to G-d in the Scriptures functions as a recognition of this power (Batto 1987a, 167).[13] One might also see in this aspect of the G-d who awaits such a call to "awake, awake, put on strength" (Isa 51:9) the "God of temporal process" that Denis Edwards also identifies, the one who "does not yet know the unformed future and interacts with

---

12. It should be noted here that in exploring this intertextuality, there is not an assumption of the later theological claim of the divinity of Jesus but rather the evocation of the sleeping one by the reference to Jesus's sleeping in the face of a *seismos megas* on the sea.

13. Batto notes that "Isa 51,9–11 is the community's lament to the effect that God has no thought for his [sic] people's plight in exile. This is followed by a series of divine assurances (51,12–16; 51,17–23; 52,1–3) that God has not forgotten his [sic] people."

history as it unfolds, responding to its development in the way so often described anthropomorphically in the Bible" (Edwards 2010, 73–74).

In Matthew, as Jesus is asleep in the boat, his bodily posture constructs him as being without fear, as if he knows more than the experience of a *seismos megas* would indicate. Like the rest or sleep of the divine one whose spirit has descended on Jesus at his baptism, Jesus's sleeping manifests his sharing in the imaging of that divinity (prerogative and power) that is with the Earth community (1:23), in right relationships (the *dikaiosynē* of Matt 3:15; 5:6, 10, 20; 6:1, 33).[14] In Jesus asleep in a boat being swamped by the waves, G-d is with the community constructed in the narrative—disciples, boat, *seismos megas*, and the waves—with the Earth community in its unfolding.

The disciples, like the people of Israel before them (Isa 51:9–11; Ps 44:24–25, 27) and those of us after them, are afraid, crying out to Jesus with the title with which readers have become familiar, *Kyrie*. This title carries abundant indicators of power, which can be claimed as power-with in the Matthean context only after it has been critiqued as power-over.[15] The invocation of the disciples—*sōson/*"save"—reminds readers for the first time in the unfolding narrative of the name and the commission given to Jesus in 1:22, the one who will save because he is, as 1:23 indicates, the one in whom divinity enters into a unique relationship *with* us/the Earth community.

Wendy Cotter draws attention here to another intertextuality, namely, that of the sea-storm stories of the Hellenistic era, which find meaning within a "new" cosmology that differed from the three-tiered universe of ancient Israel (Cotter 1997, 118–31). This new cosmology was geocentric, with the orbs of the moon and other planets circling earth. The sublunar sphere between the earth and the moon was the space in which divinely empowered heroes functioned. Augustus was one such hero, of whom Philo says, "This is the Caesar who calmed the torrential storms on every side" (Philo, *Embassy* 144–145). Cotter goes on to draw the conclusion that in the first century C.E. "both Jesus and Augustus are credited with

---

14. Carter (2000, 211) provides examples from classical literature that point to empire/emperor being "master of sea and land" (Apollonius 7.3), the one who has control or power over Earth and all its constituents.

15. This is the critique of the social imaginary of mastery called for by both Lorraine Code and Val Plumwood and discussed earlier in relation to the approach being taken in this essay.

the type of salvific activity which Psalm 107:28–33 reserves for God, ... [who] made the storm be still, and the waves of the sea ... hushed" (Cotter 1997, 126).

Prior to Jesus's calming of the *seismos megas*, however, he rebukes the disciples as being cowardly or afraid (*deiloi*), in language that occurs only here in Matthew's Gospel, and as being of little faith (*oligopistoi*). Of interest here is that the only prior use of *oligopistoi* is in the challenge to those listening to Jesus's preaching on the mountain about the G-d who clothes the grass of the field (6:30), who is concerned lovingly, as Edwards suggests, with the unfolding of all of Earth's constituents and processes (2010, 51). Jesus may be seen, therefore, as likening the cry of the disciples in the face of the *seismos megas* to exhibiting a lack of faith in the loving care of this same G-d.

Jesus's use of the same rebuke, *oligopistoi*, of the disciples, fearful before the *seismos megas* in which they are caught up, seems confronting to us in the face of the powerful movements of sea and earth that we encounter. This sends us back to look again at the *seismos megas* and its eschatological imagery in Matt 24:7: nation will rise against nation, and kingdom against kingdom, and there will be famines and earthquakes in various places. The Matthean response called for in the face of such seismic challenges is an endurance in the preaching of the *basileia*. The disciples have either not yet learned or have lost sight of their being caught up into and implicated in this preaching of the ethic of the *basileia* and the making present of this *basileia* that is of G-d or of the heavens or skies/*ouranōn* (see Matt 4:17, 23; 5:3, 10, 19, 20; 6:10, 33; 7:21). It holds together in the religious imagination of its hearers/readers the materiality of the heavens/skies, these layers of the cosmos, and the transcendent aspects of divinity.

This is the response that the Jesus who is able to sleep through the storm asks of his disciples, the recognition that in the face of the worst of disasters, the proclaiming, the doing of the ethic of the *basileia*, is what is required, because G-d is with the Earth community. This is the faith/*pistis* that this Gospel story calls for—faith that requires a healing of our anthropocentric perspectives, enabling us to enter deeply into a new way of seeing our belonging within the Earth community and, from that belonging, being in relation to the divine who is engaged with Earth in its unfolding. That unfolding will often be beyond our limited capacity to know and/ or to control, beyond the human borders and the boundaries we construct.

The text then, however, seems to move into a different mode as Jesus does, indeed, rise up and rebuke (*epetimēsen*) the wind and the sea, resulting in a great calm. Jesus acts here as does Augustus and other divinely empowered heroes within the Hellenistic cosmos: he exercises authority over the wind and the sea and brings about a great calm. Jesus seems to accede to the disciples' request, which he called faithless, with a bodily gesture of speaking with authority in a way that constructs that authority. And it has an effect—it is as if Jesus has woken up as did the G-d of Isaiah and has acted in response to the cry of distress, linking his power with that of the divine. Problematically, however, the language of rebuke is that used in relation to the demonic (12:16; 17:18) and so can function to construct the *seismos megas* as demonic or as participating in demonic power, that power which lurks in the sublunar realm of the Hellenistic cosmos. It is the narrator who uses this descriptive language, naming the movement on the lake as demonic, perhaps reflecting the inaccurate perspective of the cowardly and "little-faithed" disciples.

These hints of the demonic in understandings of the *seismos megas* and the relationships between the winds and the sea, the disciples and Jesus in this short narrative are confronting. They point to first-century thought that saw the threatening and the demonic as inheriting the sublunar realm between the earth and the moon (Martin 1987, 4–15). For contemporary readers, this hint of evil or the demonic may evoke the unethical attitudes and behaviors among Earth's human constituents that may need to be driven out if Earth's seismic activity is not to be compounded by behaviors that are destructive of the delicate interrelationships within an unfolding universe. This must be a nuanced reading, however, as I do not wish to equate Earth's unfolding in ways that are more powerful than and hence destructive of both the human and other-than-human with the demonic. Indeed, I have sought to demonstrate earlier that such Earth processes are caught up with and in the Divine. Human destruction of Earth's intricate interrelationships, bringing about unusual cosmic movements, ought, however, to be rebuked.

Intertextually, this verse can evoke again the sleeping deity who is awakened by the call of the Earth community (Isa 51:9–11; Ps 44:24–25, 27). "Get up," calls the psalmist in 44:27, "you must come to our rescue and deliver us for the sake of your steadfast love"—language very similar to that of the terrified disciples. We saw that earlier, in Matt 6:30, the ones of little faith were challenged to believe that they would be cared for by G-d, who likewise cares for the "grass of the fields." Jesus's rebuking of the winds and the sea, bringing about a *galēnē megalē*, or great calm, is in contrast to the earlier *seismos megas*, or great movement of Earth. Narratively, it invites the readers to recognize that G-d acts, as Denis Edwards's title suggests (2010), and that the human community is invited to recognize that action in the calm as in the storm. It is, however, action that is subtly caught up with and in the very movements of Earth's unfolding and not interventionist or "interruptionist," on behalf of some Earth constituents and to the detriment of others.

The exclamation of the disciples—"What sort of human person is this!"—recognizes Jesus as Emmanuel, the one in whom divine power is with the Earth community in and through the different moments and movements of Earth's unfolding. For this recognition to be named *pistis* in Gospel terms, it must be attentive to the different moments and movements with/in Earth's unfolding, Earth's breaking of borders, of opening up possibilities of new belongings. It is this that will lead to wonder (*ethaumasan*) and expand the horizons of our thinking and our knowing of G-d and the ways of G-d. This is how G-d is with G-d's Earth community in the Matthean narrative and in those communities that seek to engage with the seismic ecological crises that face us in so many different Earth communities. The power within Earth is seismic, as is that of G-d and of Jesus, who both sleep but then awake to the call of those who are engaged in the ethic of the *basileia* against forces that could destroy them.

Conclusion

This reading sends us back to our initial consideration of flood, earthquake, and tsunami, which can destroy the borders and the boundaries of human, other-than-human, and divine that we have constructed in our anthropocentric imaginary of mastery. Aspects of this mastery have been encoded into the web of our biblical narrative, shaped by the worldviews of its various authors and readers. An ecological reading of the Matthean Gospel's narrative of the calming of the storm brought us as human community to a recognition of the vulnerability of the borders we construct between the human, other-than-human, and divine. For Matthean readers, G-d is with not only the human community but the entire Earth community in Jesus, the human one of the Gospel.

Belonging to communities shaped by this unfolding Gospel story invites readers into the story of Jesus's preaching of a *basileia* of the heavens/skies, which might be envisioned in eschatological seismic activity but which revolves back into the doing of the ethic of the *basileia*. Within this ethical perspective, G-d is envisioned as caring for all Earth's constituents and intimately engaged in Earth's unfolding—not intervening on behalf of individuals or communities but rather inviting them into full engagement with the ethical unfolding of Earth and removing any human activity that would contribute to a disturbance of that unfolding.

The cry "Save us, we are perishing" evokes, therefore, as did the cry of Jason Rice in the Toowoomba flood, human engagement in communities of belonging in the face of and in response to the outcomes of Earth's unfolding movements and moments in and through which G-d is acting. This same cry brings with it the urgency of radically engaging in ecological ethics that will ensure that Earth's movements in flood, earthquake, and tsunami are not of human making. This too will shape communities of belonging, a belonging to Earth's communities, in which the right relationships of the Matthean *basileia* of the heavens/skies might be developed and maintained.

Works Consulted

Batto, Bernard F. 1987a. The Sleeping God: An Ancient Near Eastern Motif of Divine Sovereignty. *Biblica* 68:153–77.

———. 1987b. When God Sleeps. *Bible Review* 111 (4):16–23.

Carter, Warren. 2000. *Matthew and the Margins: A Socio-political and Religious Reading*. Maryknoll: Orbis.

Code, Lorraine. 2006. *Ecological Thinking: The Politics of Epistemic Location*. Studies in Feminist Theology. Oxford: Oxford University Press.

Cotter, Wendy. 1997. Cosmology and the Jesus Miracles. Pages 118–31 in *Whose Historical Jesus?* Edited by William E. Arnal and Michel Desjardins. Waterloo, Ont.: Wilfrid Laurier University Press.

Edwards, Denis. 2010. *How God Acts: Creation, Redemption and Special Divine Action*. Hindmarsh: ATF.

Elvey, Anne. 2011. Partnering the Waters in Luke 8:22–25. *Interface* 14 (1):81–94.

Fogarty, David. 2011. "Scientists See Climate Change Link to Australian Floods." Reuters, January 12. Online: http://www.reuters.com/article/2011/01/12/us-climate-australia-floods-idUSTRE70B1XF20110112.

Fretheim, Terence E. 2010. *Creation Untamed: The Bible, God, and Natural Disasters*. Grand Rapids: Baker Academic.

Horrell, David G., Cherryl Hunt, Christopher Southgate, and Francesca Stavrakopoulou, eds. 2010. *Ecological Hermeneutics: Biblical, Historical and Theological Perspectives*. New York: T&T Clark.

Malina, Bruce J. 1989. Christ and Time: Swiss or Mediterranean? *Catholic Biblical Quarterly* 51:1–31.

Martin, Luther H. 1987. *Hellenistic Religions: An Introduction.* New York: Oxford University Press.

Nun, Mendel. 1989. *Newly Discovered Harbour from New Testament Days around the Sea of Galilee.* Kibbutz Ein Gev: Kinnereth Sailing Co.

Philo. *On the Embassy to Gaius.* 1962. Translated by F. H. Colson. Vol. 10. Loeb Classical Library. Cambridge: Harvard University Press.

Plumwood, Val. 1993. *Feminism and the Mastery of Nature.* Feminism for Today. London: Routledge.

———. 2002. *Environmental Culture: The Ecological Crisis of Reason.* Environmental Philosophies. London: Routledge.

Roach, John. 2006. "Warming Oceans Are Fueling Stronger Hurricanes, Study Finds." *National Geographic News*, March 16. Online: http://news.nationalgeographic.com/news/2006/03/0316_060316_hurricanes.html.

Robbins, Vernon. 1996. *Exploring the Texture of Texts: A Guide to Sociorhetorical Interpretation.* Valley Forge: Trinity Press International.

Saulwick, Jacob. 2011. "'You're My Little Hero': Farewell to 'Weedsy.'" *Brisbane Times*, January 19. http://www.brisbanetimes.com.au/environment/weather/youre-my-little-hero-farewell-to-weedsy-20110119-19w54.html#ixzz1rh5ya7ld.

Smith, Bridie. 2011. "All the Wrong Stars Aligned for Perfect Storms." *The Sydney Morning Herald*, January 12. Online: http://www.smh.com.au/environment/weather/all-the-wrong-stars-aligned-for-perfect-storms-20110111-19mrr.html.

Stewart, Eric C. 2009. *Gathered around Jesus: An Alternative Spatial Practice in the Gospel of Mark.* The Bible in Mediterranean Context. Eugene, Ore.: Cascade.

Volohonsky, H., A. Kaplanovsky, and S. Serruya. 1983. Storms on Lake Kinneret: Observations and Mathematical Model. *Ecological Modelling* 18:141–53.

Wachsmann, Shelley. 1988. The Galilee Boat: 2,000-Year Old Hull Recovered Intact. *Biblical Archaeology Review* 14.5:18–33.

Wainwright, Elaine M. 1991. *Toward a Feminist Critical Reading of the Gospel according to Matthew.* Beihefte zur Zeitschrift für die neutestamentliche Wissenschaft 60. Berlin: de Gruyter.

———. 2010. Place, Power and Potentiality: Reading Matthew 2:1–12 Ecologically. *Expository Times* 121:159–63.

———. 2011. Beyond the Crossroads: Reading Matthew 13:52 Ecologically into the Twenty-First Century. Pages 375–88 in *The Gospel of Matthew at the Crossroads of Early Christianity*. Edited by Donald Senior. Leuven: Peeters.

———. 2012a. "Hear Then the Parable of the Seed": Reading the Agrarian Parables of Matthew 13 Ecologically. Pages 125–41 in *The One Who Reads May Run: Essays in Honour of Edgar W. Conrad*. Edited by Roland Boer, Michael Carden, and Julie Kelso. New York: T&T Clark.

———. 2012b. Images, Words and Stories: Exploring Their Transformative Power in Reading Biblical Texts Ecologically. *Biblical Interpretation* 20:280–304.

Calamity and the Biblical God—Borderline or Line of Belonging? Intratextual Tension in Luke 13

David J. Neville

Since the turn of the millennium, most years to date have witnessed what are typically described as natural disasters. Some of the more memorable, according to the crass criteria of magnitude and mayhem caused, include the 2001 Gujarat earthquake in India, the 2003 Bam earthquake in Iran, the 2004 Sumatra-Andaman earthquake and resultant Indian Ocean tsunami, the 2005 Kashmir earthquake, the 2008 Sichuan earthquake in China and Cyclone Nargis in Burma, the 2010 Haiti earthquake, and the 2011 Tohoku earthquake and tsunami that caused so much devastation in Japan. For the inhabitants of Otautahi Christchurch in Aotearoa New Zealand, 2011 was punctuated by traumatic earthquakes, and Australians are all too familiar with drought, fire, and flood (see also the essays by Rushton and Wainwright in this volume). Around the world, biological life is constantly threatened by tectonic shifts, volcanic eruptions, cyclones, hurricanes, tornados, heat waves, and droughts. Such is life on planet Earth; indeed, it would seem that such must be life.

Natural calamities tend to provoke reflection on ultimate questions, especially for people of faith and even more particularly for people of biblical faith. In view of the temptation to interpret large-scale calamities as instances of divine judgment, is the Bible blessing or bane? In other words, does the Bible sanction the interpretation of natural calamity as divine judgment or warn against doing so? Both, it would seem, which makes the task of responsible and edifying interpretation that much more difficult. Biblical authors attribute both natural and human-engineered calamity to divine agency, oftentimes in response to (alleged) wrongdoing. This might well explain why natural calamities are characterized in certain contexts as "acts of God." For various reasons, however, the purported nexus between calamity and divine agency is perplexing and perturbing. Between the "violence" of natural calamity and the biblical God, is there a dissociating borderline or a binding line of belonging? To explore the relation between calamity and divine agency, this study focuses on Luke 13, which begins with words of Jesus regarding two kinds of calamity and ends with a lament for Jerusalem, one of several prophetic warnings relating to Jerusalem in which catastrophe is apparently interpreted as divine judgment.

Jerusalem in Luke–Acts

Among the canonical Gospel writers, Luke has a particular penchant for Jerusalem. This is partly because he is the only one of the four to write a second volume concerned with the continuation of the story of Jesus in the spread of the earliest church, in which Jerusalem rather than the Galilee serves as the geographical and narrative hinge between Luke's Gospel and Acts. Even in his Gospel, however, Jerusalem is much more central to Luke's symbolic world than it is for any of his biblical counterparts. Unlike the other Gospels, Luke's Gospel both begins and ends in Jerusalem. His narrative proper begins in the sanctuary of the temple, where the priest Zechariah is visited by an angel (Luke 1:5–23). Although Jesus is born in Bethlehem, his parents honor the Torah by taking their baby to the temple in Jerusalem for presentation to the God of Israel, and later the twelve-year-old Jesus displays his precociousness within the temple precincts (2:22–52). At this early stage, Jewish hopes for the "consolation of Israel" and "liberation of Jerusalem" are invested in the infant Jesus (2:25–26, 38).

Like his synoptic counterparts, Luke has Jesus journey from Galilee to Jerusalem to meet his necessary end. (In relation to Jesus's mission, *dei*, "it is necessary," occurs in Luke's Gospel as often as in the other canonical Gospels combined. See especially 9:22; 13:33; 17:25; 22:37; 24:7, 26, 44[–46].) In Luke's narrative, however, the journey to Jerusalem features more prominently than in either Matthew's or Mark's Gospel and serves as the setting for much of Jesus's teaching on various themes. At Jesus's transfiguration, according to Luke 9:30–31, Moses and Elijah discuss with Jesus his forthcoming "exodus," which he is about to fulfill in Jerusalem. When the time for his "taking up" draws near, according to Luke 9:51, Jesus fixes his face for Jerusalem. As in the other Gospels, Jesus is crucified in Jerusalem, but Luke is both distinctive in restricting appearances of the risen Jesus to Jerusalem and its environs (24:1–42) and unique in recounting the risen

Jesus's instruction that his disciples should remain in Jerusalem (24:49). Luke's Gospel concludes with Jesus's departure from his disciples a short distance from Jerusalem, after which they return to Jerusalem to praise God in the temple (24:50–53).

Acts picks up from the Gospel's end, with the disciples in and around Jerusalem. The first seven chapters narrate the church's beginnings at Pentecost, together with both the progress and persecution of the church in Jerusalem. Only at Acts 8:1 does the story move beyond Jerusalem, although it is clear that, for Luke, Jerusalem remains the mother church (8:14–17; 11:1–18; 15:1–33; 21:17–26). Later in Acts, Paul journeys to Jerusalem and runs afoul of Jewish authorities there (19:21; 20:16–23:31), a narrative parallel to Jesus's journey to Jerusalem in Luke's Gospel.

On one hand, then, Jerusalem is central to Luke's narrative and salvation-historical concerns. Not only must Jesus go to Jerusalem, teach and die in Jerusalem, and ascend to heaven from just outside Jerusalem, but the infant church must also be gifted with the Spirit in Jerusalem, establish itself within Jerusalem, and expand outward from Jerusalem. Given the favored status of Jerusalem as the salvation-historical setting for so much of Luke's two-part narrative, however, it is disconcerting that Jerusalem's devastating demise should be emphasized more by Luke than by any of his biblical counterparts. For it is not simply that Jerusalem is accorded favored status within the timeframe of Luke's narrative; the city's imminent destruction construed as divine judgment also features more prominently for Luke than for any other Evangelist.

A series of four passages in Luke's Gospel discloses the author's theological interpretation of Jerusalem's destruction—an event still future, albeit imminent, within Luke's narrative framework but in all likelihood an event from the recent past for Luke himself.[1] Midway through Luke's central section comprising Jesus's journey to Jerusalem, some Pharisees warn Jesus of Herod Antipas's intent to kill him. Jesus responds cryptically, concluding with the hyperbolic remark that it is impossible for a prophet to perish outside Jerusalem (13:31–33). This then provokes the first of four warnings for Jerusalem (13:34–35), couched in lament form, and the only one of the four paralleled in another Gospel, albeit in a different context (cf. Matt 23:37–39).

---

1. For more detailed studies of these Lukan "omens" (13:34–35; 19:41–44; 21:20–24; 23:28–31), see Tiede (1980, 65–96), Chance (1988, 115–27), and Walker (1996, 69–80).

At the culmination of Jesus's journey, immediately preceding Jesus's entry into the temple, Luke records Jesus's weeping over the city of Jerusalem and prophesying its besiegement and destruction for failing to recognize in his arrival divine "visitation" (Luke 19:41–44). Later, while teaching in the temple, Jesus elaborates on this warning, describing the inevitable trampling of Jerusalem by Gentiles as "days of vengeance" (21:20–24; cf. Hos 9:7). Finally, en route to his crucifixion and in response to some women wailing on his behalf, Jesus recommends lamenting for themselves and for their children, because the time is near when inhabitants of Jerusalem will wish for death (Luke 23:26–31). The cryptic rationale for Jesus's response in the form of a proverbial question in Luke 23:31 is difficult to convey in English, but its gist is as follows: if this can be done to a green, living tree—Jesus himself—what is likely to happen after it has been hacked down? Implicit within the question is the forecast that the fate of the green tree will be visited upon those responsible for its felling, perhaps even that the dead, dry wood of the once-green tree will kindle the inevitable conflagration.

As the first of four warnings of disaster soon to befall Jerusalem, Luke 13:34–35 gains in clarity from being read with the set of Lukan warnings taken together. Seen in light of the later, more explicit, warnings of Jerusalem's destruction construed as divine retribution for Jewish rejection of Jesus and his mission, the lament of Luke 13:34–35 is but the first step of this textual trajectory. On the other hand, there are countervailing winds both in Luke 13 and within its broader narrative framework.

Observations on Luke 13

Luke 13 occurs midway through Luke's central section, in which Jesus meanders toward Jerusalem. A rare reference to Jesus's journey toward Jerusalem occurs at Luke 13:22, which precedes his first lament for Jerusalem by one pericope.[2] As the first explicit reference to Jesus's movement toward Jerusalem since the beginning of his Jerusalem-oriented journey (9:51–53), Luke 13:22 appears to be a literary seam dividing the earlier part of this chapter from what follows. Nevertheless, there are reasons to read

---

2. Jesus's travelogue en route to Jerusalem is provided by Luke *9:51–53*, 56–57; 10:1, 38; *13:22, 31–33*; *17:11*; *18:31*, 35; *19:1, 11, 28–45* (texts in italics explicitly identify Jerusalem as Jesus's destination). With Matera (1993, 57–58), I consider Luke 19:45–46 to be the culmination of Luke's central section.

the beginning and end of Luke 13 in light of each other. Not only is each passage in close proximity to the reminder in Luke 13:22 of Jesus's journey toward Jerusalem, but each also makes reference to Jerusalem, and in each Jesus pronounces a prophetic warning if things do not change. Also noteworthy is that Luke 13:1–5 makes reference to Pilate, Rome's representative in Judea, and 13:31–35 makes reference to Herod Antipas, Rome's vicegerent in Galilee and Perea. In other words, both passages foreground the sociopolitical context of imperial hegemony, and neither depicts the powers that be as benign.

In both Luke 13:1–5 and 13:31–35, people approach Jesus with news of current events, provoking a response on Jesus's part. On the earlier occasion, Jesus is informed about fellow Galileans slaughtered by Pilate, apparently while offering sacrifices. Jesus responds provocatively: "Do you consider that these Galileans happened to be greater sinners than all other Galileans because they suffered these things? No, I tell you, but unless you change, you will all perish similarly" (13:2–3).[3] He then reminds his audience of a calamitous episode in which eighteen people were killed at Siloam by a tower collapsing, reiterating both his question and his challenge to change in close to identical terms. In fact, the wording of his call for repentance, radical change, is identical except for the use of synonymous penultimate words. This reinforces both the rhetorical effect of Jesus's question and the urgency of his call for change so as to avoid perishing inexplicably.

In each case, Jesus's question dismantles any supposition that death came to the Galileans killed by Pilate or to the eighteen upon whom a tower collapsed because they somehow deserved their fate more than others. Not so, retorts Jesus. Instead of further undermining the logic that those who die terrible or inexplicable deaths somehow have it coming, however, Jesus unsettles his listeners by saying that similar deaths await those who refuse radically to reorient their attitudes and lives. This probably means that those who do not change will either die unprepared for eschatological judgment (Reiser 1997, 249) or experience imminent ruin by Roman forces (Schottroff 2006, 59), not that they will suffer exactly the same fate as the Galileans or the eighteen killed by a falling tower. Indeed, the repetition of the call for repentance reveals that the manner of death is not the point, since unrepentant listeners could not be both cut down intentionally and accidentally crushed. That people die prematurely and

---

3. Unless otherwise indicated, all translations of Lukan texts are my own.

unexpectedly is what we might call a fact of life, and Jesus seizes upon this reality to call for radical change.

In the wake of earthquakes, tsunamis, floods, and fire, what is most compelling about the sayings in Luke 13:1–5 is Jesus's refusal to blame the victim, his severing of the nexus between catastrophe and personal culpability. Calamities occur, but nothing can be inferred about the character or spiritual state of those who perish as a result of human malice or natural calamity. Nor, indeed, are such events attributable directly to God, because the only reason for interpreting such events as punishments of God—greater culpability—is denied. Rome's representative in Judea kills Galileans while they are worshiping God, but Jesus denies any possible inference regarding personal culpability or divine agency. The same logic holds for the eighteen killed accidentally by a falling tower; a tower collapsed and people died, but their deaths signal nothing about either their respective characters or divine involvement.

On the other hand, a rather different logic seems to undergird the lament for Jerusalem in Luke 13:34–35. Although not forthright about the inevitability of, and rationale for, Jerusalem's demise, Luke 13:34–35 nevertheless intimates envisaging Jerusalem's destruction as divine punishment. Three considerations support such a conclusion. First, Luke 13:34–35 is of a piece with later Lukan passages that more explicitly associate Jerusalem's destruction with divine judgment. Second, this lament follows hard upon Jesus's affirmation that it is incongruent for a prophet to perish outside Jerusalem. When he is warned of Herod's intent to kill him, Jesus's response does not signal a stratagem of avoidance. To the contrary, he expressly signals his intent to complete his journey to Jerusalem so that he might meet death where prophetic precursors met theirs. The reference to Jerusalem as the necessary locus for his death provokes the following lament, in which Jerusalem is pictured as resisting Jesus's determination to protect its inhabitants from impending harm. Those who have witnessed a hen calling her clutch of chicks under her wings for protection are able to appreciate what a striking image this is. According to Jesus's word picture, however, his warning of danger falls on deaf ears; the chicks scatter rather than gather under this mother bird's wings.

A third consideration in support of reading this lament as intimating calamity conceived as divine retribution is the opening statement of Luke 13:35, "Look, your [plural] house is left to you." In context, this most plausibly means that either Jerusalem as a whole or perhaps the temple (as Jerusalem's reason for being) is abandoned by God for failing to respond positively to Jesus. Taken alone, Luke 13:35a might be understood to mean that Jerusalem (or the temple at its heart) is left to its own devices rather than being the direct object of divine retribution for refusing the prophetic entreaties of Jesus. When this saying is interpreted alongside its textual siblings, however, it is difficult to avoid reading the saying as intimating divine judgment against Jerusalem. Indeed, if Luke 13:35a is intentionally reminiscent of Jer 12:7 or 22:5, abandonment into the hands of enemies is but the mode of divine judgment (Travis 2009, 217–18).

So, Luke 13 begins with sayings of Jesus that prohibit interpreting calamity as divine judgment but ends with a saying that in all likelihood envisages Jerusalem's calamitous destruction as divine payback. What is one to make of this intratextual tension? While Luke apparently understood Jerusalem's destruction by Rome in terms of divine retribution for failing to embrace Jesus and his prophetic message, most clearly articulated in Luke 19:43–44 and 21:20–24, other features of Luke's literary legacy give one pause. After all, Luke is the Evangelist of peace, and the broader literary context of Luke 13 calls into question both the logic of retribution and the possibility of inferring divine involvement from calamitous events.

Luke as the Evangelist of Peace

Various interrelated reasons can be given for designating Luke the Evangelist of peace. Willard Swartley (2006, 121–76) has demonstrated how central peace is to Luke's theological and moral vision. First, the vocabulary of peace is much more prominent in Luke's Gospel than in any of the other canonical Gospels. Swartley points out that the Greek term for peace, ἡ εἰρήνη (*hē eirēnē*), occurs fourteen times in Luke's Gospel, with only one parallel occurrence in Mark 5:34 and one parallel occurrence in Matt 10:34. The peace motif is sounded at Luke 1:79; 2:14, 29; 7:50; 8:48 (cf. Mark 5:34); 10:5–6 (three occurrences); 11:21; 12:51 (cf. Matt 10:34); 14:32; 19:38, 42; and 24:36 (Swartley 2006, 122).[4] Luke's more frequent usage of the terminology of peace signals the theological and ethical significance he attached to this theme, but it is not simply frequency of occurrence that counts. Most references to peace within Luke's Gospel are theologically and/or morally weighted.

---

4. Notably, however, the peace greeting in Luke 24:36 is textually uncertain, and both 11:21 and 14:32 lack the theological depth of the other references to peace.

Equally important is Swartley's observation that most of Luke's distinctive peace references occur at structurally significant junctures in his Gospel:

> Three uses occur in Luke's infancy narratives (1:79; 2:14, 29) and thus set the mood of peace expectancy: the announced coming one will bring *eirēnē* as a new and unprecedented historical reality. A second structurally strategic cluster comes close to the beginning and end of Luke's special section (10:5–6; 19:38, 42). Jesus' teachings on discipleship that leads to the kingdom of God are framed by peace emphases. And conversely, when *eirēnē* is refused, judgment follows (10:10–12; 19:43–46). Jesus' *eirēnē* thus brings crisis, a point clearly expressed in 12:51. The third structurally crucial occurrence is 24:36 where peace is the resurrected Lord's self-identifying greeting to his disciples. (Swartley 2006, 129–30)

The significantly greater number of references to peace, the theological and/or moral weight of most such references, and their strategic narrative plotting combine to compel the conclusion that peace is central to Luke's understanding of Jesus's identity and the significance of his mission. Moreover, although the book of Acts fails to foreground the peace theme as much as does Luke's Gospel, Acts 10:36 reinforces the tight thematic connection between Christology and peace by summing up, in a crucial speech by Peter, Jesus's mission in its entirety as God's peace proclamation to Israel.

Beyond Luke's explicit references to peace and their narrative role, Swartley identifies three other Lukan features that bolster his peace emphasis. First, even though Luke records no blessing on peacemakers (cf. Matt 5:9), Swartley (2006, 130–31) shows how the content and arrangement of Jesus's teaching in Luke 6:27–36, the central section of Luke's parallel to Matthew's Sermon on the Mount, accentuate (peacemaking and peace-promoting) love of enemies. Second, Swartley (2006, 133–34) documents that Luke's sociopolitical stance is critically countercultural in relation to deep-set Roman values but nevertheless congruent with a peaceful moral vision. Significant dimensions of this peaceful moral vision include concern for those such as the poor, the infirm, and the disreputable ordinarily disregarded by those with power, rank, and status; a critique of wealth and the wealthy; condemnation of injustice and oppression, matched by a call for social relations to be based on humble service; and repudiation of violence. And third, complementing Luke's focus on peace, Swartley (2006, 140–44) draws attention to the prominence within Luke's Gospel of the terminology of righteousness or justice (δίκαιος, δικαιοσύνη, δικαιοῦν; *dikaios, dikaiosynē, dikaioun*). In Lukan perspective, Jesus both proclaims and embodies peace with justice, whether peace-as-the-fruit-of-justice or justice-as-the-mode-of-peace.

Within a narrative featuring the theme of peace in its most pregnant christological sense, it is theologically and morally incongruent that Luke should interpret Jerusalem's destruction by Rome as divine retribution. That on this matter his perspective should resonate with that of Jewish contemporaries such as Josephus and the authors of 4 Ezra and 2 Baruch reveals that he was, unavoidably, a person of his era. Although in certain respects Luke was capable of seeing things differently from his contemporaries as a result of reflecting on Jesus's mission and message, Luke's Christology of peace seems not to have nuanced his interpretation of Jerusalem's destruction. On this point, therefore, one is entitled to question whether Luke perceived and internalized all that follows—or should follow—from his Christology of peace. If the vision of God inherent in Luke's conceptualization of Jerusalem's destruction as divine judgment is incongruent with an understanding of Jesus as God's peace proclamation to Israel, where does that leave Luke's interpreters today? Perhaps closer attention to some of Luke's peace texts brings one closer to a responsible answer.

Luke 13 within Luke's Central Section (9:51–19:46)

To reiterate, the broader narrative context of Luke 13 is Luke's distinctive central section, within which Jesus journeys toward Jerusalem and, en route, instructs his disciples regarding discipleship, prayer, wealth, and divine mercy. This central section begins at Luke 9:51–53, where Jesus fixes his face for Jerusalem, sends messengers ahead of him, and is rebuffed by Samaritan villagers precisely because he is bound for Jerusalem. Although Luke 10:38 has Jesus and his entourage going on their way, Luke 13:22 is the first explicit resumption of the motif of Jesus journeying toward Jerusalem sounded at the beginning of the section.[5] In other words, this narrative transition constitutes the first explicit reminiscence

---

5. Luke 13:22 is significant not only because it is reminiscent of Jesus's journey toward Jerusalem but also because it provides the rationale for Luke's structuring of his central section. The journey motif serves Luke's purpose of presenting Jesus's teaching in a memorable way. The way of Jesus is taught on the way to Jerusalem. In narrative terms, Luke 13:22 is reinforced by 13:31–35.

of Jesus's intentional journey to Jerusalem and thereby recalls this journey's beginnings.

Earlier, in support of identifying Luke as the Evangelist of peace, I cited Swartley's observation that references to peace enclose Luke's central section. On closer inspection, however, things are not quite so neat and tidy. First, although the peace theme is sounded three times in Luke 10:5-6, this is a pericope or two into Luke's central section, not at its outset. Moreover, although Swartley's bracketing texts, Luke 10:1–16 and 19:28–44, undoubtedly contain a number of references to peace, such peace references are juxtaposed alongside warnings of divine vengeance (10:10–16; 19:43–44), which might seem to diminish the persuasiveness of Swartley's appeal to their structural significance. For Swartley (2006, 125–26), the three peace references near the beginning of Luke's central section signal four key points: first, that peace is intrinsic to the gospel; second, that the purpose of Jesus's mission is to search out children of peace; third, that "the peace gospel is God's way in Jesus and his followers to subdue evil"; and fourth, that the worldwide mission (symbolized by the Seventy) is to spread the gospel precisely as a gospel of peace.[6] Swartley's third point, cited verbatim, is critical because in this instance he articulates something fundamentally true to Luke, even if not carried through consistently. The point is this: in Luke's presentation, Jesus's peace proclamation is not simply well meaning but is precisely the means by which God undoes antagonistic forces. This interpretive claim finds support in the passage that opens Luke's central section, which in various ways anticipates the sending of the Seventy-Two.

The phrasing of Luke 10:1 echoes that of 9:52 (literally, "and he sent … ahead of his face"), and in each instance those sent by Jesus are precursors in the sense of preparing for his coming. Moreover, the paired themes of rejection and response to rejection are prominent in each passage, provided one accepts Luke 10:13–16 as part of the pericope beginning at 10:1. As a result, Luke 10:1–16, within which occur three references to peace, may be read as anticipated by 9:51–56. At the beginning of Jesus's journey to Jerusalem, according to Luke, when Jesus sends out emissaries in the wake of his experience of rejection by a Samaritan village, he does so with a message of peace on their lips. Furthermore, in view of Jesus's rejection

---

6. Swartley accepts the textual reading of "seventy" in Luke 10:1, whereas I consider "seventy-two" to be more likely original.

of violent retaliation in Luke 9:54–55, one wonders whether his warning of judgment in 10:12–15 should not be understood as prophetic hyperbole to emphasize the seriousness of rejecting his message, which according to 10:16 constitutes a rejection of God.

Although the vocabulary of peace may not appear in the opening pericope of Luke's central section, the theme of peace does. In response to the question by James and John whether the inhospitable Samaritans deserve a bolt from the blue, Jesus repudiates the suggestion of divine vengeance for failure to welcome him (see Allison 2002, 459–78). Seen in light of this opening, anticipatory passage of Luke's central section, the instructed peace greeting in Luke 10:5 as the very first utterance on the part of the Seventy-Two takes on added significance. As if to emphasize that peace is integral to his good news, despite prior rejection and fully cognizant of vulnerability (10:3), Jesus has his emissaries speak peace and permit peace to do its work, whether by remaining or returning (10:6).

At the culmination of Luke's central section, he shares with his synoptic counterparts the story of Jesus's approach to Jerusalem on a borrowed donkey. Among the distinctive features of Luke's account, however, is the double occurrence of the peace theme. In Luke 19:38, the company of disciples praise God in these words: "Blessed be the one coming, *the king*, in the Lord's name; *in heaven peace and glory* in the highest heavens."[7] Then follows a uniquely Lukan passage in which Jesus first responds to the demand of some Pharisees that he rebuke his disciples for their song of praise and subsequently utters an oracle of doom against Jerusalem. Weeping over the city, Jesus exclaims: "If only you had realized this day those things that lead to peace, but now they are concealed from your eyes" (19:42). Twice in close compass, then, Luke's peace theme recurs at the conclusion of his central section.

For Swartley (2006, 127), "the structural function of these two *eirēnē* texts, closing off Luke's special section, underscores the prominence that Luke assigns to *eirēnē*." Perhaps so, but once again Luke's peace theme occurs alongside the threat of divine vengeance. Jesus's tearful oracle of woe against Jerusalem begins with his lament over the city's blindness *this day* to those things that lead to peace. This note of timing suggests that the things that lead to peace reside in the one who has arrived at the city *as king* in the name of the Lord (19:38a). Jesus's prophecy of Jerusalem's siege

---

7. The italicized phrases are distinctive to Luke.

and sacking, in language quite close to what occurred in 70 C.E., envisages Jerusalem's destruction as punishment for failing to recognize divine visitation in Jesus's arrival to the city (19:44). As at the beginning of Luke's central section, there are discordant notes at its end.

Most perplexing of all, perhaps, is that Jesus's oracle of doom in Luke 19:41–44 is at odds with his response to Samaritan rejection at the beginning of his journey to Jerusalem (9:51–56). Earlier, Jesus repudiated divine vengeance against the unreceptive, but now he apparently considers Jerusalem's recalcitrance worthy of divine recompense by means of destruction by its enemies.

It has been noted that the lament for Jerusalem at journey's end is reminiscent of the lament in Luke 13:34–35. Also reminiscent of the lament for Jerusalem in Luke 13, however, is the first half of the paean of praise voiced by the disciples as Jesus approaches Jerusalem: "Blessed be the one coming, the king, in the Lord's name" (19:38a). That this is not the fulfillment of the earlier conditional prophecy in Luke 13:35 is indicated by the fact that this praise is uttered only by disciples and provokes annoyance on the part of some Pharisees. Perhaps Luke envisaged Jesus's disciples as speaking proleptically for Jerusalem. It is certainly the response Luke considered appropriate upon Jesus's arrival to Jerusalem.

Whereas the first half of the disciples' paean of praise in Luke 19:38 echoes the lament for Jerusalem in 13:34–35, the second half echoes the praise of the heavenly host in 2:14, "Glory be to God in the highest heavens, and on earth peace among people (divinely) favored." In form and content, the praise of the disciples in Luke 19:38 mirrors the praise of the heavenly host in 2:14 (Mauser 1992, 46–50). As a result, the praise of the disciples may be read as an earthly echo of heavenly praise. This compositional resonance thereby reinforces the peaceable character of Jesus's mission and in doing so relativizes the note of divine vengeance. Not only so, but the visitation motif in Luke 19:41–44 is reminiscent of Zechariah's prophecy of praise in 1:68–79, in which divine visitation is closely associated with the way of peace. Thus, both compositional echoes of the lament for Jerusalem in Luke 13:34–35 also echo earlier passages in which the new work of God begun in the births of John and Jesus is characterized in peaceable terms.

Intratextual tension within Luke 13 is matched by the thematic tension between peace and divine vengeance at both the beginning and end of Luke's central section. Textual and thematic tension of this kind is hardly susceptible to neat resolution, but simply to affirm both as features of divine action within Luke's narrative world potentially leads to a schizoid theological outlook at odds with Luke's Christology of peace. To appropriate the theological and moral vision of the Evangelist of peace in a responsible and edifying way today, what interpretive resources may be marshaled?

Hermeneutical Reflections

Nearly two millennia separate Luke from his present-day readers, and the sociocultural gap between his day and ours is unbridgeable. At this distance, it behooves us to avoid crassly anachronistic interpretive maneuvers. On the other hand, to risk hermeneutical anachronism may be unavoidable in view of features of Luke's literary legacy that are central to but not wholly integrated into his theological and moral vision.

It has been argued that Luke is the Evangelist of peace principally because he articulates a Christology of peace. For Luke, Jesus's mission in its entirety constitutes a divine overture of peace to Israel (Acts 10:36). On the other hand, as Luke 13:33 reveals, Luke's Christology has a pronounced prophetic dimension to it. In one of Luke's signature stories, the encounter with the risen Jesus en route to Emmaus, not only is Jesus affirmed as a prophet but the prophetic tradition is indispensable to his explication of the necessity of his own "messianic suffering" (Luke 24:13-27; cf. 24:44-47). Even more telling is the response to the uniquely Lukan story of the raising of a widow's son near Nain (7:11-17), in which Jesus's prophetic identity is juxtaposed with Luke's distinctive theme of divine visitation: "A great prophet has arisen in our midst," and "God has visited his people" (7:16).

Within the prophetic tradition, the destruction of Jerusalem by the Babylonians in 587 B.C.E. was interpreted as divine judgment (2 Kgs 21–25; Jer 12:7-13; 13:20-27; 25:1-14; Ezek 14:12–15:8; cf. Lam 2). When Jerusalem experienced the same fate at the hands of the Romans in 70 C.E., it was perhaps natural to echo this scriptural tradition. In *An Introduction to the Gospels and Acts*, Puskas and Crump (2008, 146-47) aver that "if Luke's depiction of Jesus as Israel's final prophet reflects an authentic reminiscence of the historical Jesus, then condemning the city in which he is finally rejected and crucified, using language borrowed from his prophetic predecessors, is precisely what one would expect him to do."[8] Well and

---

8. I cite this introductory text because it illustrates how readily scholars writing for students slide over theological and moral pressure points within biblical texts.

good—provided Jesus brought nothing new to the profile of a prophet. It is one thing to affirm Jesus's foresight of the inevitability of Jerusalem's destruction, quite another to belabor that inevitable demise as divine vengeance for failing to respond positively to Jesus and his message.

Israel's prophetic heritage helps to explain why Luke may have interpreted Jerusalem's destruction as divine vengeance, but it also provides a resource for reading Luke more hopefully. Prophecies of divine judgment were sometimes conditional. Moreover, beyond destruction as divine judgment, prophets sometimes dared to hope for forgiveness and restoration. Chris Marshall (2001, 165) notes how various Lukan pronouncements of divine judgment on Jerusalem seemingly allude to Hos 9–10 and in light of this comments: "Yet just as Hosea's threats are followed by the counternote of mercy ... so Jesus' warnings of judgment are not necessarily the last word on the matter but are meant to provoke Israel to repentance."[9]

Similarly, in a study of the laments for Jerusalem in Luke 13:31–35 and 19:41–44, Bruce Fisk (2008, 147–78) argues for interpreting these forebodings of judgment against Jerusalem as similar in kind to Jeremiah's provisional prophecies of judgment followed up by promises of restoration. Fisk makes three points that bear on whether Luke's conception of Jerusalem's destruction as divine vengeance undermines his peace-oriented theology. First, Fisk follows Dale Allison (1983, 75–84) by interpreting Luke 13:35b as a contingent prophecy, thereby allowing for the prospect of hope beyond calamity, especially if the two laments in Luke 13 and 19 are read in light of each other. Second, he notes that the lament for Jerusalem in Luke 19:41–44 is restricted to the immediate future, again leaving open the possibility of restoration beyond devastation. And third, he draws attention to frequent offers of forgiveness within Luke–Acts subsequent to Jesus's prophecy of woe against Jerusalem. Together, these considerations lead Fisk to suggest that, for Luke, the judgment meted out on Jerusalem may not be God's final word for Jerusalem.

Although Marshall and Fisk detect a glimmer of hope beyond calamity, their observations do not ameliorate the theological tension for the Evangelist of peace caused by his acceptance of Jerusalem's destruction as divine judgment.[10] In this respect, Luke's thinking would seem to be

---

9. Marshall detects the following Lukan allusions to Hosea: Luke 13:6–9 / Hos 9:10, 13, 16; Luke 19:41–44 / Hos 9:7; 10:2, 4; Luke 21:22 / Hos 9:7; Luke 23:28–31 / Hos 10:8.

10. Fisk follows those who perceive Jerusalem's judgment within Luke–Acts in

shaped more by Deuteronomistic ideology than by his own christological convictions.

One way of interpreting the theme of divine judgment in the Hebrew Bible is to envisage the created order as constructed so that certain actions bring about inevitable negative consequences (see Koch 1955, 1–42). In a closely interrelated web of life, this makes ecological sense and is applicable to certain current crises such as exponential population growth, dying waterways, topsoil erosion, and global warming. Brendan Byrne (2000, 156) interprets the lament of Luke 19:41–44 along such lines: "The destruction is not so much a divine punishment as a consequence of the fateful choice that Jerusalem makes." It is doubtful, however, whether the scriptural conception of divine judgment can be wholly reduced to an act-consequence construct (see Via 2007, 14–22), even if it helpfully encourages interpreters to desist from attributing this or that natural event, calamitous or otherwise, to divine inte(rve)ntion. In *Creation Untamed*, Terence Fretheim (2010) appeals fairly frequently to the act-consequence construct, albeit within a created order in process of becoming precisely by means of natural calamities (alongside other natural agencies and processes). Insofar as human actions produce negative consequences by exacerbating natural calamities, such consequences may be interpreted as divine judgments, but natural calamities themselves are integral to a world in process of becoming. Seen from this perspective, there seems to be an inevitable association or line of belonging between calamity and the biblical God, even though this is difficult to integrate into a christologically oriented theological vision.

Reflecting upon intratextual tension within Luke 13 seems inevitably to lead to questions regarding divine action in the world. If Fretheim is correct that the biblical understanding of creation is of a world in process of becoming, then perhaps certain aspects of process thought should feature in attempts to interpret calamitous events. Or perhaps the Thomistic notion of secondary causality needs to play a greater role in biblical

---

tragic terms, e.g., Tiede (1980, 65–96) and Tannehill (1985, 69–85). Such a perspective holds out hope for Jerusalem beyond calamity construed as divine judgment and also helps to counter charges of Lukan "anti-Semitism." Anticipation of divine judgment expressed in the form of lament is also hermeneutically significant. This perspective nevertheless fails to resolve a deep-seated theological tension if, indeed, both the Christ-event ("divine visitation" in Jesus) and the wholesale destruction of Jerusalem are attributed to divine action.

interpretation. Then again, in view of the profound mystery of God, which relates to divine action no less than to God's being, perhaps what is most important to affirm in the face of natural calamity is twofold: first, the inherent goodness of life in our world, which makes life cut short by calamity so maddeningly incomprehensible; and second, hope in God's competence and capacity ultimately to bring the world to its intended end, by whatever circuitous route.

Ultimately, the intratextual tension one finds in Luke 13 and, indeed, within Luke's Gospel as a whole unsettles any easy association between calamity of any kind and divine judgment. Without denying that calamity may legitimately be interpreted as divine judgment, most especially when such an interpretation arises from *self*-examination,[11] Luke's Christology of peace would seem to support the logic inherent in those sayings of Jesus at the beginning of Luke 13, in which victims are not blamed and God is not immediately implicated, however responsible God might be for the inner dynamics of our world.

Works Consulted

Allison, Dale C., Jr. 1983. Matt. 23:39 = Luke 13:35b as a Conditional Prophecy. *Journal for the Study of the New Testament* 18:75–84.

———. 2002. Rejecting Violent Judgment: Luke 9:52–56 and Its Relatives. *Journal of Biblical Literature* 121:459–78.

Byrne, Brendan. 2000. *The Hospitality of God: A Reading of Luke's Gospel*. Collegeville, Minn.: Liturgical Press.

Chance, J. Bradley. 1988. *Jerusalem, the Temple, and the New Age in Luke-Acts*. Macon: Mercer University Press.

Fisk, Bruce N. 2008. *See My Tears*: A Lament for Jerusalem (Luke 13:31–35; 19:41–44). Pages 147–78 in *The Word Leaps the Gap: Essays on Scripture and Theology in Honor of Richard B. Hays*. Edited by J. Ross Wagner et al. Grand Rapids: Eerdmans.

Fretheim, Terence E. 2010. *Creation Untamed: The Bible, God, and Natural Disasters*. Grand Rapids: Baker Academic.

Koch, Klaus. 1955. Gibt es ein Vergeltungsdogma im Alten Testament? *Zeitschrift für Theologie und Kirche* 52:1–42. English translation: Is

---

11. Cf. Via (2007, 60–80), who offers a "hermeneutics of judgment" in relation to 9/11.

There a Doctrine of Retribution in the Old Testament? Pages 57–87 in *Theodicy in the Old Testament*. Edited by James L. Crenshaw. Philadelphia: Fortress, 1983.

Marshall, Christopher D. 2001. *Beyond Retribution: A New Testament Vision for Justice, Crime, and Punishment*. Grand Rapids: Eerdmans.

Matera, Frank J. 1993. Jesus' Journey to Jerusalem (Luke 9:51–19:46): A Conflict with Israel. *Journal for the Study of the New Testament* 51:57–77.

Mauser, Ulrich. 1992. *The Gospel of Peace: A Scriptural Message for Today's World*. Louisville: Westminster John Knox.

Puskas, Charles B., and David Crump. 2008. *An Introduction to the Gospels and Acts*. Grand Rapids: Eerdmans.

Reiser, Marius. 1997. *Jesus and Judgment: The Eschatological Proclamation in Its Jewish Context*. Translated by Linda M. Maloney. Minneapolis: Fortress.

Schottroff, Luise. 2006. *The Parables of Jesus*. Translated by Linda M. Maloney. Minneapolis: Fortress.

Swartley, Willard M. 2006. *Covenant of Peace: The Missing Peace in New Testament Theology and Ethics*. Grand Rapids: Eerdmans.

Tannehill, Robert C. 1985. Israel in Luke–Acts: A Tragic Story. *Journal of Biblical Literature* 104:69–85.

Tiede, David L. 1980. *Prophecy and History in Luke–Acts*. Philadelphia: Fortress.

Travis, Stephen H. 2009. *Christ and the Judgement of God: The Limits of Divine Retribution in New Testament Thought*. Rev. ed. Peabody, Mass.: Hendrickson.

Via, Dan O. 2007. *Divine Justice, Divine Judgment: Rethinking the Judgment of Nations*. Minneapolis: Fortress.

Walker, Peter W. L. 1996. *Jesus and the Holy City: New Testament Perspectives on Jerusalem*. Grand Rapids: Eerdmans.

On the Crossroads between Life and Death: Reading Birth Imagery in John in the Earthquake-Changed Regions of Otautahi Christchurch

Kathleen P. Rushton

The first earthquake in the Otautahi Christchurch region was magnitude 7.1 at 4:35 a.m. on September 4, 2010. There was some property damage but no loss of life. The second earthquake was magnitude 6.3 on Tuesday, February 22, 2011, at lunchtime. It was closer to the city. There were 185 fatalities and numerous injuries. The third earthquake was magnitude 6.3 on June 13, 2011. There was further property damage and some serious injuries but no loss of life. The fourth earthquake was magnitude 6.0 on December 23, 2011. There was further property damage but no serious injuries.[1] Up until April 7, 2012, 10,292 earthquakes and aftershocks have been recorded.[2] A considerable number of these have been of magnitude 5.0 and above.[3] The situation is ongoing and may take years, even decades, before the high levels of stress in the earth's crust are fully dispelled. Earthquake activity will accompany this.

The city of Otautahi Christchurch and the surrounding regions are much changed. A recent visitor noted there is a different sense of time—"before the earthquakes" and "after the earthquakes." Usually cranes on the skyline of a city indicate a construction boom, but in Christchurch they mean unprecedented destruction. The Central Business District (CBD) has fenced borders. It has been closed since February 22, 2011, with the

---

1. On major aftershocks, see "Canterbury News," GeoNet, http://info.geonet.org.nz/display/home/Canterbury+News.

2. "Christchurch Quake Map," http://www.christchurchquakemap.co.nz/all.

3. "Aftershocks," GeoNet, http://info.geonet.org.nz/display/home/Aftershocks. For a visual sequence, see http://www.canterburyquakelive.co.nz.

loss of about 8,000 businesses. By February 2012 there had been more than 970 demolitions or partial demolitions of earthquake-hit buildings out of the almost 1,400 that are required to come down either fully or partially (Gorman 2012b).[4] Included are many heritage buildings. Even those who know the city well lose their bearings amid blocks now cleared of familiar landmarks. The intense shaking of the February 2011 quake, especially in the eastern suburbs, made the damage caused by liquefaction among the most extensive in the world, as up to 500,000 metric tons of gray silt erupted from the ground. Since June of 2011, the city and surrounding residential areas are color coded according to the findings of the government land report: red for land understood to be too damaged to repair economically; orange for properties requiring further assessment; green for land where rebuilding may start; and white for land needing more geotechnical work. Churches have been affected badly, with all denominations sustaining the loss of key churches and many others.[5]

I learned much about my own sense of belonging. At the time of the earthquake of February 22, I was asleep, safely in bed, as I was on sabbatical in Cambridge, U.K. I woke up about 1:30 a.m. and switched on BBC radio, soon to hear that just over an hour ago yet another serious earthquake had hit my home city and that there was loss of life. I returned at the end of November to a region where the borders and the sense of belonging had shifted at the levels of home, street, and work and cultural, religious, and sports facilities. Welfare agencies report immense hardship and an upsurge in family stress and violence. Neighborhoods have been uprooted and abandoned. Months of waiting for assessment on the color zoning of properties leave people in a quagmire of uncertainty and entangled in insurance claims. Those on low incomes or unemployed have no such backup. The price of rental housing has skyrocketed. Distrust of local and national government is prevalent. Loss of jobs and businesses has meant that many valued citizens have migrated from the region.

Aotearoa New Zealand has Pacific Ocean borders of over fifteen thousand kilometers, making it the tenth-longest coastline in the world. In addition, there is another often overlooked border—a fiery border. Aotearoa, the Land of the Long White Cloud, is situated on the Pacific Rim's Ring of Fire, which is a forty-thousand-kilometer arc of fault lines, ocean

---

4. See also "Demolitions," Canterbury Earthquake Recovery Authority, http://cera.govt.nz/demolitions/list.

5. For a list of demolished or partly demolished churches, see Creed 2012.

trenches, and volcanoes, where about 90 percent of earth's earthquakes happen and where 75 percent of the largest have occurred.[6] Active tectonic plate movement gives rise to known and unknown faults. Before the September 4, 2010, earthquake, Otautahi Christchurch was thought to be a region of low seismicity, even though over the past 150 years the Canterbury Province has had its share of large earthquakes. The Southern Alps on its western borders are riddled with faults, including the 650-kilometer Alpine Fault. Between the Pacific Plate, on which Canterbury is situated, and the Australian Plate, this fault runs along the edge of the Main Divide and its lower ranges, which fan out through North Canterbury and Marlborough. We who live in the sight of those glorious Southern Alps also live with the speculation that as pressure builds in the activity of those massive tectonic plates, this fault is close to generating its next quake of a magnitude of about 8.0. Expert opinions are divided over when this is expected to happen.[7] However, according to retired Canterbury University active tectonics expert Jocelyn Campbell, many hidden and previously unknown faults were "basically all pointing to one place—Christchurch" (Gorman 2012a).

Where Is God?

People's relationship with space has changed. To enter an unfamiliar building is automatically in one's mind to size up how to get out. Old certainties are gone, as instanced by a man who nodded in the direction of the badly damaged Cathedral of the Blessed Sacrament and said to me as we came out of Liszt's choral Good Friday Stations of the Cross in St. Mary's Pro-Cathedral: "I thought it would always be there." People's relationship with the earth itself and the universe have changed. Underlying all of this for people of faith and many others is the question, "Where and who is God?"

---

6. Over 75 percent of all active and dormant volcanoes in the world are located in this area, which includes sections of North America, South America, Asia, Australia, New Zealand, Russia, and Antarctica. See "What Is the Ring of Fire?," InfoBarrel, April 14, 2011, edited September 14, 2012, http://www.infobarrel.com/The_Ring_Of_Fire#ixzz1oZDILTiJ.

7. The last rupture was about 1717, then 1230 (plus or minus 50 years) and 750 (plus or minus 50 years), appearing to break on average about every 480 years rather than the previously thought 300 years, which would indicate that the next rupture is still 200 years away. See Gorman 2012c and Berryman et al. 2012. For a contrary view, see Davies et al. 2012.

In his discussion of the biblical questions that natural disasters raise about God, tragedy, and suffering, Terence E. Fretheim shows that the Bible "does not shy away from linking God to natural disasters." He continues:

> God's creation is intended to go somewhere; it is a work in progress. Built into the very structure of things is its potential of becoming something more or even something different. In the development of such a universe, God chooses to involve that which is other than God, from human beings to earthquakes, tsunamis, periodic extinction of species, volcanic eruptions, and storms galore. All of these "creatures" of God participate with God in the continuing creation of the universe. *An important point for me: natural disasters are a key agent of God in the continuing creation of the world.* How might this biblical perspective inform our consideration of natural disasters in our own time? (Fretheim 2010, 150–51; italics original)

Fretheim's expansion of "creatures" to include natural disasters is helpful. However, a further horizon is needed. Jack Mahoney speaks of those who see humanity's relationship with God "as a continual border dispute," which he argues is a false position. Instead, he develops the image of created being and uncreated being that are not "in some form of demarcation dispute, like tectonic plates jostling against each other" (Mahoney 2011, 107–8). Rather, created being shares in or participates in uncreated being to a derived degree. The personal and local crises that envelop so many in the earthquakes and their aftermath take place against the wider horizon or aspect of a universal crisis of reconciling the impact of the evolutionary universe in the tension between science and theology. In this theological vision informed by science, the great story of the evolving universe is not only our story but God's story—the story of God's created universe. Denis Edwards reflects that God "must be a Creator who not only enables but respects and waits upon the processes by which things evolve in more and more complex ways. It seems that it is characteristic of God to create in an emergent and evolutionary way" (2010, 4–5). In this theological view, through the evolution of time, movements of the tectonic plates on which Otautahi Christchurch and its regions are situated have given birth to a variety of landscapes of unimaginable beauty *and* to immense pressure released through earthquakes and the considerable readjustments that result in aftershocks.[8]

---

8. David Neville, in the conclusion of his essay earlier in this volume, makes the link between a world in process of becoming and natural disasters.

In the Otautahi Christchurch region this evolutionary process has been, and still is, costly. People have been living on the crossroads between life and death in actual and metaphorical terms. This is no time for glib solutions, religious or otherwise. A poem in Liz Pearce's "The Christchurch Stations of the Cross" challenges: "Can you bring ... hope out of the pulpit ... a triumphant risen Christ is offensive, / for Christchurch is an eternal Good Friday" (2011, 21). She continues, quoting Ruth Burgess: "We are not ready for hope—not yet—and some of us are not sure that we will recognise it when it comes" (Burgess and Polhill 2003). This evolutionary context, which I have outlined above, suggests resonances for the imagery of birth. I shall revisit my previous work on Johannine birth imagery in dialogue with Claudia Bergmann (2008), whose work on ancient and biblical birth imagery gives me two ways to extend my interpretation of John 16:21 as an image for the death-resurrection of Jesus. I parallel the experience of earthquakes with her three-phase exploration of the biblical birth metaphor and her placing of biblical birth imagery explicitly within the experience of crisis—local, universal, and personal.

Biblical Birth Metaphor

When earthquakes are found in the New Testament, it is in metaphorical speech, as in the imagery of the apocalyptic genre of the book of Revelation (11:13, 19; 16:18) and in the so-called synoptic apocalypses (Mark 13:8; Matt 24:7; Luke 21:11). Further, Alan Cadwallader argues that the shaking of the earth contributes to the significance and meaning of the death and resurrection of Jesus in Matthew (27:51, 54; 28:2), because these accounts are constructed in connection with the scientific worldview of the day: the three-tiered universe. For Matthew, there is no understanding of new life without links to the total cosmic setting (Cadwallader 2004, 52–53).[9] Earthquakes are not found in the Gospel according to John. However, I seek to explore the possibility that the birth imagery that threads through this Gospel evoking the experience of the actual birth process has cosmic implications as well as parallels with the experience of earthquakes.

Bergmann and I use different theories of metaphor; nevertheless, we both agree strongly about the power of metaphor. I shall not review her theory of metaphor but illustrate how her work on the birth metaphor

---

9. On *seismos*, see also the discussion in Wainwright's chapter, above.

in ancient Near Eastern literature and the Hebrew Bible links into mine and reflect on a crucial point of difference in our surveys of the latter. My approach to metaphor follows Janet Martin Soskice, who sees metaphor as bringing to expression that which cannot be brought to expression in literal speech. Metaphor is that figure of speech whereby we speak about one thing in terms that are seen to be suggestive of other (Soskice 1992, 15). When the birth metaphor of the woman in childbirth of John 16:21 is read with Soskice's interanimative theory of metaphor, networks of sets of associations enable me to link two complete birth images, which are the only complete birth images I found in my survey of both testaments (Rushton 2011, 38–43; 2003).

Birth imagery in John begins in the prologue, where it is stated that all who receive the Word, the true light, and believe in his name are given power to become children of God, who are born of God (1:12–13). Embedded in the prologue, the lens through which the Gospel is to be read, is a cosmology drawn from biblical traditions and contemporary ancient cosmology (Painter 2002). The birth imagery found here, namely, those who become the children of God, who are born of God, needs to be considered within that cosmology. Where darkness has sway the Logos, the true light,[10] became flesh, flesh on the way to death, which is the lot of all flesh (Painter 2002, 79). There is a tragic perspective portrayed in the prologue that is foreshadowed (1:10–11). The centrality of the ongoing work of creation is the context from which John tells the story of Jesus. This is signaled in the prologue's link with the Genesis creation story, which culminates with the garden setting in the passion narrative (John 18:1; 19:41) and the resurrection (20:1–18). In this movement, the prologue fits the cosmologies of the Hellenistic age that are dynamic and future oriented and imply change (Painter 2002, 74). Thus, in the prologue, being born of God is related to the passion and resurrection. So also is the image of the woman in childbirth of John 16:21, which evokes the birth imagery of the

---

10. On birth as coming out of darkness into light in ancient Near Eastern text, see Bergmann 2008, 44–45, 59. On the concept of birth as coming out into light, which continued into medieval Christian Europe, see Elsakker 2000 (e.g., "For pain in childbirth. Say to the woman. Anna bore Samuel. ... Whether man or woman, come out. Our saviour calls you into light. ... Christ calls you to be born, draw yourself out, draw yourself out, draw yourself out!" [2000, 183].)

Isaian "daughter of Zion," as I shall now describe and set in the context of other ancient birth images.[11]

Birth, Crisis, and Earthquakes

The birth metaphor of John 16:21 has five metaphoric elements: a woman, pain, the childbirth process itself, the offspring, and joy after childbirth:

> When a woman is in labor,
> she has pain,
> because her hour has come.
> But when her child is born,
> she no longer remembers the anguish because of the joy
> of having brought a human being into the world.

While all the elements of birth appear to be present in this text, all is not as it seems when this metaphor is explored through an interanimative theory of metaphor. There are sets of association evoked by natural birth (pain [*lypē*], labor, child, born), Johannine theological themes (her hour has come, human person, into the world), biblical intertextuality (pain [*lypē/ lypeō*], anguish [*thlipsis*], joy [*chara*]), and sociocultural associations. The "daughter of Zion" and John 16:21 are two complete birth images that bring new hope and new beginnings, yet these remain birth images that move through the process of birth: a woman, pain, the childbirth process itself, the offspring, and joy after childbirth.

The transformation evoked in these two images does not take away from the pain involved or the fact that both the woman and the child may be on the threshold of life and death. In addition, it does not discount the three-phase process of the experience of birth that Bergmann identified and that I suggest parallels the experience of earthquakes: (1) once the reality is underway it is unstoppable, (2) there is no other option than to bear the reality, and (3) both realities are on the crossroads between life and death (Bergmann 2008, 68). Inherent in this sequence is the story of the processes by which the universe is created in an emergent and evolutionary way. For Bergmann, birth imagery and terminology are

---

11. Here my focus is on the "daughter of Zion" in relation to the portrayal of "the servant of God" in Isaiah, not on her portrayal as a city, which has potential to be developed in the context of the city of Christchurch.

used in "descriptions of crisis where birth becomes the lens by which the reader understands a crisis so terrible that it leads people to the crossroads between life and death" (2008, 80). The moment of a difficult birth process when the mother and child are at this crossroads is highlighted rather than the entire birth process. Further, Bergmann points out that reactions to the biblical birth simile ("like a woman giving birth") are part of the semantic field of shock rather than the semantic field of birth (2008, 70).

Bergmann has identified that there are patterns and conventions in ancient Near Eastern texts (my sociocultural associations) that discuss childbirth from many different angles (2008, 9–59). In contrast, the birth image in the Hebrew Bible (my biblical intertextuality associations) neither describes many birth events nor gives much detail (2008, 59, 67–68). Some examples illustrate that only aspects of the birth process are mentioned when used exclusively for crisis and applied to people in crisis:

> I writhe in pain … For I heard a cry as of a woman in labor, anguish as of one bringing forth her first child, the cry of daughter Zion gasping for breath. (Jer 4:19, 31)

> Like a woman with child, who writhes and cries out in her pangs when she is near her time, so were we because of you, O LORD; we were with child, we writhed, but we gave birth only to wind. We have won no victories on earth, and no one is born to inhabit the world. (Isa 26:17–18)

This would seem to be also similar in the New Testament, where, for example, the birth metaphor is used to evoke the beginning of a crisis: "For nation will rise against nation, and kingdom against kingdom; there will be earthquakes in various places; there will be famines. This is but the beginning of the birthpangs" (Mark 13:8; cf. Matt 24:8). Hebrew Bible birth imagery is used exclusively for crisis and applied to people in crisis. There is a relationship between two apparently unrelated concepts, *birth* and *crisis*. The concept of birth itself is redescribed. Relating *birth* to the concept of *crisis* rather than of *new beginnings* places "a certain twist on birth because it highlights the possibility of tragedy and death and focuses on the threshold between life and death rather than that of joyful expectation" (Bergmann 2008, 6). Further, the biblical birth metaphor is used for situations of local, universal, or personal crisis (Bergmann 2008, 114, 125–26, 162–64). These crises provoke fear and anxiety when individuals or groups suffer personal oppression, historical events such as wars, or events that are universe-changing related to the coming of "that day" or the "day of the Lord" (Bergmann 2008, 67–68). A. Joseph Everson explains about those days: "Events such as war, earthquakes or plagues, which mark the eras or turning points in the life of a nation, are the kind of events, which can be described as days of Yahweh. They are events which have the potential for turning history in various directions" (1974, 337). Further, in her review of the birth metaphor, Bergmann notes that the joy and new beginnings that most modern people associate with birth are not found, because it is associated with crisis (2008, 68). She does not mention that in the biblical texts there is no reference to the child who is the outcome of a birth. This lack matches my findings with one exception in a text that Bergmann does not review, namely, the "daughter of Zion's" mysterious offspring(s) of Isaiah 66 (Rushton 2003, 80–82).

In summary to this point, the actual experience of birth has parallels with the experience of earthquakes: (1) once the reality is underway it is unstoppable, (2) there is no other option than to bear the reality, and (3) both realities are on the crossroads between life and death. Biblical birth imagery is used for situations of local, universal, or personal crisis. I shall explain further how the biblical images of the Isaian "daughter of Zion" and the woman in childbirth of John 16:21 are, unlike other birth metaphors, complete birth images. I shall summarize the significance of John 16:21, a birth image making meaning of the death-resurrection of Jesus in preparation for suggesting how this may be read when the personal, local, and universal crises precipitated by the ongoing situation of earthquakes in the Otautahi Christchurch region are placed in a theological evolutionary vision of God.

John 16:21—An Image for the Death-Resurrection of Jesus

We have seen how in its metaphorical power John 16:21, and the "daughter of Zion" that it evokes, creates associations between the two apparently unrelated concepts of *birth* and *crisis*. However, unlike the incomplete birth imagery discussed above, there is another dimension in that these two birth images move through the *birth* and *crisis* to *new beginnings*, arguably still located in situations of ongoing *crisis*. John 16:21 follows a biblical tradition that has reinterpreted the motif of the barren woman and adapted it to the changing circumstances of Israel's sacred story. The transformative story of the "daughter of Zion" (Isa 40–66) functions in extent and prominence as a paradigmatic suffering one.[12] The birth of her children (66:8–9) is framed by references to the creation of the new heavens and the new earth (66:22). Birth and fecundity contrast with previous passages when birth pains evoke a catastrophic situation or a birth that could not come to fruition. The birth(s) of 66:7–13 follows the promise of the creation of new heavens and a new earth (65:17) where "no more shall there be ... an infant that lives but a few days" (65:20). Further, "they shall not labor in vain, or bear children in calamity; for they shall be offspring blessed by God" (65:23). Her story evokes new Johannine nuances (Rushton 2003, 82). Her distress (*thlipsis*), which transformed into joy (*chara*) at the birth of her children, is evoked in the image of John 16:21.

In its essence, the metaphor of the parable of John 16:21 is a transformative image. The woman brings new life through her suffering and childbirth. Her "ordinary experience" is layered. Her suffering (*lypē*) evokes the relative equality that woman and man share in the hardship of life in Gen 3:16–17 (Rushton 2011, 163–75).[13] The Johannine text echoes this multiple relatedness: the woman (16:21); the tree of the cross, that is, the lifting up motif (3:14; 8:28; 12:32, 34) and the cross/tree itself (19:17–19, 25, 31); the serpent (3:14); the situating of the death-resurrection of Jesus in the garden (18:1; 19:41; 20:15); and the prominence of water (19:34). All these feature in the Johannine death-glory of Jesus. The woman of John 16:21 evokes the birth of people in the context of re-creation. The phrase "her hour has come" associates her with "the/my hour" of Jesus. The phrase "into the world" recalls God's coming into the human story. Johannine symbolism functions at two levels. At the primary level, Jesus is the one who brings transformation by accomplishing the works of God. At the secondary level, the Johannine disciples in a situation of crisis are transformed by their participation in the birth process of death-resurrection of Jesus.

Intratextually, through the underlying model of birth, the transformative image of John 16:21, which moves through crisis and birth to new beginnings as I have outlined above, forms networks of associations with other Johannine birth images (1:12–13; 3:3–8; 7:37–38;

---

12. For how her story (Isa 49:14, 21, 24; 51:17–52:2; 54:1–10; 66:7–14) parallels and departs from "servant" texts (42:1–7; 49:1–7; 50:4–9; 52:13–53:12), see Rushton 2011, 147–63.

13. In the LXX and elsewhere in the New Testament, *lypē* is used not for physical pain but for hardship and mental anxiety.

19:34). Those believing in the Word become children of God (1:12) and are born of God (1:13). The Spirit will abide forever with the disciples (14:16). The Spirit ensures that they remember what Jesus told them (14:26) and leads them into the fullness of truth, which they were not able to bear previously (16:12–13). As Swetnam (1993) argues, on the cross Jesus hands over the Spirit to all believers (19:30). This outpouring of the Spirit is connected closely with the outpouring of the blood and water from the side of Jesus (19:34) and the birth of the new people of God (Swetnam 1993). Blood and water are elemental symbols of birth. Those born of God are to accomplish the works of God through being sent into the world (4:31–36; 17:18; 20:31) to gather all the scattered children of God (11:50–52; cf. 4:39–42; 10:15–16; 12:11, 19, 20–24, 31–32). The children of God are those born of God who have received Jesus and believed in his name (1:12). Jesus draws all to himself when he is lifted up (12:32). Throughout the Gospel, there are assertions that the understanding of the disciples has been transformed after Jesus's death and resurrection (2:17, 22; 12:17; 14:25–26; 16:12–13). This is evoked in the transformative image of John 16:21. According to Macgregor, "John intends us to understand that the New Testament church is actually born at the Resurrection out of the travail of the Cross" (1928, 301). In the allusive language of the writer, the human being (*anthrōpos*) who is born into the world is a new creation, a new people (Stevick 2011, 266–67). The transformation has enabled the new relationship between God and human persons that is shown in the command of the Risen One (20:18) to Mary Magdalene (Okure 1992). Jesus, who alone prior to this birth called God "my God" and "my Father," indicates to disciples that God is now "your God … your Father." In other words, the birth imagery of the Isaian "daughter of Zion" is evoked in the joy of his disciples. Further, the suffering and death of Jesus is connected with the epochal "Day of the Lord," referred to previously, out of which something living and new is born (Stevick 2011, 266).

Conclusion

We have seen how the actual experience of birth has parallels with the experience of earthquakes: (1) once the reality is underway it is unstoppable, (2) there is no other option than to bear the reality, and (3) both realities are on the crossroads between life and death. In situations of local, universal, or personal crisis, birth imagery was used to express what cannot be expressed in other ways. Can this ancient metaphor that describes the concept of *crisis* by means of the concept of *birth* as in the Hebrew Bible and the New Testament still be understood today? Does its reinterpretation and extension in John 16:21, drawing on the "daughter of Zion" in the context of ongoing creation and the death-resurrection of Jesus, offer the concept of *crisis* by means of the concept of *birth* the possibility of *transformation* in situations that have been, and are, on the threshold between life and death? Is birth an appropriate image? Without in any way denying or minimizing the hardships experienced in the region of Otautahi Christchurch, which I overviewed in the first part of this chapter, there is evidence of birth, of movement and interconnection, in the aftermath of the earthquakes and ongoing aftershocks.

Responses to local crises have birthed new life in extraordinary circumstances, thereby opening new beginnings, as instanced in the following examples. An inner-city secondary school, with years of low National Certificates of Educational Achievement (NCEA) results and which spent most of last year site-sharing with a school on the other side of the city, produced NCEA results among the highest in the region (Law 2012). The relationship between the city and tertiary students reached an all-time high through the extraordinary practical generosity of the Student Volunteer Army. One student, via social media, rallied hundreds of others time and again to remove the heavy silt spread by tons of liquefaction from homes and properties, especially in the eastern suburbs. The Re-Start Mall, built mainly of shipping containers, enables citizens and visitors to experience that the heart of the city still beats. In this instance, business-led recovery is not just a matter of economic urgency but contributes to the community's wider sense of well-being (Dalziel 2012). Shipping containers function as the Inner-City Bus Depot and as beautifully decorated cafes, giving birth to simplicity, ingenuity, and creativity. Shipping containers? Borders have been crossed here, for in other contexts these provide housing for the poor in such places as the townships of the Republic of South Africa. Yet in other contexts, shipping containers are suggestive of migration. Each year, hundreds pack these with their possessions to leave the shores of Aotearoa New Zealand for higher wages in Australia, while many from Oceania cross borders perceiving the former to be the land of opportunity.

A recent visit to L'Aquila in Italy by Paul Dalziel, Professor of Economics in the Agribusiness and Economics Research Unit at Lincoln University, draws us into the universal and reminds us that Canterbury is not the only community recovering from natural disaster.[14] An Organisation for Economic Co-operation and Development and University of Groningen–hosted forum drew on representatives not only from Christchurch but also from New Orleans in the United States, Tohoku in Japan, and the Van Province in Turkey to share their respective experiences of how their communities are recovering from natural disasters (Dalziel 2012). In the main, these countries share my context of upheaval and uncertainty in a well-resourced nation, a context that differs greatly from recent earthquakes and tsunamis in the ecologically and economically vulnerable nations of Samoa,[15] Haiti, and Sumatra.[16] This divide is a universal crisis that presents urgent moral dilemmas concerning poverty and the distribution of wealth. For example, on June 12, 2010, an earthquake of 7.1 magnitude hit Haiti, the same magnitude as the one in Otautahi Christchurch on September 4, 2010, which had no loss of life, in contrast with the loss of over two hundred thousand Haitian lives. Human responsibility is a factor in that impoverished nation because of international and local unjust economic systems. Similarly, human choice in the form of nuclear power and contamination has compounded the destruction of the Honshu earthquake and tsunami.[17]

The stories of the bravery, resilience, and big-heartedness of the human spirit in individual crisis is exemplified by Russian Orthodox immigrant Alec Cvetanov, who located his medical doctor wife, Tamara, after the February 22 earthquake in the Canterbury Television (CTV) building, where

---

14. On April 6, 2009, L'Aquila was struck by an earthquake that claimed 309 lives. Three years later its historical center is still closed (Dalziel 2012).

15. An 8.1 earthquake on September 29, 2009, followed by a tsunami with a 4.5-meter wave, left 135 dead and 8 missing in Samoa, 32 dead in American Samoa, and 9 dead in Tonga. Two recent earthquakes are among the strongest ever recorded. See "Deadly Tsunami Strikes in Pacific," BBC News, September 30, 2009, http://news.bbc.co.uk/2/hi/8281616.stm.

16. On December 26, 2004, a 9.1 earthquake off the west coast of Northern Sumatra left a total of more than 283,100 people killed, 14,100 missing, and 1,126,900 displaced by the earthquake and subsequent tsunami in ten countries in South Asia and East Africa. See "Magnitude 9.1 off the West Coast of Northern Sumatra," USGS, http://neic.usgs.gov/neis/eq_depot/2004/eq_041226/.

17. Near the east coast of Honshu, Japan, a 9.0 earthquake resulted in a tsunami that struck Tohoku on the eastern coast of Japan on March 11, 2011. A fifteen-meter-high wave destroyed coastal communities, killing more than 15,700 people and leaving about 3,300 missing (Heather 2012).

115 lives, including those of 65 foreign students, were lost. He found where she was trapped, tried to alert rescue workers, spoke to her on a cellphone 31 times over 12 hours, yet in vain. He watched as diggers began the delayering process on the place where she was trapped. In a recent television documentary, Cvetanov, an engineer trained in firefighting in his native Serbia, declared with compassion for the volunteer rescuers: "I can't blame those people, they are still my heroes.... I cannot blame anyone."[18]

For believers, I indicated earlier that the ongoing work of creation in the Johannine prologue's link with the Genesis creation story culminates with the garden setting in the passion narrative (John 18:1; 19:41) and the resurrection (20:1–18). Thus, being born of God (1:12–13) is related to both the passion and resurrection in the prologue and to the image of the woman in childbirth of John 16:21. In this scenario, Otautahi Christchurch is part of something bigger, which is an aspect of the universal crisis precipitated by our present context. Those tectonic plates that have led to the movement of hidden faults are connected with 13.7 billion years of the evolutionary universe, which is unstoppable and endured by us, and we are shaken on the threshold of life and death. We emerge born with a new sense of our own created vulnerability, yet such events have, as Everson pointed out earlier, "the potential for turning history in various directions" (1974, 337). Dalziel warns "against approaches based on rebuilding the city as it was and only then looking for ways to move forward" (2012). In the grief and loss of what was, many citizens realize that they will not see what will come to be in the rebuilt city. It will be for the next generation.[19] Borders have shifted and still shift, yet, paradoxically in evolutionary terms, there are not borders between created and uncreated reality. The image of transformation at the core of the birth imagery evoking death-resurrection offers the potential of re-creation, new priorities, and new ways of belonging in the borderlessness of God's emergent and evolutionary way.

Works Consulted

Bergmann, Claudia. 2008. *Childbirth as a Metaphor for Crisis: Evidence from the Ancient Near East, the Hebrew Bible, and 1QH XI, 1–18*. Bei-

---

18. "The Longest Night," *Sunday* (TV ONE), April 15, 2012.
19. Jeanette Mathews, in her essay later in this volume, makes this point in her discussion of the hope of return among Karen refugees.

hefte zur Zeitschrift für die alttestamentliche Wissenschaft 382. Berlin: de Gruyter.

Berryman, Kelvin, et al. 2012. Late Holocene Rupture History of the Alpine Fault in South Westland, New Zealand. *Bulletin of the Seismological Society of America* 102:620–38.

Burgess, Ruth, and C. Polhill. 2003. *Eggs and Ashes: Practical and Liturgical Sources for Holy Week.* Glasgow: Wild Goose.

Cadwallader, Alan. 2004. "And the Earth Shook"—Mortality and Ecological Diversity: Interpreting Jesus' Death in Matthew's Gospel. Pages 45–54 in *Biodiversity and Ecology: An Interdisciplinary Challenge.* Interface 7.1. Edited by Denis Edwards and Mark Worthing. Adelaide: ATF.

Creed, Philip. 2012. Churches Pummelled, in Taking Stock: One Year On. *The Press*, February 23, 8.

Dalziel, Paul. 2012. Quake Lessons Shared in L'Aquila. *The Press*, April 9, A15.

Davies, Tim, et al. 2012. Over-Optimistic to a Fault. *The Press*, April 13, A17.

Edwards, Denis. 2010. *How God Acts: Creation, Redemption and Special Divine Acts.* Hindmarsh: ATF Theology.

Elsakker, M. 2000. "In Pain You Shall Bear Children" (Gen 3:16): Medieval Prayers for a Safe Delivery. Pages 179–209 in *Women and Miracles Stories: A Multidisciplinary Exploration.* Edited by A.-M. Korte. Leiden: Brill.

Everson, A. Joseph. 1974. The Days of Yahweh. *Journal of Biblical Literature* 93:329–37.

Fretheim, Terence E. 2010. *Creation Untamed: The Bible, God, and Natural Disasters.* Grand Rapids: Baker Academic.

Gorman, Paul. 2012a. Primed for a Show of Force. *The Press*, February 20, The Year That Was Supplement, 6.

———. 2012b. Changing Face of Shattered City. *The Press*, February 20, The Year That Was Supplement, 7.

———. 2012c. Threat of Quake in Alps Wane. *The Press*, April 3, 1.

Heather, Ben. 2012. A Slow Road to Recovery. *The Press*, March 3, C1–3.

Law, Tina. 2012. Pupils Excel Despite Quakes. *The Press*, April 2, 1–2.

Macgregor, G. H. C. 1929. *The Gospel of John.* Garden City: Doubleday Doran.

Mahoney, Jack. 2011. *Christianity in Evolution: An Exploration.* Washington, D.C.: Georgetown University Press.

Okure, Teresa. 1992. The Significance Today of Jesus' Commission to Mary Magdalene. *International Review of Mission* 81:177–88.

Painter, John. 2002. Earth Made Whole: John's Reading of Genesis. Pages 65–84 in *Word, Theology and Community in John*. Edited by John Painter, R. Alan Culpepper, and Fernando F. Segovia. St. Louis: Chalice.

Pearce, Liz. 2011. The Christchurch Stations of the Cross. *Marist Messenger*, April, 15–24.

Rushton, Kathleen P. 2002. The (Pro)creative Parables of Labour and Childbirth (John 3:1–10 and 16:21–22). Pages 206–29 in *The Lost Coin: Parables of Women, Work and Wisdom*. Edited by Mary Ann Beavis. Sheffield: Sheffield Academic Press.

———. 2003. The Woman in Childbirth of John 16:21: A Feminist Reading in (Pro)creative Boundary Crossing. Pages 77–90 in *Wholly Woman, Holy Blood: A Feminist Critique of Purity and Impurity*. Edited by Kristin de Troyer, Judith A. Herbert, Judith A. Johnson, and Anne-Marie Korte. Harrisburg: Trinity Press International.

———. 2011. *The Parable of the Woman in Childbirth of John 16:21: A Metaphor for the Death and Glorification of Jesus*. Lewiston: Mellen.

Schneiders, Sandra M. 1999. *The Revelatory Text: Interpreting the New Testament as Sacred Scripture*. 2d ed. Collegeville, Minn.: Liturgical Press.

Soskice, Janet Martin. 1992. *Metaphor and Religious Language*. Oxford: Clarendon.

Stevick, Daniel B. 2011. *Jesus and His Own: A Commentary on John 13–17*. Grand Rapids: Eerdmans.

Swetnam, James. 1993. Bestowal of the Spirit in the Fourth Gospel. *Biblica* 74:556–76.

The Prologue of John: Bridge into a New World

John Painter

My chosen image to describe the function of John's prologue is a "bridge," a bridge from the world of Moses into the narrative world of this Gospel. Others have chosen to speak of the prologue as an "entry" into the Gospel, which implies no bridging function. Harnack adopts a view consistent with the image of a bridge but differs from the approach developed in this chapter, which features British scholars from Westcott to Barrett and some recent objections to commonly held views. Dealing with their objections allows me to develop aspects of my position. Scholars in the Westcott tradition responded to the challenges posed by Harnack, and Barrett places Bultmann first of the three primary influences on his work (Barrett 1955, vii). My focus on these scholars reflects my scholarly foundation, which was also shaped by the impact of the then newly discovered Qumran texts. It helps me to clarify and develop my view of the prologue as a bridge.

Identifying the Prologue

P. J. Williams (2011)[1] rejects the recognition of a distinct prologue, because the earliest sources show no paragraph break between John 1:18 and 19, though they attest a break after 1:5. The opening paragraph (1:1–5) forms a discrete phase, focused on prehistory, or the history of creation, while 1:6–8 signals the beginning of the Gospel story encapsulated in 1:6–18, so that 1:1–18 enigmatically establishes a conceptual framework to interpret 1:19–20:31 in the context of the worldview expressed in 1:1–5, and in the light of 1:6–18. Williams's article fails to justify his title, "Not the Prologue of John," implying his rejection of any prologue as a distinct literary unit.

---

1. Williams, of Tyndale House, Cambridge, first gave this paper, "Not the Prologue of John," at the British New Testament Conference, September 2006.

Jo-Ann Brant (2011, 26–27) uses the substance of Williams's article (in its 2007 form), not to reject any prologue, but to argue that the prologue consists of 1:1–14 and that 1:15–18 belongs with 1:19–34. She asserts:

> Some ancient witnesses treat 1:14 as the prologue's conclusion (see Irenaeus, *Haer.* 1.8.5) and 1:15–18 as the words of John the Baptist (see Origen, *Comm. Jo.* 2.29 …). This commentary follows this early tradition and treats 1:1–14 as the prologue proper and 1:15–18 as the beginning of John's witness, which continues in 1:19–34.

Contrary to her view, I find nothing in these references to show that Irenaeus took 1:14 to be the conclusion of the prologue or that Origen identified 1:15–18 with 1:19ff. *rather than* with 1:1–14.

First, Irenaeus (*Haer.* 1.8.5) reports the teaching of Ptolemy, one of the disciples of Valentinus, on John's teaching about the origin of all things. Not surprisingly, there is no mention here of the witness of John (the Baptist) in 1:6–8, or 1:15–18. The commentary of Ptolemy apparently moved from 1:1–5 to 1:14. This should not be taken to mean that the "prologue" (not named, of course) ended at 1:14. Rather, Ptolemy's prologue commentary was concerned only with the cosmological/mythological elements. His selection reveals more about Ptolemy than the scope of the prologue. Further, the Valentinian Commentary of Heracleon on John implies that 1:15–18 belongs with 1:1–14 (Pagels 1973, 37, 51–52), though Heracleon ascribes 1:18 to the Evangelist (narrator), not to the Baptist (Pagels 1973, 37, 51–52).[2]

Second, Origen's commentary (*Comm. Jo.* 2.29) is developed thematically (not verse by verse), and section 2.29 deals with "the six testimonies of John (the Baptist)" beginning not with John 1:15 but with 1:7, "John came to bear witness of the light," before going on to 1:15–18, 23, 26, 29–31, 32–34, 35–38. This does not support the view that 1:15–18 belongs with 1:19ff. It reflects a thematic treatment overlapping 1:1–18 and 1:19–38 and beyond. The way 1:6–8, 15 connect the prologue to the witness of John in 1:19ff. suggests that the prologue was designed to link into the following narrative.

---

2. These Valentinian Commentaries provide the earliest surviving evidence concerning the *interpretation* of the prologue. They do not specifically identify its scope or name it "prologue" or "proem."

Contemporary analysis of the prologue in relation to classical rhetoric (Aristotle) supports the recognition of 1:1–18 as a discrete literary unit and the naming of it as "prologue" or "proemium." Elizabeth Harris notes that Jerome "refers to these verses as *proemium*" (2004, 12 n. 1). She notes that πρόλογος is "derived from the verb προλέγειν in the sense of 'to announce beforehand' [and] means 'the statement announced in advance.'" She refers to the practice of using a prologue in Greek epic dramas and elsewhere, announcing the plot to the audience at the very beginning. This provides a precedent for those who first used the word "prologue" to describe 1:1–18 and its relationship to the body of the Gospel (E. Harris 2004, 12–16, 21–25). In Aristotle's *Rhetoric* (1415a), he says that the *prooimia* of forensic speech produce the same effect as the dramatic *prologoi* and epic *prooimia* and describes the function as announcing beforehand what the story is about. The Johannine prologue fits this influential contemporary understanding. The privileged knowledge the prologue gives readers allows the Gospel to develop a deep irony and the use of double entendre, because the reader knows more than the characters in the story.

That the prologue involves 1:1–18 is obvious, because the interaction between characters in the story begins in 1:19.[3] John 1:1–18 is addressed directly and exclusively to the reader, not to characters in the story, even when the voice of the narrator gives way to the voices of witnesses (1:14) and the voice of the foundational witness (1:15). Heracleon ascribes 1:18 to the Evangelist (narrator), not to John (the Baptist). I am inclined to ascribe 1:16–18 to the narrator also, leaving only the words common to 1:27 and 1:30 as words of the witness John (1:15). In that case, without notice, the voice of John gives way to the voice of the narrator in 1:16–18, just as it does in the course of 3:27–36, probably in 3:31–36. Whatever voices we hear in the prologue, they are addressed only to the reader. That is the mark of a dramatic prologue. It is addressed to the audience.

The unity of the prologue is subtly held together by μονογενὴς θεὸς ὁ ὢν εἰς τὸν κόλπον τοῦ πατρός, in 1:18, forming an impressive Johannine *inclusio* with 1:1, ὁ λόγος ἦν πρὸς τὸν θεόν, thus explicating the meaning of πρὸς τὸν θεόν. The relationship of the λόγος to God is further revealed in language suggestive of the Father/Son relationship. The mystery of God

---

3. At times in the Gospel narrative the narrator intervenes to address the reader directly, as in 2:21–22 and 12:16.

beyond sight and knowledge is revealed, yet the mystery remains, because "no one has ever seen God."

The Prologue as an Entry: Brooke Foss Westcott (1825–1901)

While Westcott does not use it himself, the image of an entry was adopted by later scholars indebted to his work. His work lends some weight to its use. In the English-speaking world, his commentary on John dominated the field from its publication in 1880 at least until the publication of J. H. Bernard's International Critical Commentary in 1928. Even then, Adam Fox's introduction to the 1958 edition reveals that it was still in demand.[4] Westcott argues that the author of John's Gospel was a Jew of Palestine, an eyewitness of Jesus, an apostle, John bar-Zebedee, but he recognizes that John was writing not for a Jewish audience but for a more general audience in the empire. Westcott argues that the Gospel reflects a time remote from the events it describes. From tradition, he dates the Gospel in the last decade of the first century, in Ephesus, in a church shaped to some extent by the Pauline mission. Though it contained Jews and Gentiles, it was predominantly a Gentile church. Chronologically, John was the fourth Gospel, written with awareness of the Synoptics, and it reflects emerging early Christian theology at the turn of the century (1958, xxxvi). Although the tradition was shaped in Palestine, it was now addressed to readers/hearers of the Graeco-Roman world in the cosmopolitan city of Ephesus. Thus the Jewish influence of the author on the character of the Gospel is minimized, because the followers of Jesus to whom it was addressed were making their way in the Roman world (1958, xxxv–xl).

Westcott says that his view that the prologue (1:1–18) forms an introduction to the Gospel is generally acknowledged, though it "is not marked off by any very distinct line" from the body of the Gospel. "This conclusion appears to be completely established by a careful analysis of the contents of the section, which present in a summary form the main truths that are illustrated by the records of the history" (1958, 1). The prologue "summarizes" the main themes of the rest of the Gospel (1:19–20:31), announcing them in advance, but there is no suggestion of a cultural border to be bridged for the reader by the prologue. Each part is based on Palestinian

---

4. In 1905 William Sanday said: "Westcott's commentary remains, and will still for long remain, the best that we have on the Fourth Gospel" (1905, 14).

tradition, just as each part is expressed in terms of the theology of the last decade of the first century. Westcott implies that the prologue is a suitable introduction to the body of the Gospel. His view plays down the distinctive features of the prologue and the role they might play in adding a dimension to the reading of the Gospel.

Nevertheless, Westcott notes that the christological use of λόγος is found only in John 1:1 and 14. He argues that it is derived not from Philo of Alexandria but from the Palestinian concept of the *Memra* (1958, 2–3).[5] He also notes John's dependence on Gen 1:1 and the development of a similar early Christian understanding in Paul, Hebrews, and Revelation. Thus, he has interpreted as a common feature of Christian theology at the end of the first century what others have seen as the distinctiveness of the prologue and of John, and he has recognized Paul, John, and the author of Hebrews as exponents of individual theologies that influenced the emerging church in different ways. In so doing he fails to treat seriously the significantly different language used by these different authors.[6]

Against the influence of Philo on the Johannine λόγος theology, Westcott argues that, in Philo, the meaning of λόγος is "Reason," but in John and the New Testament generally it is always "Word," even in John 1:1, where Westcott refers to "the immanent word (λόγος ἐνδιάθετος)," language that John does not use, though Westcott argues that the thought is present and that the prologue develops in the direction of Christian Trinitarian thought (1958, 2–3). His case for the Palestinian origin of John's use of λόγος is weakened by the failure to recognize evidence of John's use of Israel's Wisdom literature in the prologue, where the parallel use of "Wisdom" and "Word" is evident, as it is in Philo. Further, in the Wisdom literature, "Wisdom" has the role attributed to the λόγος ἐνδιάθετος alongside the dynamic and active role of the creative and prophetic "Word." J. Rendel Harris (1917), Rudolf Bultmann (1923), C. H. Dodd (1953), and John Painter (1991, 115–17; 1993a, 145–47) have shown how the statements in the prologue concerning the λόγος are replete with "Wisdom" parallels. Just as Wisdom and λόγος motifs have interpenetrated each other in the Wisdom literature, so Wisdom motifs have added a dimension to the use of λόγος in the Prologue.

---

5. This view has been given new impetus by the recent work of John Ronning (2010). See also Martin McNamara (1972, 2010).

6. See Dodd's caution against such harmonization (1953, 5).

Though Westcott does not make the point, he implies that the Gospel as a whole *bridges* the border between the world of the message of Jesus in Palestine (as in the Synoptics and the Jesus tradition used in John) and the world, message, and theology of the early church at the end of the first century in the Roman Empire. The prologue, like the body of the Gospel, gives expression to that transformation while retaining roots in the Palestinian tradition. In this respect his work foreshadows that of C. H. Dodd. For Westcott, the prologue announces in advance the main themes of this late first-century Gospel. John does in a Gospel, rooted in Palestinian tradition, what Paul and the author of Hebrews, as exponents of the theology of the emerging church, do in a less historically rooted fashion. Westcott's influence is to be seen in the work of other British Johannine scholars, such as William Sanday (1905, 13–14), J. S. Johnston (1909, vii), and J. H. Bernard (1928, clxxxvii).

The Prologue as an Attractive Buffer: Adolf von Harnack (1851–1930)

The question of the relationship of the prologue to the body of the Gospel was explicitly raised, perhaps for the first time in a serious critical fashion, by the great scholar of early Christianity Adolf von Harnack (1892, 189–231). He argues that the prologue emerged as an afterthought and concludes that it was placed at the beginning as a kind of bridge or buffer connecting cultivated Hellenistic readers to what was, for them, a strange Hebraic Gospel. Harnack epigrammatically remarks that whereas, for modern readers, the prologue is the mysterious part of the Gospel, for first-century readers in the Graeco-Roman world it was the body of the Gospel that was a mystery ([1894] 1961, 1:328–29 n. 1). The prologue was not an essential part of the Gospel but was added to attract cultivated Hellenistic readers. This takes account of those elements found only in the prologue but gives too little weight to the inclusion of significant Johannine terminology, which, to some extent, prepares the reader for what is to come. Apparently Harnack does not consider this to be enough to provide a significant orientation to reading the following narrative. Thus, for him, the prologue is not the key to the following narrative but an enigma, leaving a gulf between these two parts. At best, it invites enlightened Hellenistic readers to enter the world of the Gospel in the hope that, having begun, they would continue to read. This approach suggests the image of the prologue as a bridge connecting educated Hellenistic readers to an Hebraic Gospel. If Harnack is right about the lack of significant connection between the prologue and the body of the Gospel, this bridge is flimsy and inadequate, doing little more than to delay the shock of entry.

Does the evidence of the prologue show closer and more substantial connection to the body of the Gospel than Harnack has allowed? In my view, that is the case.

First, unlike Gen 1:1, before narrating the act of creation John establishes the most important relationship in the Gospel, which finds expression in the words "and the Word was with God" (John 1:1), and in 1:18 foreshadows the language of the "Father"/"Son" relationship of the Gospel.

Second, in the worldview established in John's rereading of the Genesis creation story, it soon becomes evident that there is a struggle between light and darkness (1:5; and see 3:19–21; 8:12; 9:4–5, 39–41; 12:35–36, 46); God and the world (1:10); belief and unbelief (1:10–13).

Third, key Johannine terms, expressing Johannine motifs, emerge in the prologue: "light" and "darkness," "truth," "glory," "believing," "receiving," "not receiving," "rejecting," "grace"/"love," and "witness."

Fourth, there is an overlapping theme of *the* key human witness of the man named John (1:6–8, 15[16–18]), whose witness is narrated in 1:19–34; 3:27–36; 5:32–36; 10:40–42. Even the witness of Jesus's disciples emerges on the basis of the witness of John (1:35–37).

The Prologue as an Entry: Westcott's Influence after Harnack

Using an Egyptian temple as an image of this Gospel, William Sanday refers to the prologue as a "pylon," that is, an entry to the temple (1905, 185). This image was picked up from him by J. S. Johnston (1909, 7), who refers to the prologue as "a vestibule that admits us to a stately temple." The image is not clearly elaborated and may mean little more than an appropriate way into the Gospel. Like Westcott, they treat the prologue as a common part of the Gospel, affirming that the Johannine λόγος teaching is of Palestinian origin, being dependent on use of the term *Memra*. However, they also appeal to the Wisdom literature and allow for overlap with the Alexandrian λόγος of Philo, who also made use of the Wisdom literature. Wisdom provides a more obvious tradition for understanding the λόγος with God before the creation. Philo shows that the overlap or parallelism of "Wisdom" and "Word" (λόγος) in the Wisdom literature, where both are images of the Law (Torah), was intelligible to Greek readers along

Stoic-Platonic lines, a view later adopted by C. H. Dodd. The Palestinian λόγος teaching of John may have appealed to readers sharing Philo's Middle Platonic understanding. Harnack's assessment of the acceptability of the complete prologue for Greek readers is overstated. Augustine states that he has not read the substance of John 1:11–12, 14 in the Platonic sources, and in particular, he has not read there that the Word (λόγος) became flesh (*Confessions* 7.9). He implies that this part of the prologue would have scandalized Platonic readers.

Both Sanday and Johnston refer to Harnack's article somewhat dismissively and fail to deal seriously with the evidence of the distinctiveness and differences of the prologue from the rest of the Gospel. The concentration of distinctive language in only eighteen verses (especially vv. 14–18) undermines the view that the prologue provides an introductory *summary* of the whole Gospel.[7] This notion, introduced by Westcott, will not do. Even common elements, like the overlapping treatment of the witness of John in the prologue and the body of the Gospel (1:6–8, 15[16–18]; 1:19–42; 3:22–36; 4:1; 5:33–36; 10:40–42), are not a matter of summary (prologue) and detailed account (body of the Gospel). Rather, the prologue provides a dimension that transforms the reader's understanding of what follows in the body of the Gospel. In the prologue, the witness of the man called John to the light is made the basis of universal belief (1:6–8). Following the announcement of the incarnation (1:14), the response of believing witness identifies the incarnate Word with Jesus Christ. He is the one who actualizes loving-kindness and faithfulness (grace and truth [חסד ואמת]) in human life, revealing on Earth the character and reality of the hidden God (1:14–18). We may suspect that, after 1:15, the voice is no longer that of John (the Baptist) but the voice of the narrator of the prologue. If that is the case, it seems that the narrator's voice has been allowed to blend with John's, suggesting that they speak from a common point of view and in the same voice.[8] In 1:29 (cf. 1:35–36) John identifies Jesus as

---

7. See especially the christological use of λόγος restricted to 1:1 and 14 in the Gospel. Other words and expressions found only in the prologue: φωτίζει (1:9), ἐσκήνωσεν, μονογενοῦς παρὰ πατρός, πλήρης, χάριτος καὶ ἀληθείας (1:14), πληρώματος, χάριν ἀντὶ χάριτος (1:16), χάρις καὶ ἀλήθεια (1:17), μονογενὴς θεός, ὁ ὢν εἰς τὸν κόλπον, ἐξηγήσατο (1:18). The name "Jesus Christ" (1:17) is uncharacteristic of John and found elsewhere only at 17:3 in the Gospel.

8. See also John 3:22–36. Somewhere in 3:31–36 the voice of John, introduced in 3:27 and continuing at least to 3:30, becomes the voice of the narrator. In this Gospel,

"the lamb of God who takes away the sin of the world." But this turns out to be an enigmatic and unexplained identification.[9]

The perspective of the prologue has impacted the shaping of tradition in the narrative, not only the *reading* of the text of the body of the Gospel (1:19–20:31). The narrative maintains contact with the Jesus tradition known also in the Synoptics, but the reader has the advantage of the perspective of the prologue with its worldview framing the story of Jesus, which is told from the perspective of the glorified Jesus. Hence the prologue is not simply an entry to the Gospel but a bridge to enable the reader to cross into the world of the Gospel, which is a literary-theological creation.

A Bridge for Readers "Nurtured in the Higher Religion of Hellenism": C. H. Dodd

C. H. Dodd argues that the Gospel is addressed to outsiders (1953, 8–9) and identifies them as a public nurtured in the higher religion of Hellenism, whose views are representative of the Middle Platonism (stoicizing Platonism) found in the Corpus Hermeticum and the writings of Philo (1953, 10–11). Such a public could be found in varied cosmopolitan Hellenistic cities such as Ephesus (1953, 133). He thinks that Johannine thought has affinities with the Platonic doctrine of Ideas, the conception of the world of invisible realities where the visible world is an imperfect transitory copy. Dodd says that the λόγος of the prologue "is also the divine Wisdom, the Hebrew analogue at once of the Platonic world of Ideas and of the Stoic Logos: it is that thought of God which is the transcendent design of the universe, and its immanent meaning." The prologue is based on the philosophy of two orders, that of the transcendent, eternal thought of God and the imperfect empirical world that is real only to the extent it embodies the eternal thought. For John, "in one single area of the universe of space and time phenomena have completely absorbed the reality of the

---

the only other voice with which the narrator's voice blends is that of Jesus. See John 3:10–21. In 3:10 Jesus responds to Nicodemus, who makes no further contribution to the conversation. Somewhere around 3:13 Nicodemus seems to have vanished from the scene so that the only person addressed from there on is the reader. In this Gospel, Jesus, the narrator, and the man called John speak with the same voice.

9. See Painter 2004, 291–94; Bieringer 2007, 199–232.

eternal archetypes, and that this area is co-extensive with the life, death and resurrection of Jesus Christ..., ὁ λόγος σὰρξ ἐγένετο" (1953, 295).

"The Logos-doctrine is placed first, because, addressing a public nurtured in the higher religion of Hellenism, the writer wished to offer the Logos-idea as the appropriate approach ... through which he might lead them to the historical actuality of its story, rooted as it is in Jewish tradition" (Dodd 1953, 296).[10] The λόγος idea provides the key to reading the prologue, and it provides a philosophical introduction to the narrative of the Gospel, which is at once "factually true and symbolic of deeper truth," because events of this world derive their reality from the eternal ideas they embody. The symbolism of the Gospel is an expression of the worldview of this philosophy in which things and events are a living, moving image of the eternal, a world in which the Word was made flesh (1953, 142–43).

Dodd impressively shows how the language of the Gospel raises questions concerning the universe of discourse within which its thought moves (1953, 3). His outline of the interpretative process is similar to Bultmann's understanding of the hermeneutical circle ([1950] 1955a, 235–36; Painter 1987a, 56–66). An example of this issue is Dodd's recognition that John's use of λόγος in the prologue is not a matter of lexical meaning but belongs to a philosophy, comprehended in understanding the Gospel as a whole (1953, 3). Only when its *Weltanschauung* is grasped can the Gospel be understood deeply.[11] Though I find Dodd's work impressive and persuasive in principle, I am not persuaded that the Platonic doctrine of Ideas, linked with the Stoic λόγος, is the world within which this Gospel moves.[12] Nevertheless, I agree that the prologue is the means of creating a bridge to enable readers to understand and to encourage them to receive the understanding conveyed in the Gospel. I also think that the λόγος of the prologue is related to the Johannine symbolism and the presentation of the signs of Jesus.

---

10. Dodd's identification of audience may explain why there is no reference to Gen 1:1 in this book, including Scripture Index (1953, 455). Only Wisdom parallels are provided for the prologue (1953, 274–75), because it is Wisdom that provides the Hebrew analogue to the Platonic world of Ideas and of the Stoic λόγος.

11. Bultmann argues that a failure to grasp the *Weltanschauung* leads to a distortion of meaning.

12. See Bultmann's (1954) review of Dodd's *Interpretation of the Fourth Gospel*.

Dodd insists that the Fourth Gospel is a theological work *rather than a work of history* but also insists that this work is rooted in history, though in "the process ... of bringing out the symbolical value of the facts he [the Evangelist] has used some freedom" (1953, 444). The result is a work quite original and creative, revealing a masterful, independent mind, faithful to the tradition while expressing it in terms of a different worldview and philosophy (1953, 6). Dodd's primary stress is on the success of the Fourth Gospel as an achievement of communication, expressing an Hebraic gospel tradition in terms of Middle Platonism, a work Bultmann called "translation," which I clarified as "hermeneutical translation" (Painter 1987a, 51–55). If this was the Evangelist's primary concern, the Gospel is a work of apologetics, which, as a by-product, produced significant theological insights. Thus, for Dodd the λόγος idea of the prologue is a bridge enabling a public nurtured in the higher religion of Hellenism to enter the world of the Gospel.

A Wide-Open Entry: Peter M. Phillips

Peter Phillips, in his lightly revised Sheffield University Ph.D. thesis, done under the supervision of Professor Loveday Alexander, makes suggestive use of the image of the prologue as an entry ("threshold") to a temple to illuminate the function of the prologue in relation to the Gospel (2006, 1–4, 221–22). Apparently unaware of the work of Sanday (1905), or Johnston (1909), he appeals to an article by Frederick Brenk (1993) as the inspiration for his use of the image (Phillips 2006, 1). He describes the prologue as an open, inviting, and public access to the Gospel that implies that the Gospel was written for a wide range of outsiders. This broadens Dodd's apologetic reading, though they both see the Gospel addressed to "outsiders." The open text in 1:1–5 uses no proper nouns that demand special knowledge. Its language is accessible to readers from a wide variety of backgrounds and can be read meaningfully without recourse to either intertextual or intratextual references. New readers can proceed sequentially, knowing only what the text has already revealed. Only at the end of the prologue is the λόγος identified with Jesus Christ, linking the prologue to the narrative of the body of the Gospel, where the reader learns more about who Jesus Christ is. This understanding of the prologue as an entry implies a bridging function, from an open view of λόγος to an identification with Jesus Christ as the ὁ λόγος σὰρξ ἐγένετο in 1:14, 17.

Normal reading is sequential, from the beginning to the end. In some reader-oriented approaches to the text it is common to assume that the *implied reader* is a first-time reader who progressively learns what is in a book. Phillips assumes first-time readers with no knowledge of the content of John and rejects all intratextual references to parts of the Gospel yet to be read. But does the text of the prologue imply that the readers know more than they have yet been told?[13] In the case of readers of the Gospels, was the "story" generally unknown? The prologue raises this question in an acute fashion. The witness of John (the Baptist)[14] is introduced in 1:6–8, but John's actual words of witness are not reported until 1:15, where John is reported as saying, "This *was* [he of] whom I said, 'After me is coming ... ,'" *quoting* his words as yet to be narrated in 1:27 ("The one coming after me…"), and repeated again in his report in 1:30, "This *is* he concerning whom I said, 'After me comes….'" The reports of 1:15 and 30 are of words actually spoken in the narration of 1:27. The two reports agree more closely with each other than with the words in the narrated event. In all three instances, John (the Baptist) introduces his words differently. I conclude from the different use of tenses that 1:30 retains the perspective of Jesus's ministry in the narrative but the prologue adopts a postresurrection, postglorification perspective, because the incarnate λόγος has already returned to the bosom of the Father (1:18). That perspective is open to the narrator and reader (see 2:21–22; 12:16) but not the disciples and other participants in the events narrated.

Some texts like Gospels contain well-known stories and are read repeatedly. This Gospel bears the marks of long reflection and often presupposes that the readers know more than the text contains. I take this evidence to cast doubt on Phillips's view that the implied readers of John are "outsiders" from a wide variety of backgrounds. Rather, the evidence suggest that they are "insiders" who already have a basic grasp of the Gospel

---

13. No reader begins to read with a head empty of ideas and expectations (Bultmann [1957] 1961, 289).

14. He is simply called "John," the only John named in the Gospel. Do readers know that he is John the Baptist (or baptizer)? Do readers know of the baptism of Jesus by John? They will read of the baptizing activity of Jesus (perhaps of his disciples) and John in 3:22–26; 4:1–2. These references imply more knowledge than is given in the text.

story and are being challenged to grasp a deeper and fuller understanding and faith as revealed by the Jesus *of John*.

It may seem that Phillips has a strong case for rejecting any intertextual relationship between John 1:1 and Gen 1:1. He suggests that the supporting case, based on two common words in Greek and just one in Hebrew, is flimsy. In spite of this, C. K. Barrett writes, "That John's opening verse is intended to recall the opening verse of Genesis is certain" (1955, 126–27; 1978, 151). This conclusion can be justified convincingly, even if based on few words. It is not just any few words, and it also involves common context, and common theme. Although John begins by speaking of the relation of the λόγος to God, this is in order to speak of God's creation of all things by God's λόγος. Psalm 33:6 shows that the creative "and God said" of Genesis was widely understood as a reference to "the Word of the Lord." Thus John and Genesis both speak of God's creation of "all things" (the heavens and the earth in Genesis) "in the beginning" and by the Word. In the light of the common words, that should be enough to indicate intertextuality. But there is more! In the ancient world, books/texts were often known by their *incipit*, or opening word(s). Genesis was known as *bĕrēšît* (בראשית). In Greek this is ἐν ἀρχῇ. Hence, use of this one word, or these two words (LXX and John) *at the beginning* of each book, is an unmistakable intertextual reference, and that is why it has been widely recognized. But this does not exhaust the scope of intertextual evidence.

The work of J. Rendel Harris (1917), Rudolf Bultmann (1923), C. H. Dodd (1953), C. K. Barrett (1955, 1978), John Painter (1991, 1993a), and others has demonstrated the way the Wisdom tradition has interpreted Gen 1, and John's prologue intertwines Wisdom and Word traditions from the Wisdom literature in building on the Genesis creation. In the ancient world, the creation story of Genesis was widely known, as is attested by the Poimandres Tractate. Just as it uses Genesis for its own purpose, John has interpreted Genesis using Wisdom tradition to express the Johannine faith in Jesus. In Gen 1, God creates an orderly sequence of light and darkness, day and night (Gen 1:3–5; see Ps 104:20–23), but in John light and darkness portray a life-and-death struggle (1:5; 3:19–21; 8:12; 9:5; 11:9–10; 12:35–36, 46), which impinges on the symbolism of day and night (3:2; 13:30; 9:4; 11:9–10; 20:1). Nicodemus comes to Jesus (the light) from out of the darkness of night (3:2). Judas departs from Jesus into the darkness of night (13:30). The resurrection is reported as dawn is breaking (20:1). A world in which there is a struggle between light and darkness is the world in which the Johannine story takes place. In the world created by God's λόγος there is darkness and rejection. Nevertheless, this is God's world, and the fulfillment of God's purpose is the goal of the drama of the Gospel. At the very beginning of the Gospel we learn that the prologue forms a bridge, from the world of Genesis (John 1:1) and Moses (1:17) to the world to be made whole through the λόγος made flesh and now returned to the bosom of the Father (1:14–18).

C. K. Barrett:
The Theological Achievement of Prologue and Gospel

Though completed before the publication of Dodd's *Interpretation of the Fourth Gospel* (1953), Barrett's commentary on the Greek text of John was first published in 1955. It dealt with all textual, historical, and theological issues. Reviewers recognized it as a classic commentary that assured his reputation as a leading New Testament scholar and theologian. In the *first edition* he acknowledges his indebtedness, especially to three outstanding scholars: Rudolf Bultmann, and his teachers Sir Edwyn Hoskyns and C. H. Dodd. These three are set apart in this order, though his debt to another seventeen international scholars is noted. Barrett stands in a line of remarkable British Johannine scholars that includes, in addition to his teachers, Westcott and Bernard. They recognized that the Gospel was a literary unity. At the same time, his work bears the mark of an independent mind and an openness to learn from Bultmann in a critical manner at a time when English New Testament scholarship either ignored or disparaged his work. Barrett, like Dodd, acknowledges the Evangelist's use and mastery of sources in writing a Gospel to express his own theological vision. Where Dodd argued that this happened as the Evangelist sought to express the gospel in Middle Platonic terms for Greek readers, Barrett argues that the Gospel was the product of the Evangelist's struggle to overcome inherent tensions and limitations that had emerged in the tradition by the end of the first century. Barrett argues that the finished Gospel shows evidence of contact with Mark, and probably Luke, but Dodd argued that John was independent of the Synoptics, uncovering Synoptic-like tradition in John. For both, the Gospel is a profound interpretation of the tradition rather than a straightforward transmission of it. Barrett is closer to Westcott than Dodd, in seeing John's use of Jewish Jesus traditions and interpreting them in a Christian context at the end of the first century. It is an internal Christian theological work. A mark of Barrett's reading is to identify the dialectical character of the Evangelist's thought, holding together future and realized eschatology, human freedom and divine determination. See Barrett's essays on "The Dialectical Theology of St John" (1972, 49–69), and "Paradox and Dualism" (1982, 98–115).

Though recognizing the literary border between the prologue and the body of the Gospel, like Westcott, Barrett argues for the unity of the Gospel as the composition of the Evangelist. The prologue is a customized beginning of the Gospel using an echo of Gen 1:1 (not mentioned by Dodd), and an elaboration of creation tradition concerning the Word of the Lord and Wisdom found in the Psalms, Proverbs, Wisdom, and Sirach. In these traditions both the Word of the Lord and Wisdom are identified with Torah as agents of God's creative activity (Barrett 1955, 126–27; 1978, 151–52). The Gospel "was produced by normal literary processes" that were probably "complex rather than simple" (1978, 25).[15] The unity of language and thought is an expression of the author's "grasp of the theological significance of the earlier gospel tradition as a whole." From the fragments of tradition the author produced a unified vision of Jesus in word and deed (Barrett 1978, 51–54), "setting forth the faith once delivered to the saints in the new idiom" to overcome shortcomings in the fragmentary tradition, and errors in emerging Gnosticism, to win new converts, to strengthen "those who were unsettled by the new winds of doctrine," and to provide a "more adequate exposition of the faith itself" (1978, 25–26).

In John, Jewish and Hellenistic elements are "fused into a unitary presentation of the universal significance of Jesus" (Barrett 1978, 39). Although the Evangelist did not work in a vacuum, the Gospel is not addressed to specific groups in response to particular problems (1978, 139). Rather, the Evangelist "wrote primarily to satisfy himself" and "the traditional material … cried aloud for rehandling; its true meaning had crystalized in his mind, and he simply conveyed this meaning to paper." Evidence of the lack of concern for publication is found in "that the gospel had an obscure origin," and John 21:24–25 suggests that it was not published in the lifetime of the Evangelist. It is not surprising that the masterly response turned out to be relevant (1978, 133–35 [cf. 26]). On the whole, Barrett emphasizes the theological achievement, which has practical benefits. Unlike Westcott, Barrett recognizes this as the outstanding achieve-

---

15. This is set in a wider hypothesis concerning the Johannine literature (Barrett 1955, 113–14; 1978, 133–34, 577).

ment of the Evangelist and not as a feature of late first-century theological development. As with Westcott, the achievement is made by the Gospel as a whole.

Conclusion

The prologue of John has a distinct and special purpose in the Gospel. The rich concentration of intertextual evidence in the prologue provides a basis for recognizing it as a bridge from the understanding of God and the world found in the first creation story (Gen 1:1–2:4a) to the one established in the prologue. From the God who speaks to bring creation to completion, where night harmoniously follows day, the Evangelist has used Wisdom tradition to develop a more complex view of God, beginning with the relation of the λόγος to God. This prepares the way for speaking of incarnation and return of the λόγος/Son to the bosom of the Father. Only after introducing the λόγος does the prologue speak of the creation of all things (the world) by the λόγος.

The world too has changed. It is not complete, a harmony of day and night, but is dominated by the darkness. Though the life of the λόγος is the light, the world is not luminous with the presence of God, and it was necessary for the λόγος to become flesh to reveal the underlying goal of creation in the loving-kindness and faithfulness of God, to make creation whole (see Painter 1987b; 1993b, 27–42; 2002, 65–84). The prologue is a bridge from the worldview of Genesis and Moses (John 1:17) to reveal that creation is not complete and that the λόγος became flesh to make creation whole.

This bridge provides the conceptual transformation to enable Jewish and Christian Jewish readers to enter into the narrative world of the body of the Gospel. It is thus a bridge from something like the synoptic tradition to the Johannine telling of the story of Jesus. The point at which the prologue ends provides the perspective from which this Gospel tells the story of Jesus. It is the perspective open to the readers of the Gospel but not to participants in the story apart from the Jesus of John, and the man called John. It is the perspective of the narrator/Fourth Evangelist, and hence that of the prologue. Because the man called John also bridges the prologue and the body of the Gospel, it is also his perspective. Elsewhere in the narrative the narrator reminds the reader of the postresurrection perspective of the Gospel (2:21–22; 12:16), which is laid out in the theological paradigm of the prologue.

Bultmann relates the Johannine understanding of signs to the creative λόγος in the context of the darkness of the world. There are five key passages where he deals with the signs linked to the perception of the dynamic action of the divine creative λόγος.[16] From these passages (Bultmann [1941] 1971, 114, 452, 698; 1955b, 59–61), the following can be said. Like Dodd he notes that "miraculous" actions of Jesus are called "signs" only in John, where they are interpreted symbolically in Jesus's discourses. He concludes that the signs, like the words of Jesus, are ambiguous, and their meaning is accessible only to faith. The signs are visible words (*verba visibilia*), "deeds that speak." The words of Jesus are "divinely effected event, as ῥήματα ζωῆς (6:63, 68)" for those with faith. The signs reveal the presence and activity of God, but in a way that is accessible only to faith. In the signs the lovingkindness of the faithful God is present as a token, or as firstfruits, of God's purpose to make creation whole.[17]

Works Consulted

Barrett, C. K. 1955. *The Gospel according to St John: An Introduction with Commentary and Notes on the Greek Text*. London: SPCK.
———. 1972. *New Testament Essays*. London: SPCK.
———. 1978. *The Gospel according to St John: An Introduction with Commentary and Notes on the Greek Text*. 2d ed. London: SPCK.
———. 1982. *Essays on John*. London: SPCK.
Bernard, J. H. 1928. *A Critical and Exegetical Commentary on the Gospel according to St. John*. International Critical Commentary. Edinburgh: T&T Clark.
Bieringer, Reimund. 2007. Das Lamm Gottes, das die Sünde der Welt hinwegnimmt (John 1:29). Pages 199–232 in *The Death of Jesus in the Fourth Gospel*. Edited by G. Van Belle. Leuven: Leuven University Press.
Brant, J.-A. 2011. *John*. Paideia Commentaries on the New Testament. Grand Rapids: Baker Academic.

---

16. See Bultmann 1962, 78–79, 160–61, 346, 540–41; 1971, 113–14, 217–18, 452, 697–98; and (1951) 1977, 412–14; 1955b, 2:59–61.

17. For the relationship of the Johannine dynamic creative λόγος to the Johannine symbolism, see Painter 1979, 29–41; 1986, 41–61; 1991, 272–85; 1993b, 35–37; 2002, 65–84, and especially 2014, 44–46.

Brenk, Frederick E. 1993. A Gleaming Ray: Blessed Afterlife in the Mysteries. *Illinois Classical Studies* 18:147–64.
Bultmann, Rudolf. 1922. Karl Barth's Römerbrief in zweiter auflage. *Die Christliche Welt* 36:320–23, 330–34, 358–61, 369–73.
———. 1923. Der religionsgeschichtliche Hintergrund des Prologs zum Johannes-Evangelium. Pages 27–46 in *Eucharisterion: Festschrift für H. Gunkel*. Göttingen: Vandenhoeck & Ruprecht. English translation: The History of Religions Background of the Prologue to the Gospel of John. Pages 27–46 in *The Interpretation of John*. Edited by John Ashton. 2d ed. Edinburgh: T&T Clark, 1997.
———. 1941. *Das Evangelium des Johannes*. Göttingen: Vandenhoeck und Ruprecht.
———. (1950) 1955a. The Problem of Hermeneutics. Pages 234–61 in *Essays Philosophical and Theological*. London: SCM. Translation of Das Problem der Hermeneutik. *Zeitschrift für Theologie und Kirche* 47:47–69.
———. (1951) 1977. *Theologie des Neuen Testaments*. 7th ed. Tübingen: Mohr Siebeck.
———. 1954. Review of C. H. Dodd, *Interpretation of the Fourth Gospel*. *New Testament Studies* 1:77–91. English translation: *Harvard Divinity Bulletin* 27 (1963): 9–22.
———. 1955b. *Theology of the New Testament*. London: SCM. Translation of Bultmann (1951) 1977.
———. (1957) 1961. Is Exegesis without Presuppositions Possible? Pages 289–96, 314–15 in *Existence and Faith*. London: Hodder and Stoughton. Translation of Ist vorussetzungslose Exegese möglich? *Theologische Zeitschrift* 13:409–17.
———. 1962. *Das Evangelium des Johannes*. 17th ed. Göttingen: Vandenhoeck und Ruprecht.
———. 1971. *The Gospel of John*. Oxford: Blackwell. Translation of Bultmann 1941.
Dodd, C. H. 1935. *The Bible and the Greeks*. London: Hodder and Stoughton.
———. 1946. *Johannine Epistles*. London: Hodder and Stoughton.
———. 1953. *Interpretation of the Fourth Gospel*. Cambridge: Cambridge University Press.
Harnack, Adolf von. 1892. Über das Verhältnis des Prologs des vierten Evangeliums zum ganzen Werke. *Zeitschrift für Theologie und Kirche* 2:189–231.

———. (1894) 1961. *History of Dogma*. Translated by Neil Buchanan. London: Dover.

Harris, Elizabeth. 2004. *Prologue and Gospel: The Theology of the Fourth Evangelist.* 2d ed. London: T&T Clark.

Harris, J. Rendel. 1917. *The Origin of the Prologue to St. John.* Cambridge: Cambridge University Press.

Johnston, J. S. 1909. *The Philosophy of the Fourth Gospel: A Study of the Logos-Doctrine; Its Sources and Its Significance.* London: SPCK.

McNamara, Martin. 1972. *Targum and Testament: Aramaic Paraphrases of the Hebrew Bible; A Light on the New Testament.* Shannon: Irish University Press.

———. 2010. *Targum and Testament Revisited: Aramaic Paraphrases of the Hebrew Bible; A Light on the New Testament.* 2d ed. Grand Rapids: Eerdmans.

Pagels, Elaine. 1973. *The Johannine Gospel in Gnostic Exegesis: Heracleon's Commentary on John.* Nashville: Abingdon.

Painter, John. 1979. Johannine Symbols: A Case Study in Epistemology. *Journal of Theology for Southern Africa* 27:26–41.

———. 1986. John 9 and the Interpretation of the Fourth Gospel. *Journal for the Study of the New Testament* 28:31–61.

———. 1987a. *Theology as Hermeneutics: Rudolf Bultmann's Interpretation of the History of Jesus.* Sheffield: Sheffield University Press.

———. 1987b. Text and Context in John 5. *Australian Biblical Review* 35:28–34.

———. 1991. *The Quest for the Messiah: The History, Literature, and Theology of the Johannine Community.* Edinburgh: T&T Clark.

———. 1993a. *The Quest for the Messiah: The History, Literature, and Theology of the Johannine Community.* 2d ed. Edinburgh: T&T Clark; Nashville: Abingdon.

———. 1993b. Theology, Eschatology and the Prologue of John. *Scottish Journal of Theology* 46:27–42.

———. 2002. Earth Made Whole. Pages 65–84 in *Word, Theology, and Community in John.* Edited by John Painter, R. Alan Culpepper, and Fernando F. Segovia. St. Louis: Chalice.

———. 2004. Sacrifice and Atonement in the Gospel of John. Pages 287–313 in *Israel und seine Heilstraditionen im Johannesevangelium.* Edited by Michael Labahn et al. Paderborn: Schöningh.

———. 2007a. Memory Holds the Key: The Transformation of Memory in the Interface of History and Theology in John. Pages 229–45 in vol. 1

of *John, Jesus, and History*. Edited by Paul N. Anderson, Felix Just, and Tom Thatcher. Atlanta: Society of Biblical Literature.

———. 2007b. The Death of Jesus in John: A Discussion of the Tradition, History, and Theology of John. Pages 327–61 in *The Death of Jesus in the Fourth Gospel*. Edited by G. Van Belle. Leuven: Leuven University Press.

———. 2008. Review of Peter M. Phillips, *The Prologue of the Fourth Gospel: A Sequential Reading*. *Review of Biblical Literature*, November 29. http://www.bookreviews.org/pdf/5271_6646.pdf.

———. 2014. The Prologue as an Hermeneutical Key to Reading the Fourth Gospel. Pages 37–60 in *Studies in the Gospel of John and Its Christology: Festschrift Gilbert Van Belle*. Edited by Joseph Verheyden et al. Bibliotheca Ephemeridum Theologicarum Lovaniensium 265. Leuven: Peeters, 2014.

Phillips, Peter M. 2006. *The Prologue of the Fourth Gospel: A Sequential Reading*. Library of New Testament Studies 294. London: T&T Clark.

Ronning, John. 2010. *The Jewish Targums and John's Logos Theology*. Peabody, Mass.: Hendrickson.

Sanday, William. 1905. *The Criticism of the Fourth Gospel*. Oxford: Clarendon.

Westcott, Brooke Foss. 1958. *Westcott's St. John: A Reissue of a Famous Commentary*. London: James Clark. Reissue of *The Speaker's Commentary* of 1880.

Williams, P. J. 2011. Not the Prologue of John. *Journal for the Study of the New Testament* 33:375–86.

Jewish Readings of the Fourth Gospel: Beyond the Pale?

Ruth Sheridan

In Bernard Malamud's award-winning novel *The Fixer*, a familiar historical tale is dramatized in narrative form. Set in Tsarist Russia, the story tells of Yakov Bok, a Jewish artisan against whom a "blood libel" is taken out over the brutal murder of a Christian boy. Repeatedly interrogated by equally brutal prison guards, Bok refuses to confess to the crime, which he did not commit. In an attempt to endure his interminable prison stay, one day Bok breaks open the phylacteries left in his cell. He reads the scrolls found within "with excitement and sadness" until, one day, the prison guard Zhitnyak catches Bok in the act of reading, confiscates the scrolls and broken phylacteries, and hands the "new evidence" over to the Deputy Warden. But Zhitnyak is not entirely heartless. Assuming that Bok likes to read, Zhitnyak surreptitiously brings Bok a well-worn copy of the New Testament. When Bok questions the guard over why he has not brought an "Old Testament," Zhitnyak replies, "The Old won't do you any good at all. It's long been used out." Bok's impressions upon reading the New Testament surprise him. Initially wary, he comes to feel a strange empathic connection with the crucified Jew, who cried out to God on the cross but who was not heard. Bok wonders why, in a Christian land, he is kept in prison, when he is (like Jesus) innocent.

The other prison guard, Kogin, notices that Bok recites from memory the words of Christ. Perplexed, Kogin asks him why "a Jew who killed a Christian child" would memorize the Gospels. After Bok again denies that he even touched the boy, Kogin says that Jews consider it no crime to kill Christians. Kogin adds, "All that blood and matzo business is an old part of your religion," to which Bok replies, "In the Old Testament we're not allowed to eat blood. It's forbidden." Then ensues a most intriguing exchange. Bok goes on to question Kogin about the puzzling words of Jesus, wherein the believer is enjoined to "eat the flesh of the son of man and drink his blood" (cf. John 6:35). Kogin explains that these words of Jesus refer symbolically to the eucharistic elements: "Ah, that's a different load of fish altogether. It means the bread and the wine, and not the real flesh and blood." The exchange continues, with Kogin speaking first:

> "Besides, how do you know those words that you just said?
> When the Devil teaches scripture to a Jew they both get it wrong."
> "Blood is blood. I said it the way it was written."
> "How do you know it?"
> "I read it in the Gospel of John."
> "What's a Jew doing reading the Gospels?"
> "I read them to find out what a Christian is."

Reading this narrative exchange again now, in light of the recent advances in confessed "Jewish" scholarly readings of the Fourth Gospel, I am struck by its pointedness. Bok's final response in this exchange touches upon the observation voiced in literary-rhetorical criticism that reading is an ethical undertaking: accepting a readerly "contract" shapes our subjectivities (Booth 1988; Phelan 1996, 2004). Applied to sacred texts, or religiously canonical texts like the New Testament, similarly expressed premises suggest that the reader encounters a text with a transformative potential to shape him or her into the *imago Dei* (Schneiders 1999). In this light, Kogin's question, "What's a Jew doing reading the Gospels?" stands out. Is Jewish identity shaped by reading the New Testament? Does not "Jewish identity" stand opposed to the faith claims of the New Testament—at least its "high" christological ones, like those found in the Gospel of John? And Bok's response is that he wants to find out "what a Christian is." Bok is interested in discovering, we might say, how the Fourth Gospel shapes Christian identity.

These introductory remarks lead me into the topic of this essay. I want to discover if, and how, "Jewishness"—as a constructed social and religious identity—functions to create particular positions from which to read the Gospel of John. I am able to propose this topic because of the steady increase in the number of Jewish scholars who specialize not only in the New Testament generally but in the Fourth Gospel specifically. Two of these scholars will be examined in this essay: Daniel Boyarin and Adele Reinhartz.[1]

---

1. More could be named: Claude Montefiore (1894) was the first; see also Michael

Whether there is a particularly "Jewish" way of reading the Gospel of John is open to debate. This depends, in part, on how "Jewishness" is defined. Does it refer to the Jewish (religious and/or ethnic) identity of the scholar? Even if it does, there is the prior question of whether this identity should have any impact upon the apparently objective task of scholarship. Does "Jewishness" refer to the Jewish sources used (such as rabbinic literature) to read the New Testament?[2] And what might be said to attract Jewish readers to the Gospel of John (or to repel them from it)? Does the well-noted paradox that the Gospel of John is at once "anti-Jewish" and "most Jewish" have some part to play in this (Barrett 1947, 155–69)? It is difficult to answer these questions generally, because to do so would be to assume that "Jewishness" (an identity marker that is not homogeneous) conditions a certain kind of interest in the Gospel or guarantees certain results in the research.

Yet the two scholars I have chosen to examine in this essay identify the relevance of their Jewish identity for their interpretation of the Gospel of John. There is a consciousness expressed by each writer of reading from outside the borders of the Christian faith community. What is more, at least one of these writers concentrates specifically upon reading as a member of a group (in John, "the Jews") that is explicitly "othered" by the Gospel itself. These two scholars identify themselves as Jews in the literary context of what I will call autobiographical confessional narrative.[3] As such, my interest in this essay is not only in interpreting the *content* of their scholarship but also—and perhaps more so—in interpreting their prefacing narratives about themselves that situate aspects of their Jewish identity as highly relevant to their scholarship. These autobiographical narratives are, of course, not complete; they are fragmentary and tailored

---

Kraus (2006) and Sheridan (2012). Other Jewish scholars who have written on (or are writing on) the New Testament more broadly include Samuel Sandmel ([1956] 2005), Michael Cook (2008), Amy-Jill Levine (2006), and Joshua Garroway (2009).

2. For Kraus (2006), Jewish readings ought to refer only to the former, i.e., the affiliations/sensitivities, identities of the interpreter, not to the fact that the scholar uses Jewish sources. For the editors of the new *Jewish Annotated New Testament* (Levine and Brettler 2011), "Jewish" refers to both of these, and to other factors as well (xi–xiii).

3. This genre is said to have begun with Rousseau, but some scholars look back to Augustine. Bosch (2008, 141) looks back to the ancient Greek epic as the archetype for the autobiographical script—the testing of the hero and his homecoming (cf. Homer's *Odysseus*).

to the purpose at hand. But, I wish to ask, what is the discursive function of these fragmented confessional narratives? How do they frame the scholarship that they introduce? As narratives, how do they work in shaping a Jewish identity that then meets and interacts with the persuasive invitation to a Christian identity narrated in the Gospel itself?[4] I want to posit that the fragmented confessional mode of autobiographical narrative exhibited in the prefaces to the works of two scholars analyzed below (Boyarin and Reinhartz) aptly suits the content of those narratives, namely, some degree of concern over the *perception* of crossing a boundary that does not want to be crossed.[5] The confessional exigency is curiously expressed by both Boyarin and Reinhartz as "coming out"—for the former, exposing his (perhaps perceptibly) illicit "love" for Christianity as an Orthodox Jew, and for the latter, exposing her Jewish identity when the pressures of the academy were such that she felt she needed to keep this identity hidden behind a veneer of scholarly objectivity. Moreover, in each scholar's work, it is evident that the boundaries between Judaism and Christianity at the time of *the composition* of the Fourth Gospel were more fluid and porous than scholars have previously realized. The balancing of the bounded Jewish identity of the scholar with the porous Jewish/Christian identities found in the text of the Fourth Gospel creates a tension that adds both to the prefacing confessional narratives and to the scholarship of these authors.

The subtitle of this essay also warrants explanation. When I question whether Jewish readings of the Fourth Gospel are "beyond the pale," I do not use this proverbial term in its current sense of the abrogation of agreed standards of decency (although Boyarin once encountered an emotional response from a Christian student that might be said to have matched this definition!); much less do I mean it in its "urban" sense of someone who comes from a lower social class or intellectual capability. Rather, I use the expression in its archaic sense, which understands a

---

4. On telling the narrative of our lives in ways that make us who we are, see Eakin 2004. On the distinction between the subject who is *telling* and the subject who is *being told*, see Redman 2005 (32).

5. Note this theme in Harold Brodkey's illness autobiography: Avrahami (2003, 168) cites Ricoeur's remark about confession calling the audience to understanding while simultaneously seducing the audience by means of narrating a "scandal." The issue here is that some boundary that *should not* be crossed is crossed or is about to be crossed.

"pale" to be a geographically bounded region cut off from larger districts inhabited by those living in accord with hegemonic social and cultural discourses and practices.[6]

My use of the phrase and its geographical meaning is metaphorical and aims to fit with the subject of this edited book about "Bible, borders, and belongings." Jewish scholars are a minority within the field of Fourth Gospel studies—and within the global post-Christian culture of the Western world more generally. While there is no "pale" prohibiting Jewish scholarship on the Fourth Gospel, the relative newness of Jewish scholarship seems to require prefacing "confessions" that suggest a "pale" of sorts still exists. As "outsiders" to the faith that the Fourth Gospel vigorously promotes, Jewish scholars like Reinhartz and Boyarin are effectively shifting boundaries with their innovative readings of the text.

Daniel Boyarin

In a seminal article published in the *Harvard Theological Review* in 2001, Daniel Boyarin investigates the parallels between Johannine Logos Christology and the Aramaic articulation of the function of the *Memra* (Word) in the Targumim. Boyarin's aim in doing so is not to underscore the great theological differences between Aramaic-speaking Jews of Palestine and early (Johannine) Christians but rather to show how similar they were (2001, 244). Instead of espousing the long-held scholarly view that John's Philonic-inflected Logos Christology drove a wedge between Jews and Christians and was a key factor in the "parting of the ways" from an early date, Boyarin argues that John's Logos theology had important points of continuity with the first-century Jewish world, which were not cut off until well into the "second half of the second century" (2001, 246).

Boyarin pays specific attention to the prologue of the Fourth Gospel against the background of Philo's treatise on the *Migration of the Soul*, where the Logos is described both as a part of God and somehow distinct from God, with God in the beginning; he then analyzes the Targum fragments where the *Memra* is personified and depicted as performing roles similar to that of John's Logos: creating light at the beginning of time; speaking to humans; acting on behalf of God; saving and redeeming God's

---

6. We might also think of the Pale of Settlement in Russia, where Jews were settled in the *shtetl* culture in the seventeenth to nineteenth centuries.

people; and so on (2001, 256–57). What is more, *Targum Neofiti 1 identifies* God with the *Memra*, in the revelation of the divine name to Moses, reading, "I, my *Memra*, will be with you" (*Targum Neofiti* Exod 3:12–15; Boyarin 2001, 258). A poetic homily extant as a targumic fragment, called the "Four Nights," signals the probative conclusion for Boyarin. The "first night" of creation depicted in this homily has the *Memra* of God functioning as the agent through which "light and illumination" are created. Insisting that this cannot be a Christian interpolation because of various ancient witnesses to the Palestinian Targum, Boyarin concedes with the much earlier opinion of McNamara that the author of the Fourth Gospel would have heard this homily used in the synagogue and would have been influenced by it (Boyarin 2001, 259–260).

To substantiate his claims, Boyarin contends against consensus views that the genre of the Fourth Gospel's prologue is that of a hymn. Rather, like the Targumim, it is an example of proto-rabbinic midrash: an exegetical *narrative* on the opening of Genesis, a "synagogue homily of the Proem variety" (Boyarin 2001, 267). The first five verses of the prologue in particular fit this bill. According to Boyarin, the divergence between "Jewish" views and emergent "Christian" views comes only in verse 14 of the prologue, with the announcement of an incarnational Christology. But a binitarian view of the Godhead is not "un-Jewish" in this era: the Philonic Logos and the Targumic *Memra* indicate as much. It is when this separate "aspect" of God becomes incarnate in the man Jesus that we begin to see something categorically new in the thought world of early Judaism. Moreover, the midrashic homily was characterized by the way it played upon another text from the Nevi'im or the Ketuvim to expand and interpret the Torah text. For Boyarin, this second text was Prov 8:22–31, on the personification of Wisdom and her role in the creation of the world (2001, 269). To draw his argument together, Boyarin distinguishes between the preincarnate Logos (the *Logos Asarkos*), who in various other rabbinic texts was said to have appeared to Abraham (Gen 15:1 LXX), and the incarnate Logos (the *Logos Ensarkos*), in the Johannine view, the person of Jesus (2001, 257). Early Christians such as Justin Martyr drew a line of continuity between the activity of the preincarnate Logos and the Logos incarnate in Jesus (2001, 257). For Boyarin, the poetic homily that is the prologue begins with an exegetical narrative on Genesis (1:1–5) and a discussion of the appearance of the *Logos Asarkos* on earth (1:6–13) and concludes with a narrative of the *Logos Ensarkos* (1:14–18; Boyarin 2001, 276–77). The rejection of the Logos by "his own" in John 1:10 refers *not* to the rejection of Jesus in his lifetime but to the rejection of the *Logos Asarkos* before the birth of Jesus. This is precisely what necessitates the incarnation: the *Logos Asarkos* is perceived (by the Johannine author) to be an insufficient "teacher"; but the *Logos Ensarkos*—Jesus—will be a more effective teacher. Instead of reading this temporal movement as one of supersession, Boyarin reads the incarnation of the Logos in John's framework as a kind of complementary act to God's work in the world via the preincarnate Logos (2001, 278–79). The emergence of the *Logos Ensarkos* begins, however, the "specifically 'Christian' kerygma" (2001, 279).

Perhaps Boyarin's 2001 article illustrates that there is no specifically "Jewish" scholarly standpoint from which one reads this Gospel. Boyarin does not explicitly address issues of contemporary Jewish identity in this article. But in his 2004 book, *Border Lines*—a book based upon his 2001 article—Boyarin does raise this topic in all its exceedingly fraught dimensions. He writes, "Some Jews, it seems, are destined by fate, psychology, or personal history to be drawn to Christianity. This book won't let me be done with, or so it seems, until I come clean and confess that I am one of those Jews" (Boyarin 2004, ix). This "confession" leads Boyarin to ponder the difference between his two great "loves"—Rabbinic Judaism and Christianity—and how these loves inform his identity.

Boyarin hints that his motivation in analyzing the discursive practices of early "Christians" and Rabbinic Jews—the ways in which they created heresiological categories that effectively defined who was "in" and who was "out" and so "created" their respective faiths—proceeds in part from the need he feels to "discover the meaning of my work *to me*" (2004, xii). This need arises from the problematic of his desire for Christianity. He states that he has no desire to *convert* to Christianity, that he does not believe Jesus to be the Messiah, much less to be eternally begotten of God; he is not a "Jew for Jesus," but neither does he consider himself to be "a Jew *against* Jesus" (2004, xii). He is, rather, an Orthodox Jew. But the reception of his work in a variety of public forums raised the difficult question of his "place." In one forum, when Boyarin was presenting his reading of the Fourth Gospel just outlined above, "a very upset undergraduate" interrogatively asked him, "Who are you, and why are you taking our Gospel away from us?" (2004, x). Boyarin narrates his disengagement from the question of his personal identity at that time and what implication it might have had for his scholarship. His answer was, "I'm just trying to figure out what really happened!" Later, Boyarin became aware of his inability to evade the undergraduate's question: he needed to preface his work with an answer to the question "Who am I?" in order to properly explain his attraction to Christianity and to do justice to the Jews and Christians who would read his work (2004, x).

In a candid passage, Boyarin writes, "Something seems to frighten me here, either some boundary that I am afraid ... that I am threatening to breach or perhaps a fear that I will be perceived to have breached ... and be ... excluded from a community to which I still fervently desire to belong" (2004, xi). This desired community is Orthodox/Rabbinic Judaism, his "greater love" (2004, x). Today boundaries between Judaism and Christianity are clearly delineated. There is no middle ground—unless messianic Judaism is to be counted as such. Yet the period under analysis in Boyarin's work (ca. second–fifth century C.E.) attests to the fact that these "religious" identities were fluid and unsure and were being worked out as they developed, through heresiological practice. Hybridity, that curious and fearfully contagious mix of "Judaism" and "Christianity"—what is referred to in Christian writings as "Judaizing"—is the monstrous entity to be "othered." Early Christian and Jewish "orthodoxy" allowed no admixture of the "Other" to taint their perceived purity; heresy was hybrid (Boyarin 2004, xii). Boyarin finds himself "speaking for the monsters" in his book, the hybrid heretics that were both Jewish and Christian, *not* because he secretly "believes in Jesus" or wishes to revive some Jewish-Christian middle-ground, but because this "monstrous" position "is close enough to my own to call me to it, to identify with it as my place" (2004, xii). The complexity involved in the writing of a history in which the borders to belonging (to either Judaism or Christianity) were not fixed sits uncomfortably with Boyarin's professed and lived Orthodox Jewish identity. He writes from a "conventional form of Jewish identification," but his writing calls into question, historically, the terms of conventional, "orthodox" identities (2004, xii).

Boyarin's compulsion to "come out" in such a way in the book's preface, his felt need to "tell about [his] love" for Christianity as an Orthodox Jew, is expressed in metaphoric language also. The geographical metaphors used (borders, place, ground, boundary) and their related verbs (exclude, belong) are significant. Reader-response theories speak of the inescapability of reading from a "location," a geographic metaphor that describes the whole complex subjectivity that the author/scholar brings to the task of interpretation. In the interest of exposing one's presuppositions that may lead to bias in interpretation, reader-response critics are often upfront about their "place"—their nationality, sex/gender, personal history, faith commitments, and so on—which motivates the *questions* they ask of a text. This is not just about preempting criticism or providing a critical "disclaimer." Boyarin's brilliant analysis indicates that the work of finding a "place" is performed in the "placing." Heresiological discourse—in Althusserian terms, "interpellation"—"names" an Other and calls an Other into existence (Boyarin 2004, 1–33). The adventure of scholarship itself can often force one to carve out a "place" that is rather unique; it can often call one into existence. This fact seems to inhere in Boyarin's "confession": he writes as much to answer "Who am I?" as to answer "What really happened?" And as a historian, he knows that the answers to both questions often have a rich, complex, and confounding dialectical interplay.

Adele Reinhartz

The most well-known and influential work in the field of Fourth Gospel studies undertaken from a Jewish perspective is the book *Befriending the Beloved Disciple: A Jewish Reading of the Gospel of John* by Adele Reinhartz (2001b). Indeed, before Reinhartz's book there was no monograph in the field that considered or used a "Jewish perspective" as a hermeneutical framework. I will return to a more detailed analysis of Reinhartz's book in a moment, but for now I want to briefly look at another article written by Reinhartz that was later partially reworked and incorporated into the book. This article clearly sets out some of the questions that Reinhartz personally struggled with in terms of the relationship between the subject of her scholarly enterprise and her Jewish identity.

The article in question is entitled "John 8:31–59 from a Jewish Perspective" (Reinhartz 2001a). Reinhartz begins by saying that "rarely a week goes by" when she does not put the question to herself, "How *did* you end up in New Testament studies?" (2001a, 787). The underlying assumption of incongruity between Reinhartz's Jewish identity and her commitment to New Testament studies is influenced by a few factors. The first is a perceived incompatibility between the two, resulting from a "theological gulf" between the contemporary religious identities of Christians and Jews (2001a, 787). The second factor is a certain "suspicion" on the part of fellow Jews who have questioned Reinhartz about her decisions to study the New Testament (2001a, 787). These suspicions, and maybe even fears, arise from the view that engaging with the New Testament might lead Jews to reject their Jewish identity and adopt the

Christian faith (Reinhartz 2001b, 787). The third factor of confusion that Reinhartz notes is that "many Jews believe that the New Testament is in some way implicated in the roots and development of anti-Semitism and therefore helped to lay the groundwork for genocide" (2001a, 787). This final point is important for the ethical assumption it reveals—for a Jew to engage in New Testament scholarship after the Shoah must entail some kind of commitment to either exposing, refuting, or otherwise explaining this root anti-Semitism. For a Jewish scholar to shy away from the question of Christian anti-Semitism would be—in this view—to have no valid reason for studying the New Testament in the first place.

The evolution in Reinhartz's approach to the Gospel of John is detailed in a fascinating manner in her article. Citing a large section from the work of J. L. Martyn, she comments upon her efforts to situate herself in the place of the Johannine community, to hear the Fourth Gospel as its earliest readers would have heard it, so as to glean from the Gospel what the author intended "*in his own terms*" and not read into the text what she may want to hear instead (Reinhartz 2001a, 787). Martyn's mandate facilitated a "complete disengagement" between Reinhartz's Jewish identity and the Gospel text—between herself as an interpreting subject and the text as scholarly object (2001a, 787). She speaks of her acceptance of this scientistic approach to the text as a "complacency" that she later began to question (2001a, 787). The impossibility and even undesirability of scholarly objectivity as articulated in feminist and postmodern criticism motivated Reinhartz to change her stance toward the Fourth Gospel. Considering what it might mean to read the Gospel "ethically," Reinhartz asked, "Is there a way to read the Gospel that takes *the questions raised by one's Jewish identity* seriously and yet does not compromise the scholarly integrity of the enterprise?"(2001a, 788).

In her book *Befriending the Beloved Disciple*, Reinhartz elaborates upon this shift in perspective. She admits her difficulty in pinpointing the moment when this shift occurred, relating a gradual awareness of a "sense of vocation" in confronting the disturbing presentation of the Jews in the text of the Fourth Gospel (Reinhartz 2001b, 12). For a long time beforehand, Reinhartz had "studiously avoided those aspects of the New Testament that concerned Jews and Judaism most directly" (2001b, 13). A kind of "desensitization" occurred for Reinhartz in this time, as she bracketed out her Jewish identity from the process of interpretation and also bracketed out of her mind the negative portrayal of the Jews in the Gospel of John. She narrates that she became so good at this "bracketing" of her identity that even in her teaching her students were not always aware that she was Jewish: indeed, one class was under the general impression that Reinhartz was a Roman Catholic nun. Somewhere around this time, Reinhartz narrates, she became aware of her need to "'come out' as a Jew" (2001b, 13). But only when the field of New Testament studies opened up to reader-response approaches did Reinhartz realize the important role that her Jewish identity "should play" in her "work as an exegete of the Fourth Gospel" (2001b, 14).

One of the most impressive parts of Reinhartz's "confession" in her prologue to the book is her admission of what she found most disturbing about the Fourth Gospel when taking into full account her Jewish identity and commitments. For earlier Jewish scholars of the New Testament in general and the Fourth Gospel in particular (such as Montefiore, but also Samuel Sandmel) the "offense" of the text to Jewish sensibilities was primarily the kerygma that Jesus is God incarnate and that he is Messiah. The implications drawn from this by the Fourth Gospel were also held to be problematic: frequently the Gospel claims that there is no way to God other than through Jesus (14:6) and often the Law/Torah is presented as something from which Jesus distances himself (8:17; 10:34; 15:25). Montefiore especially found some of these implicit assertions affronting, arguing that scholars sometimes extrapolated harmful claims from the text, such as that Judaism post-70 C.E. was entirely off course for "rejecting" the Messiah (1894, 43–44, 63). For Reinhartz, these christological statements were not the bane of the matter. Instead, what bothered her was "the prominent and often hostile presentation of Jewish characters, Jewish laws, and Jewish practices" (2001b, 13).

I think that Reinhartz has identified the nub of the problem here. One does not need to be Jewish to cringe at the stark, largely unnuanced, and almost entirely pejorative use of the term "the Jews" in John. The repetition of the term alone is grating (just over seventy times in twenty-one chapters). The connotations of the term "the Jews" in John are almost irreducibly negative. This is, to be sure, a rhetorical victimization of the Jews. But the term "the Jews" is an historically continuous term that even today describes people who are ethnically Jewish and/or commit to some denominational form of Jewish communal religious expression. Then, as now, "*the* Jews" tends to lump *all* Jews together, ignoring the variegated and diverse nature of Jewish cultures and identities, but the term still functions as a marker of identity for a large global population.[7] This

---

7. Sometimes I read or hear people use the expression "the Jewish people" almost

observation makes it easier to see how a Jewish reader of the Gospel, like Reinhartz today, may hear the possibility of a transfer of what is ascribed to the Jews in John's Gospel to all Jews as Jews of every time and place. It may even suggest that "the Jews" today (let us say, any Jewish reader) might hear themselves addressed (or interpolated) as "the Jews" of the Gospel and be rightfully indignant. To be sure, much of this has to do with the issue of how *hoi ioudaioi* has been and perhaps should be translated. The literature on this question is enormous, and I will not enter into discussion of it here (see Sheridan 2013).

Reinhartz develops a careful interpretive analytic based on Wayne Booth's idea of reading as "relationship," that is, of reading as a mode of exchange between the ethos of the text and the ethos of the reader (Booth 1988). Reinhartz's framework of analysis has been explained at length in other publications, and this obviates the necessity of doing so here (Kraus 2006). I will give a brief summation. Reinhartz asks *what kind of people we become* when we read the Gospel of John, and this adequately expresses what it is that makes her attempted reading strategy "ethical" (2001b, 30). She identities four reading positions that any real reader of the Gospel may adopt. The first is a "compliant" reading of the Gospel that simply "accepts the gift" that the Beloved Disciple offers to his reader: eternal life in Jesus's name. The terms upon which this gift is offered are problematic for the Jewish reader, however: acceptance requires belief in Jesus as "Christ and Son of God" (cf. 20:31). A resistant reading, on the other hand, views the Beloved Disciple less as a teacher/mentor than as an "opponent." This stance reproduces—but in inverse fashion—the binary categories of the compliant reading: those who *resist* the "overtures of the Beloved Disciple" are presumed to be superior to those who accept them, as they are also resisting an anti-Jewish worldview. Neither a compliant nor a resistant reading of the Gospel breaks through the dualistic rhetoric of the Gospel. But a third possibility may perhaps do so: this is the sympathetic reading position. Inhabiting this position requires being able to temporarily put aside those points of difference between the reader and the text that are so discomfiting for the Jewish reader and instead to concentrate upon the points of commonality, without the reader accepting the central premises of the "gift" offered (Reinhartz 2001b, 27). This is a fruitful means of

---

as a euphemism in place of "the Jews" because the latter term has so much baggage. The definite/indefinite article seems to sharpen the problem in the case of "*a* Jew/*the* Jews." People often ask me, "Are you Jewish?" rather than, "Are you a Jew?"

enabling two radically different ethical visions to meet, but it kind of evades the problem and might even lead the Jewish reader back into the deliberate "bracketing" out of experience that Reinhartz describes so well in her prologue (2001b, 29). The fourth reading position articulated by Reinhartz is called an "engaged" reading. This approach addresses "the difficult and painful issues that stand between us"—that is, between the Gospel text and Reinhartz as a Jewish reader. An engaged reading positions the reader as one capable of recognizing the ethos of the Gospel while being able to resist its gift, without "othering" those who do accept it (2001b, 29).

Reinhartz then divides her attention between three "distinct but interrelated levels" at work in the narrative. These she calls the "historical tale," the "cosmological tale," and the "ecclesiological tale" (2001b, 34–53). The first deals with the Gospel narrative about Jesus and his disciples; the second deals with the theological narrative of the Logos entering the world in Jesus, and the gift of life through the Spirit-Paraclete; and the third concerns the story of the Johannine community as it can be glimpsed in the narrative. The combination of four reading positions across three tales generates twelve readings of the Gospel text. This makes Reinhartz's analysis nuanced and well rounded. For Reinhartz, "friendship" with the Beloved Disciple is not possible from either a "compliant" *or* a "resistant" reading position. To adopt the former is to compromise too much of her Jewish identity, with the ways it has come to understand how God is One (*Adonai echad*), but to adopt the latter is to reject all possibility of dialogue with the Gospel outright (Reinhartz 2001b, 162–63). A sympathetic reading is valuable but compromises too much on the role of readerly identity; and an engaged reading is a suitable point from which to "befriend" the Beloved Disciple, but Reinhartz finds that the terms of this friendship can never be "equal," so to speak. An *understanding* of, for example, the "ecclesiological" reasons for the Beloved Disciple's dualistic rhetoric (such as the community's possible exclusion from synagogues and felt sense of being "othered") is surely possible from this last reading position (2001b, 156). But as a Jewish reader, Reinhartz cannot feel "accepted" by the Gospel when reading from outside the boundaries of its system of belief—and hence the "unequal" terms of the friendship.

Reinhartz's scholarship has, for the most part, been positively received. Still, her "Jewish voice" remains a minority voice. When a minority voice is marginal (or marginalized) in the scholarship, if it is heard, it expresses realities that the majority voice is unable to express, precisely because the majority voice upholds the status quo by virtue of certain privileges that it has been accorded. In light of the momentous developments in philosophical and literary hermeneutics that have taken place in the last sixty years, it is no longer possible to deny validity to readings that foreground the active role of the reader in the process of interpretation. To hang on to historicist readings as though the intention of the author alone gives us clues to the meaning of the text is somewhat disingenuous: authorial intention is always *imputed* to a text by a reader. This imputation necessarily involves the interpreter's concerns and alerts us to the fact that authentic interpretation can and does take place when a reader's social location or particular bias is acknowledged rather than deliberately put aside in pursuit of objectivity. Reinhartz does not try to speak with a new authoritativeness for the Gospel of John; what she does attempt, however, is to read with authenticity.

Conclusions

The fragmented confessional (autobiographical) narratives of Boyarin and Reinhartz perform an important function in framing their scholarship. It is notable that Boyarin (in his preface to *Border Lines*) expresses something of the same concern as Reinhartz. It will be recalled that Boyarin wrote that the "frightening" aspect of his scholarly commitment was in the threat of the possible perception that he has breached a boundary that should not be breached. This perception, he wrote, could lead to his exclusion from his faith community. The Jewish "fear" of reading the New Testament that Reinhartz observes on the part of others is likewise expressed as a fear of crossing a boundary: that of the scholar possibly leaving Judaism for Christianity. The understanding of contemporary communal faith identities as a boundary marker is brought to the fore in the works of both Boyarin and Reinhartz. The perceived danger of boundary crossing (and the scandal it invokes) that inheres in a Jewish scholar's decision to investigate Christian sacred texts accounts for the apparent need both Boyarin and Reinhartz feel to confess their Jewish identity and the particular questions that this identity raises. These confessional autobiographical narratives, partial as they are, preface these scholars' forays into Gospel narratives that proclaim a Christian kerygma that evolved from a Jewish thought world. For Boyarin, there is fluidity in Jewish/Christian identities in the first several centuries of the Common Era that is virtually nonexistent today; yet he is drawn to this ancient hybrid place. For Reinhartz, her struggles with the anti-Judaism of the Johannine rhetoric (which has theological and historical layers) leads her to produce a work that is richly nuanced in its approach.

This essay has hopefully raised further questions about the idea of canon as boundary, and of faith community as bounded by canon. In this light, what does it mean to make a scholarly inquiry into the canon of the Other? What message does it perhaps send to others? What fears might it raise? Although there is much to contradict (or even to aggravate) modern Jewish readers in the Fourth Gospel, there is also much with which to sympathize, as previous scholars like Montefiore have shown, and as Boyarin and Reinhartz also indicate. Yakov Bok, in Malamud's novel *The Fixer*, feels this sympathy himself, as he ponders the words of Christ and even identifies with Christ's sufferings. Perhaps the work of Boyarin and Reinhartz will shift some boundaries in Johannine scholarship. Perhaps the question of Kogin to Bok, "What's a Jew doing reading the Gospels?" will not be a question that needs to be put so incredulously in the future.

Works Consulted

Avrahami, Einat. 2003. Impacts of Truth(s): The Confessional Mode in Harold Brodkey's Illness Autobiography. *Literature and Medicine* 22:164–87.

Barrett, C. K. 1947. The Old Testament in the Fourth Gospel. *Journal of Theological Studies* 38:155–69.

Booth, Wayne. 1988. *The Company We Keep: An Ethics of Fiction*. Berkeley: University of California Press.

Bosch, Mineke. 2008. Telling Stories, Creating (and Saving) Her Life: An Analysis of the Autobiography of Ayaan Hirsi Ali. *Women's Studies International Forum* 31:138–47.

Boyarin, Daniel. 2001. The Gospel of the *Memra*: Jewish Binitarianism and the Prologue to John. *Harvard Theological Review* 94:243–84.

———. 2004. *Border Lines: The Partition of Judaeo-Christianity*. Philadelphia: University of Pennsylvania Press.

Cook, Michael. 2008. *Modern Jews Engage the New Testament: Enhancing Jewish Wellbeing in a Christian Environment*. Woodstock: Jewish Lights.

Eakin, Paul John. 2004. What Are We Reading When We Read Autobiography? *Narrative* 12:121–32.

Garroway, Joshua. 2009. The Invasion of a Mustard Seed: A Reading of Mark 5.1–20. *Journal for the Study of the New Testament* 32:57–75.

Kraus, Michael. 2006. New Jewish Directions in the Study of the Fourth Gospel. Pages 141–66 in *New Currents through John: A Global Perspective*. Edited by Tom Thatcher and Francisco J. Lozado Jr. Resources for Biblical Study 54. Atlanta: Society of Biblical Literature.

Levine, Amy-Jill. 2006. *The Misunderstood Jew: The Church and the Scandal of the Jewish Jesus*. New York: Harper One.

Levine, Amy-Jill, and Marc Zvi Brettler, eds. 2011. *The Jewish Annotated New Testament: New Revised Standard Version*. Oxford: Oxford University Press.

Malamud, Bernard. 1966. *The Fixer*. New York: Farrar, Straus, and Giroux.

Montefiore, Claude. 1894. Notes on the Religious Value of the Fourth Gospel. *Jewish Quarterly Review* 7:24–74.

Phelan, James. 1996. *Narrative as Rhetoric: Technique, Audiences, Ethics, Ideology*. Columbus: Ohio State University Press.

———. 2004. *Living to Tell about It: A Rhetoric and Ethics of Character Narration*. Ithaca: Cornell University Press.

Redman, Peter. 2005. The Narrative Formation of Identity Revisited. *Narrative Inquiry* 15:25–44.

Reinhartz, Adele. 2001a. John 8:31–59 from a Jewish Perspective. Pages 787–97 in vol. 2 of *Remembering for the Future 2000: The Holocaust in an Age of Genocides*. Edited by John K. Roth and Elisabeth Maxwell-Meynard. London: Palgrave/Macmillan.

———. 2001b. *Befriending the Beloved Disciple: A Jewish Reading of the Gospel of John*. New York: Continuum.

Sandmel, Samuel. (1956) 2005. *A Jewish Understanding of the New Testament*. 3d ed. Woodstock: Jewish Lights.

Schneiders, Sandra. 1999. *The Revelatory Text: Interpreting the New Testament as Sacred Scripture*. Collegeville, Minn.: Liturgical Press.

Sheridan, Ruth. 2012. *Retelling Scripture: The Jews and the Scriptural Citations in John 1:19–12:15*. Biblical Interpretation Series 110. Leiden: Brill.

———. 2013. Issues in the Translation of *Hoi Ioudaioi* in the Fourth Gospel. *Journal of Biblical Literature* 132:671–95.

Mapping the Boundaries of Belonging: Another Look at Jacob's Story

Merilyn Clark

Border or boundary crossings expose us to new lands and new cultures. Whether the border crossing is forced or voluntary, legal or illegal, welcomed or resisted, we risk challenging our established values, identities, and lifestyles. The longer the stay across the border, the more likely one needs to wrestle with the issue of belonging.

Oceania is no stranger to border and boundary crossings. An important element of Oceania's history is that of migrations and settlements, with all the dislocation, disorientation, and new beginnings that accompany those. Contemporaneously, voluntary, legal, and welcomed migration persists into and within Oceania. Some of these migration patterns are causing political upheaval and are accused of generating social and economic difficulties in targeted nations such as Australia. One problematic pattern of migration concerns "illegal" immigrants, either "boat people" claiming refugee status or, more frequently, "fly ins" who overstay visas. This often results in migration into Oceania. The issue of boat people has become a vexed issue in Australia. A second problematic pattern that is just beginning to emerge is that of island states of Oceania slowly being drowned under rising sea levels due to global warming. Their citizens are forced to seek host nations; their survival demands they be accepted elsewhere as their situation becomes critical. This is likely to see migration movements within Oceania.

All immigrants are likely to experience alienation, that sense of being strangers within host nations, among often very different cultures, religions, languages, worldviews, and identities. But illegal immigrants and those forced by rising waters to leave homelands face additional pressures. The former are often not welcomed and must undergo additional dangers in crossing borders and further isolation and uncertainties in trying to prove refugee status in order to be allowed to remain. The latter must effectively deal with the physical loss of their homeland to which they may never be able to return. How will these new immigrants learn again to belong?

In Israel's long story, as told in Scripture, the motif of alienation is an important one. Israel remembered, in her sacred texts, being aliens and strangers in strange lands. In the face of these memories, her people were also called to care for the aliens and strangers within her own land. In his book *From Sacred Story to Sacred Text*, the canonical critic James Sanders argues that the canonical texts of sacred Scripture are at the center of belonging that bind communities of faith together. He contends that they address two fundamental questions: "Who are we?" and "What shall we do?" (Sanders 1987, 17). The answers to these questions shape the identity and lifestyle or praxis of the communities of faith that share them. Sanders argues that these texts acquired their canonical status within faith communities over time. They had to prove flexible and adaptable throughout the contingencies and exigencies of successive generations of faith, capable of answering these fundamental questions in whatever circumstances these faith communities found themselves (Sanders 1987, 11, 18–19). The texts revealed core relationships: relationships to God, to one another, to a land, and to the world in general. The relationship central to this network of belonging was their relationship with God: they were God's people, and he was their God. These relationships both shaped and were shaped by their sense of identity and behavior, which marked their uniqueness as individuals, families, tribes, and finally a nation.

Within the stories of the patriarchs Robert Alter argues that "Jacob in general is represented as a border crosser, a man of liminal experiences" (1996, 149). In the biblical texts Jacob is presented as an alien and stranger in all the lands in which he dwells. He crosses borders in order to save his life from his brother, whom he has cheated, and later in order to preserve his family from a terrible prolonged drought. He is never assimilated. His northern kin exploit him. He works long and hard to build their wealth and has to negotiate his freedom to return "home" to the land of his birth. Although he is an alien in his birth land, his destiny, shaped by covenantal promises from God and numinous encounters, shapes a sense of belonging to that land that he calls "home." Even in the promised land he differentiates himself from the host culture and his brother's community. There is a marked resonance between Jacob's experience and that of many modern migrants, including refugees. For this reason I have chosen this story as a relevant prism through which to seek insight into the issue of migration. In this paper I will explore the impact of boundary crossings in shaping identity and ethos, and ultimately belonging, in the Jacob texts, using a rhetorical-critical reading of those texts. Of particular interest is how identity, values, and lifestyle are challenged by border crossing; how belonging is shaped; and how difference can be negotiated and honored.

On Belonging

Belonging is a complex concept that is as much about nonbelonging as belonging, for it implies a distinctive and unique quality that defines a family or group. It is useful to consider Charles Taylor's notion of the politics of difference (in Gundry-Volf and Volf 1997, 6). This recognizes "the unique identity" of families or groups and "their distinctiveness from everyone else" (Gundry-Volf and Volf 1997, 6). If the authenticity of their identity, their belonging, is to be preserved, such distinctiveness must be preserved from assimilation into dominant or host cultures in which such families or groups dwell (Tromp 2011, 8). In exploring the dynamics of belonging, Miroslav Volf affirms Elie Wiesel's words that the stranger "represents what you are not, what you cannot be, simply because you are not *he*.... The stranger is *the other*. He is not bound by your laws, by your memories; his language is not yours, nor his silence" (Volf 1997, 41). Volf argues that distancing and belonging are crucial dimensions of the dynamic of strangers learning to belong in the lands and nations of others: "belonging without distance destroys, distance without belonging isolates" (1997, 42). He maintains that "belonging" in the midst of other cultures requires embrace that does not connote assimilation or inferiority and is more than reconciliation or giving the other their due. Rather, it involves reaching out to others (1997, 55–58) while remaining true to oneself; "living *in* a culture, *for* a culture" (1997, 43; Volf's own emphasis) but distinct *from* that culture. Difference requires separation as well as critique of self and other, but not exclusion (1997, 48–50). Volf argues that for communities of faith, belonging must center on God (1997, 45–47). God is central to the identity and ethos of any community of faith.

In the story of Jacob that sense of belonging emerges while the family is embedded in different cultures as aliens and strangers. Bound to the promises made to his grandfather, Jacob's life stories would contribute to the traditions that would consolidate and develop a distinct identity, lifestyle, and belonging that centered on Yahweh while dwelling as aliens in host cultures: "Israelites' identity was shaped by their history of transient existence; of landlessness in strange settings" (Tromp 2011, 24). They belonged to a land, and their destiny was tied to it while they were yet aliens in it.

The Abrahamic Context

The Jacob story is canonically situated in the early stages of patriarchy as told in Genesis. God's promises to Abraham of a multitude of descendants and a land wind through three generations of a family to become a key tenet of belonging. Central to their identity, as recorded in these texts, is Yahweh, their God. Yahweh is variously known as the God of Abraham, the God of Isaac, the God of Jacob, and later the God of Israel, where Israel, the name given to Jacob at the Jabbok, comes to name the people, the land, and the nation. Their identity, this sense of belonging, emerges tenuously, becoming consolidated amid dysfunctional and troubled family relationships over three generations. This forging of identity is further complicated by the experience of alienation: "Israel's lineage, tradition and self-identity is grounded in the setting of alienation" (Tromp 2011, 15). Abraham is removed from his birth land, kin, and culture by God to sojourn (*gûr*) for the rest of his life in lands far away both as stranger and as resident alien (*gēr*). A common root in the Hebrew links this verb (*gûr*) and noun (*gēr*): *to sojourn involves alienation*. Within the dominant host cultures in which they sojourn, Abraham and his family gradually acquire a new identity and lifestyle that is slowly forged into its distinctive, unique character. Without traditions or sacred texts for support, and alienated from past familial cultures and present host cultures, this marginalized and vulnerable small group has to resist pressures for assimilation into the dominant host cultures they encounter, while being protected by the One they are just learning to know. Separation and protection prove crucial for new ways, new worldviews, a new culture, and a new identity to emerge within a transitory lifestyle marked by alienation.

Inextricably linked to this process of forging a new identity and ethos are God's covenant with Abraham and God's promises of land and of being a people. The fulfillment of these promises lies in a distant future. Therefore, it is necessary to foster resistance to host cultures and maintain alienation and sojourning. The shaping of their sense of belonging is fraught. The journey of the promises through the first three generations is precarious, dangerous, and tentative. The carriers of the promise are flawed human beings. Yet, as Israel's storytellers remembered and wrote of their past, they stood at the cusp of the story of Israel's formation as a people and location within the promised land. This is a boundary story, a beginning story about belonging. It is a story that allowed Israel to survive exile and eventually to develop lively diasporan communities that contributed to their host nations' well-being without the need for assimilation.

The Jacob Story

In the story of Abraham it is God who identifies the son of the covenantal promise as Isaac (Gen 17:16–21). A wife for Isaac is chosen from among kin rather than from the host Cannanite community in which they sojourn. Isaac, however, comes to his deathbed without the next son of promise being identified, without the blessing of promise being passed on. While one may anticipate that Isaac's deathbed blessing will address this matter, it does not. Isaac wishes to direct this final blessing to his favored older son, Esau. But the twins' mother, Rebekah, conspires with her favored younger son, Jacob, to steal it. The conspiracy involves a complex and cunningly planned deception of Jacob's frail, old, blind father, Rebekah's husband. Commanding Jacob's obedience, Rebekah pits brother against brother and son against father. But Jacob is knowingly and willingly complicit, especially after his mother accepts full responsibility: "Let your curse be on me, my son" (Gen 27:13). Nowhere does Jacob evince concern for God's view of his and his mother's behavior. Nowhere does his mother invoke the deity, referring to God only when she misreports Isaac's words to Esau as "so that I may bless you before the Lord before I die" (Gen 27:7). Isaac's words, however, do not include "before the Lord," in Gen 27:4 (cf. Gen 27:10). Perhaps her willingness to lie to Jacob signifies her attempt to impress upon Jacob the importance of this blessing. Kass argues that through her words Rebekah compels "a reluctant Jacob to acknowledge for the first time the importance of his father, when she forces him to seek his father's blessing" (2003, 412). Importantly, Isaac's words to Esau, literally translated "so that my *nepeš* may bless you before I die" (Gen 27:4), point to the blessing being rooted in the core of Isaac's being. Both Isaac's and Rebekah's words and deeds suggest that this is a struggle for power, for worldly power within the next generation.

Throughout, Jacob owns close familial relationship with the participants through pronominal usage, referring to "*my* brother" and "*my* father." However, when he addresses his father's suspicions at the beginning of the deception, Jacob not only directly lies to his father about his identity—"I am Esau, your firstborn" (Gen 27:19)—but also cunningly and deceivingly attributes the reason for his quick hunt to "because the Lord *your* God granted me success" (Gen 27:20). This pronominal usage suggests not only that Jacob does not own relationship to this God but also that he does not respect the power of this God to impact upon him for his lying and impious words to his father. It further implies that Jacob is aware of his father's relationship to the Lord God, who is also the God of his grandfather Abraham. This may also be inferred by his later references to "the God of Abraham and the fear of Isaac" (Gen 31:42, 53).[1]

When Isaac finally overrides his suspicions and blesses Jacob with Esau's blessing, it is revealed that the blessing at Isaac's core is not about God's covenantal promises but about worldly prosperity and power, regionally and within the family, in the land where they sojourn as aliens, despite being clothed in formulaic religious sentiments: "May God give you…" (Gen 27:28). When Esau's arrival heralds the realization of Jacob's deception, father and son are utterly distressed, Esau pleading: "Bless me, me also, my father" (Gen 27:34, 38). This finally elicits a blessing, in which the possibility of Esau throwing off his brother's lordship is canvassed (Gen 27:39–40). This blessing is clothed in no religious sentiments. It also seems to come from Isaac's core, expressing his heartfelt hope for this son. But Esau promises revenge upon Jacob after their father's death (Gen 27:41).

Aware of Esau's fury, Rebekah insists Jacob flee to her brother's house in faraway Mesopotamia until Esau's anger dissipates and "he forgets what you have done to him," so that Jacob can return to them (Gen 27:42–45). To secure approval for her plans, she discusses with Isaac the need for a suitable wife for Jacob, as she does not like Esau's local wives (Gen 27:46). Thus she is able to criticize Esau and disguise Jacob's flight as a legitimate search for a wife (Alter 1996, 145). After Isaac orders Jacob to Rebekah's brother's house to get a wife, he, surprisingly, takes up his patriarchal authority and blesses Jacob with the blessing of promise. In the identification of Jacob as the son of promise, both prongs of the blessing, land and a people, are addressed. Perhaps Esau's choice of Canaanite wives suggests some assimilation with Canaanite culture, and perhaps

---

1. This may allude to Isaac's near sacrifice on Mount Moriah (Gen 15).

Isaac recognizes the need to preserve their distinction as embodied in the blessing of promise.

> And may El Shaddai bless you
> And make you fruitful and multiply,
> So you become an assembly of peoples.
> And may He grant you the blessing of Abraham,
> To you and your seed as well,
> That you may take possession of the land of your sojournings,
> Which God granted to Abraham. (Gen 28:3–4; Alter's translation [1996])

Unlike Jacob's earlier reference to "the Lord *your* God," Isaac does not own direct relationship with this God in this blessing. Rather, he locates the authority of the blessing within the Abrahamic tradition, appearing almost an intermediary between Abraham and Jacob. However, Isaac does not confine the blessing of promise to Jacob but extends it to his seed, his offspring, affirming perhaps a belief that this nuclear family will become an "assembly of people." In Brueggemann's words, this story deals with "the transmission of the promise and the inheritance from one generation to the next. There is in Genesis no one-generational faith. There is always the problem of the promise being safely entrusted to the next generation. Here as elsewhere, that vertical move from *generation to generation* causes a crisis" (1982, 226). However, in this family the "safely entrusted" promise passes very precariously on to the next generation. At this stage we are not sure that the promise has been "safely entrusted" into the hands of Jacob. Finally, the blessing acknowledges that Isaac and Jacob yet remain aliens, resident aliens in the land of promise. This is not yet "their" land by possession, but rather it is their land only in promise; they will continue to be sojourners in it.

Although Jacob leaves Canaan twice blessed by Isaac, he does not leave provisioned or protected, as did Abraham's servant who conducted Isaac's bride search. Jacob has to flee for his life, embarking on a long and dangerous journey north to Mesopotamia, on foot, alone, to live by his wits: "He is a fugitive from all the usual claims of family and propriety. He is a fugitive from the well-ordered world of law" (Brueggemann 1982, 236). Although no law codes are enunciated in the Torah until the Ten Commandments at Sinai, there are stories throughout Genesis where behavior is judged and individual rules to govern human behavior are specified. The flood story is one such example. Alan Dershowitz, a law professor at Harvard, argues that

> The entire Book of Genesis is about the early development of justice in human society. Jacob is born into a world with few rules and many inconsistent precedents regarding deception. His father and grandfather, Isaac and Abraham, pretended their wives were their sisters in order to save their own lives.... The biblical narrative goes out of its way to show that Jacob's deceptions against others are turned back against him—over and over again. Moreover the deceptions inflicted upon Jacob are strikingly symmetrical with those he inflicted upon his brother and father. (2000, 138–39)

This issue of law is more complex than Dershowitz suggests. Living in Canaan, this alien family has to deal with a host culture with its own laws, norms, and customs, and its familial (Mesopotamian) culture with its laws, norms, and customs. Further, despite his father's and his grandfather's deceptions, which God addressed and Pharaoh complained about, it is clear that Jacob's behavior evokes practical and emotional reactions within the family. Jacob fears the consequences of his actions, even recognizing his sin (Gen 27:11–12); his mother too recognizes the validity of his fears and takes them upon herself (27:13); his father is devastated (27:33); Esau clearly feels a terrible sense of loss, begging for a blessing (27:34), weeping (27:38), raging, and determined to seek redress by killing Jacob (27:41). All this suggests that Jacob's behavior is outside acceptable family norms. Through his deception, lies and theft, Jacob forfeits claims on family and has to pay the consequences of his actions. His departure from the family without support is a sanction the father invokes upon this son. If this son of promise is indeed to father a people, he has to find a suitable wife, and do it alone and unaided. He will never see his mother alive again.

However, this God, as yet unclaimed by this fugitive exile and alien, approaches Jacob in the night, when he is alone and very vulnerable: "It is the wonder, mystery, and shock that this God should be present in such a decisive way to this exiled one. The miracle is the way that this sovereign God binds himself to this treacherous fugitive" (Brueggemann 1982, 242). In his dream that God visits upon Jacob, God confirms to Jacob the blessing of promise conferred on him by Isaac (Gen 28:13–16).

A fuller blessing than his father's version, God's words assure that the transmission of the promise will move through Jacob's descendants. It also contains formidable and extraordinarily gracious personal assurances of God's care and presence in Jacob's journey and life. He will be protected, preserved, and brought safely home. The dream astonishes Jacob: "Surely the Lord is in this place" (Gen 28:16). But despite this numinous liminal experience and his fears, Jacob's vow in response is cautious, conditional, and self-protective, his conditions reflecting his concerns for his safety and his material needs. Jacob is still not prepared to trust this God. Curiously, the language shifts toward direct address to God as Jacob work through his bargain:

> If the Lord God be with me and guard me on this way that I am going and give me bread to eat and clothing to wear, and I return safely to my father's house, then the Lord will be my God. And this stone that I set as a pillar will be a house of God, and everything that You give me I will surely tithe it to You. (Gen 28:20–22; Alter's translation [1996])

While Jacob appears in no hurry to make Abraham's and Isaac's God his own, Jacob's bargain places him consciously on the boundary of faith with this God.

During his sojourn with uncle and later father-in-law Laban, Jacob finds himself up against another shrewd bargainer and deceiver. Little wonder Laban early expostulates, "Surely you are my bone and my flesh" (Gen 29:14). This does not foster a sense of belonging in Jacob but rather hints of competitiveness between the two men in seeking to fulfill their needs and wants, until finally Jacob yearns to return to the land where his father and brother live.

While Jacob is not portrayed as speaking much of this God in his years with Laban's family, Leah's words suggest that he does. In naming her own sons, she provides comments that imply a relationship with this God of Abraham and Isaac: regarding Reuben, she says, "Because *the Lord* has looked on my affliction…" (Gen 29:32); regarding Simeon, she says, "Because *the Lord* has heard that I am hated, he has given me this son also" (29:33); and regarding Judah, she says, "This time I will praise *the Lord*" (29:35). Rachel refers to God when her handmaid bears a son (30:5) but does not refer to him as "the Lord" (*Yhwh* in Hebrew) until she herself bears Joseph (30:24). Laban has also learned something of Yahweh, for in bargaining for further service from Jacob, he says, "I have learned by divination that *the Lord* has blessed me because of you" (30:27), which Jacob affirms (30:30). After Joseph's birth, Jacob asks Laban to be allowed to return "to my own home and country" (30:25–26) with his wife and children. It becomes clear that though he and his father and brother have dwelled in that land as aliens, it is the land with which Jacob identifies, his home. It is the land promised through Esau's final blessing. It is the land that God has assured him at Beth-el he will return to. Despite long years of hard work for uncle Laban in Laban's lands as shepherd and animal husband, and his marriages to Laban's daughters, Jacob belongs neither with uncle Laban nor in his land. He is sufficiently marked as different for his growing wealth to raise the ire of his brothers-in-law (31:1), and even Laban's attitude toward him becomes more hostile over time (31:2). As he advises his brother in his first message to him, "I have sojourned with Laban" (32:4), the verb (root *g-w-r*) clearly identifying him as an alien (*gēr*) while with Laban.

In the end Jacob's departure from Laban is precipitated by God's command to return to the land of promise (Gen 31:3), Jacob acknowledging to his wives that "the God of my father has been with me" (31:5). It appears that Jacob is still coy about owning God as his own God. Having persuaded his wives to accompany him, with his children, Jacob leaves secretly (31:4–21). Their flight triggers pursuit by an angry Laban (31:22–23). The text now refers to Laban as "the Aramean," a term that further distances Laban from Jacob and his family. The outcome of their final encounter might be very different were it not for the dream God visits upon Laban the night before their final encounter (31:24). Jacob acknowledges: "If the God of my father, the God of Abraham and the Fear of Isaac, had not been on my side, surely now you would have sent me away empty handed" (31:42). Despite the acrimony that Laban first expresses and then Jacob, they prove able to negotiate a covenant of peace between them, a covenant that recognizes borders and allows embrace in their separation. There is a clean separation of Jacob from Laban, and from Laban's gods and his culture with Jacob's own wives, children, and stock intact. Jacob's identity is slowly resolving itself. In this covenant Jacob has not followed Laban's example but "swore by the fear of his father Isaac" (31:53). He also initiates a sacrifice, including a sacrificial meal with his kinsfolk (31:54). This is the first recorded act of this kind undertaken by Jacob. Acting with an authority that he has not previously employed, Jacob stands as an equal with Laban, no longer his servant, nor subordinate in family rank. In doing so he moves even closer to the God of his fathers.

After the two parties separate, Jacob tersely reports an encounter with angels of God (Gen 32:1–2), a numinous experience resonating with his dream of angels at Beth-el. When Esau replies to Jacob's message that he is coming with four hundred men, a threatening display of power, Jacob's fear erupts again. He seeks to protect his family and his flock, using various tactical strategies, including prayer to God. This is the first time that the text shows Jacob at prayer directly addressing this God of his fathers since Beth-el:

> A God of my father Abraham and God of my father Isaac!
> > B Lord who has said to me, "Return to your land and your birthplace, and I will deal well with you."
> > > C I am unworthy of all the kindness that you have steadfastly done for your servant.
> > > > D For with my staff I crossed this Jordan, and now I have become two camps.
> > > C' O save me from the hand of my brother, from the hand of Esau, for I fear him, lest he come and strike me, mother with sons.
> > B' And You Yourself said, "I will surely deal well with you, and I will set your seed like the sand of the sea multitudinous beyond all count." (Gen 32:9–12; Alter's translation [1996])

After the opening salutation (A), which owns God's familial place in the lives of his father and grandfather, the prayer is structured as a chiasm. In this prayer Jacob rehearses part of the promises made by God (B, B') and the care that God has shown him (C), acknowledges his fears, asks God to protect him and his family, that is, to show him further undeserved care (C'), and finally acknowledges himself to be God's servant. The turning point (D) recognizes Jacob's precarious and vulnerable position. This prayer too reveals something of the bargainer that Jacob is. There is no biblical account of God assuring Jacob that he will do him good. Kass contends:

> Jacob cannot inherit the covenant of his fathers without addressing the enmity of his brother, Esau, and the lurking danger of fratricide.... But confronting Esau is more than a practical inevitability; it is also a moral imperative. Failure to settle accounts with Esau and to make amends for his conniving past would leave a permanent blot on Jacob's supremacy. It would cast grave doubts on his fitness as the next patriarch under the covenant. For under God's new way—in contrast to the uninstructed human way—a man cannot properly take his father's place by denying or destroying his father's other sons, that is, his brothers.... The ambiguous relationship between brothers bespeaks one of the deepest problems inherent in all family life: the tension between family of origin and family

of perpetuation, and more generally, between the claims of the past and the claims of the future. (2003, 446–47)

In the long night of waiting by the river, Jacob has a further numinous experience when he struggles with a stranger all night. During the encounter in that liminal space, Jacob, deceiver and thief, is wounded but hangs on tenaciously. He does not lose heart and is blessed and given a new name: "You shall no longer be called Jacob, but Israel, for you have striven with God and with humans and have prevailed" (Gen 32:28). This new name signals a new identity, freeing him from all that has defined him in the past. Although his assailant refuses to identify himself, Jacob himself interprets the experience: "And Jacob called the name of the place Peniel, meaning 'I have seen God face to face and I came out alive'" (Gen 32:30; Alter's translation [1996]). The man who waits on the border at nightfall for his brother is, at dawn, no longer the same man. A limping new creation, Jacob advances to successfully encounter his brother, gifting him with wealth and blessing. His behavior restores Esau's birthright blessing, for Jacob, in a reversal of positions, bows to his brother, speaks respectfully to him, and offers him gifts. Jacob in turn is embraced, apparently forgiven. He returns in peace and is received in peace. Thus, throughout his journey to, sojourn in, and return from Northern Mesopotamia, Jacob's character is "tested and refined, his personality moulded and transformed by the experience" (Sarna 1989, 197).

This is not the end of Jacob's story or boundary crossings. He will be deceived by his own children and know much sorrow over Joseph's reported death and Benjamin's later detention in Egypt. He will spend the final years in Egypt under the protection of Pharaoh and Joseph. But his demand that his body be returned to the land of promise, his home, the land in which he belongs, and be buried in the cave that Abraham bought and in which many of his forebears lie, will be fulfilled.[2]

Concluding Reflections

The story of Jacob proves a complex and highly nuanced reading of the experience of border and boundary crossings and their challenges to iden-

---

2. Compromises between Egyptian burial practices and the family's burial practices are evident in these arrangements (Berman 2006), as Joseph struggles with the demands of his father's culture and those of his host nation.

tity, values, and practices, which shape belonging. Whether permanent or temporary, border crossings are not just an external experience; they also foster inner journeys. Even temporary border crossings may challenge an alien or stranger's identity, values, and lifestyle.

From Jacob's story we find that kinship ties of extended and nuclear families and close common family histories and experiences are of themselves not enough to ensure belonging. Belonging is not simply inherited but needs lifelong renegotiation. Further, being an alien or stranger in a land may prove no impediment to the formation of a sense of belonging to that land. Notions of destiny and religion also mediate belonging.

The story acknowledges that border crossings may be fraught with threat and danger: of provoking hostile responses, of loss of wealth, of being wounded, of alienation and isolation, and of a need to deal with challenges to personal identity, values, and practices, and hence belonging. There is a need for careful, respectful, and honest negotiation with the Other. Border crossers may preserve and develop a distinctive and different identity and lifestyle from the dominant host and other cultures. While inhibiting assimilation, differentiation and separation can be negotiated without violence and alienation and may be marked by embrace and peace.

The story suggests that if border crossers are open to the experience and are given the space they need by the host culture, border crossing can prove life enriching and life changing rather than destructive or diminishing. The story shows borders to be liminal places where the numinous may break through. Encouragement to process such experiences within religious contexts may allow border crossers to better negotiate their crossing. In speaking about Jacob, Joan Chittister refers to the crucial role the inner self plays in enabling people to survive radical reorientation:

> The whole question becomes, what, if anything, is there inside us to carry us through this period of social and personal disorientation, of social and personal malaise, of personal and social relativism, not just in order to make the confusion bearable but to vindicate the struggle?
>
> At the same time, there is another side to this whirligig of swift social twists and harsh personal changes. There is the awareness of unlimited possibility, of certain growth, of life-giving change, both around us and within us. Life may feel precarious at times but life is also, we know, made up of a series of miracles. (2003, 12)

Border crossings may prove enriching, rewarding, and sustaining for all if there is mutual negotiation of difference between new immigrants and host cultures; a willingness to critique and be critiqued, especially in determining acceptable practices within the wider community; a recognition that life changes us all and challenges who we are and how we are to live; encouragement to personally process the experience of border crossing; respect of different spiritual and worship traditions; and ongoing intergenerational negotiation of peace and embrace between the various communities who share a land and nation. Like the Israelites of old, we who belong in Oceania and embrace her need to hear again the demand that we care for aliens and strangers in our lands, and that we do this compassionately, wisely, and innovatively.

Works Consulted

Alter, Robert. 1996. *Genesis: Translation and Commentary.* New York: Norton and Coy.

Berman, Joshua. 2006. Identity Politics and the Burial of Jacob (Genesis 50:1–14). *Catholic Biblical Quarterly* 68:11–31.

Brueggemann, Walter. 1982. *Genesis.* Atlanta: John Knox.

Chittister, Joan. 2003. *Scarred by Struggle, Transformed by Hope.* Grand Rapids: Eerdmans.

Dershowitz, Alan M. 2000. *The Genesis of Justice: Ten Stories of Biblical Injustice That Led to the Ten Commandments and Modern Law.* New York: Warner.

Goldingay, John. 2003. *Israel's Gospel.* Vol. 1 of *Old Testament Theology.* Downers Grove, Ill.: InterVarsity.

Gundry-Volf, Judith M., and Miroslav Volf. 1997. *A Spacious Heart: Essays on Identity and Belonging.* Harrisburg, Penn.: Trinity Press International.

Kass, Leon. 2003. *The Beginning of Wisdom: Reading Genesis.* New York: Free Press.

Moyers, William. 1996. *Genesis: A Living Conversation.* New York: Broadway.

Sanders, James. 1987. *From Sacred Story to Sacred Text: Canon as Paradigm.* Philadelphia: Fortress.

Sarna, Nahum M. 1989. *The JPS Torah Commentary: Genesis.* Philadelphia: Jewish Publication Society.

Tromp, K. J. 2011. Aliens and Strangers in the Old Testament. *Vox Reformata: Australian Journal for Christian Scholarship* 76:5–24.

Volf, Miroslav. 1997. Exclusion and Embrace: Theological Reflections in the Wake of "Ethnic Cleansing." Pages 33–66 in Gundry-Volf and Volf 1997.

Slipping across Borders and Bordering on Conquest: A Contrapuntal Reading of Numbers 13

Judith E. McKinlay

Numbers 13: spy story in the book of Numbers. It fits well in this tale of a landless people, escapees from Egyptian imperial power, making their slow, relentless way to another land, anOther people's land. A tale of a people and a land—to which they are traveling but which remains out of reach, inhabited by Others. It is, as has been long recognized, one episode within the overarching theme of conquest. Of course, it is not nearly as simple as this, for this is sacred Scripture, a work of religious faith. Yet it is also inherently political, a justification for land taking, written long after the event, with a carefully devised rationale for a people already long identified as Israel. It is a tale of borders to be crossed and boundaries that rebuff, yet borders and boundaries are by their very nature always and inherently permeable. So enter the spies, whose role in slipping across and gaining knowledge of what lies beyond is pivotal, if variously interpreted.

I pause, considering the fact that, as it is told, it is YHWH who is the instigator, sending in the spies and ordering Moses, with the reminder that this land is to be a divine gift for his landless people. Already I find myself baulking at the use of this motif of God's gifting to sanction the taking of other people's land. I am interrupted by the Deuteronomist insisting, "You've got it wrong. In this instance, it was the people who proposed this. Moses simply agreed" (see Deut 1:22–25). I look again at the text: "In the book of Numbers the divine word clearly gives the command," I tell him, "although three times I am told that Moses sends the men out." Certainly it is significant that three times Moses is the subject of the verb of sending (Num 13:3, 16, 17), yet, as I gently remind him, the Priestly writer is as aware as he is that Moses is YHWH's faithful servant. He, however, interrupts again: "What's with this word 'spies'?[1] Haven't you read my account (Deut 1:22–25)? It was a simple matter of working out the best route and noting the placing of the cities—a reconnaissance, not a CIA, MI6 mission!"

I look to the writer of Numbers but see shadows, of Priestly scribe and ancient storyteller(s?). I recognize that different hands have penned this tale, that I am reading a carefully woven final form.[2] The early storyteller, not to be put down, steps forward in reply: "Of course it wasn't simple. Moses wanted a lot more information, about the state of the land, of the people, and of their cities (Num 13:17–20). For that he needed spies, good spies. And that is what I have written: a spy story."

It is now my turn to interrupt. "There's still a problem," I tell him. "I can't work out which part of the land they were checking. It seems to be the south, around Hebron (Num 13:22–24), but verse 21 implies the whole of Canaan." I hear the Priestly scribe muttering about making the story conform "with the priestly delimitation of the Promised Land" (Levine 1993, 347). He is referring to Num 34:1–15. For if this is the promised land, he tells me, he needs to make sure that the people who read this scriptural account know its exact boundaries. As they are now the true and rightful people of this land, this is an important matter, with significant ramifications for their sense of self-identity, their sense of belonging. The early storyteller was writing for a different sector, the tribal people of the Hebron area. As I listen to these two I quietly mull over the fact that I am not hearing the voices of the Amalekites, Hittites, Jebusites, Amorites, or Canaanites whom the spies encountered. Their stories are well hidden. For, as Merilyn Clark writes elsewhere in this volume, "belonging is a complex concept that is as much about nonbelonging as belonging, for it implies a distinctive and unique quality that defines a family or group" (see also the essay by Jenks in this volume).

I remind myself that not only is this final version carefully written—or, more accurately, rewritten—it is also theologically driven. I may ask

---

1. Milgrom (1990, 102–3) sees the use of the verb *tûr*, rather than *rāgal*, implying gathering information as against a more military spying exercise. Although Levine (1993, 348–49) acknowledges its basic meaning as "encircle, traverse," he translates it in this context as "scout."

2. Although I am following the division of Knierim and Coats (2005) for the drama of the presentation, I am fully aware of the difficulties in assigning verses to sources, as noted by Levine (1993, 347) and others.

questions about borders and boundaries, but it is not possible to verify the historicity of any of its details. Certainly there were sophisticated intelligence services in action in the ancient Near East. Peter Dubovsky's recent work on the Assyrian spy system in the period 745–645 B.C.E. is witness to that (Dubovsky 2009).[3] I am not interested, however, in whether or not these events actually took place. My interest lies in what the narrative reveals of attitudes to land and the seizure of Other people's territory, particularly in the spies' report. I turn to the early storyteller: "Your spies report a *land flowing with milk and honey*, but—and your 'but' (*'epes kî*; v. 28) is the crux—this was a land of fierce people, and fortified cities. So why that phrase of promise, *a land flowing with milk and honey*, when the spies seem so ambivalent, if not fearful?" He is quick to reply: "How else describe such divinely gifted land?"

A Contrapuntal Turn

But I am still pondering the lack of any mention of how the Amalekites, Hittites, Jebusites, Amorites, or Canaanites reacted and decide to add, in contrapuntal style, another history, that of the Tuhoe peoples and their remote, rugged land, Te Urewera, within the larger entity of Aotearoa New Zealand, a people whose land was also entered, and their borders and boundaries crossed by an intrusive colonizing power who also planned and presumed to make it theirs. The relatively recent past of Aotearoa New Zealand is, of course, far removed both from the histories claimed in Numbers and those experienced by its writers. Am I nudging this biblical spy story too far beyond its own textual borders, even as I am aware, with Jione Havea, that stories are always "drifting in a sea of stories" (see Havea, "Bare Feet Welcome," below)? I turn to Sugirtharajah and hear him claiming that "by and large, the world of biblical interpretation is detached from the problems of the contemporary world" (2002, 16). That he considers a failure. I hear Musa Dube advocating "reading sacred and secular texts, ancient and contemporary texts … side by side," to highlight their "imperializing or decolonizing" ideologies (2000, 199–200). I am reas-

---

3. Nor does this spy account stand alone in the biblical narratives: Moses sends out spies in Num 21:32, as does Joshua in Josh 2, and the Danites in Judg 18, while further references to spies are found in Gen 42:9 and 2 Sam 10:3.

sured: postcolonial criticism makes its mark by not closing down these critical boundaries.[4]

Tuhoe also were a people experiencing the full force of an imperializing power within their land. They, too, struggled to keep its borders intact. For Tuhoe, also, their boundaries were of paramount importance. For them, it was not *promised* land, it *was* their land. It was the "Rohe Potae," meaning the "Area of the Hat," in the sense that it lay enclosed as a hat covers what lies beneath, imbued with all the sacredness of the head. Of course, for the Amalekites, Hittites, Jebusites, Amorites, or Canaanites, it was also not *promised* but their *inhabited* land. Promise, as in the divine gifting (Num 13:1), was simply the Israelite coded catchphrase.

I turn to Judith Binney, whose history I am now reading. She states, as if in conversation with Sugirtharajah, that her work is certainly not "detached from the problems of the contemporary world." As she explains, "the Rohe Potae, the encircled lands of the Urewera, is an 'imagined community' that is real. It existed on the ground in the nineteenth century; it exists in the minds and hearts of the Maori people who live there today." Just as recounting the boundaries of their land, as they understood these to have been, was essential for the sense of self-identity and belonging for the people of Yehud, so in the effort of Tuhoe "to sustain their way of life and their autonomy," the boundaries of the Rohe Potae were key (Binney 2009, 7; cf. Anderson 1991).

Tuhoe, too, experienced spies sent into their land. Not that they were called spies. Indeed, as Judith Binney tells me, the first official to enter the Urewera was a newly appointed resident magistrate, sent there in 1862 by the governor, not only "to test the 'political atmosphere' and discover 'the Native mind,'" but also "to assess the potential fighting forces … and explore the possibilities for European settlement." How very like Moses's spies. The Tuhoe were not deceived. He "encountered suspicion everywhere … taunted" with the accusation of "coming to take land" (Binney 2009, 61–63). Others, even if not technically "spying," met similar opposition. Samuel Locke, another resident magistrate, visiting the area in 1889, was told in no uncertain terms that Tuhoe were "very annoyed by the manner in which the surveyors around them had been carrying on for some time past without their knowledge or consent." Tuhoe were insis-

---

4. Jeanette Mathews (see her essay in this volume) gives another example of a contrapuntal postcolonial reading that takes its text outside the contours of the Bible, as do most of the essays in this volume.

tent "they would not have people, without their consent and knowledge, 'wandering about their country'" (Keenan 2008b, 84).[5] Is there a hint of the flowing milk and honey in the assumption, or, more probably, wishful thinking that the Urewera was a land of gold with a wealth of minerals? Whichever it was, it spurred government interest in the 1890s. The Tuhoe response was sharp: "searching for gold would not be agreed by them."[6]

Meeting the Complications

I return to Num 13 (vv. 27–29), noting that reporting the people as fierce and cities as fortified implies a warlike and militarily prepared people. So, too, the government agent writes in 1864 that "the Uriwera [sic] have openly avowed their determination to attack ... and from their wild savage state and revengeful feelings ... there is every reason to expect they will soon carry this threat into execution." Yes, says Judith Binney, "such was the framework of thought" (2009, 95).[7] She is referring to the colonial powers.

My eye, however, keeps returning to that biblical listing of the peoples who do inhabit the land. As Carolyn Sharp comments, "a foundational irony involved in colonization ... [is] that domination of the colonized inevitably requires a shift in the identity of the colonizer" (2009, 99). There is now no question: to be Israelite, as a self-defined people, is to be distinct from these Other peoples, whose lands they will eventually seize, settle, and possess. Randall Styers, writing of postcolonial theory in another context, also notes "how dependent the identities of the colonizer and the colonized are on their foils and how unstable every identity ultimately is" (2009, 852–53).

I do, however, get the spies' point: the land may be fertile, but there are obstacles aplenty in any attempted border crossing. Yet according to Num

---

5. With references to the Maori Census Report, Appendix to the Journals, House of Representatives, 1896, G-I, 95, and the Land Purchase Report, Appendix to the Journals, House of Representatives, 1889, G-6, 1. See also Binney (2009, 265) for Locke's description of the meeting.

6. From the report delivered by Numia Te Ruakariata to the Premier Richard Seddon, quoted by Binney (2009, 345) with reference to Appendix to the Journals, House of Representatives, 1895, G-I, 52.

7. Her note regarding McLean's letter is that this was a "draft letter to the governor, 11 May, 1864."

1, the Israelites are traveling with an "enormous army of over 600,000 warriors ... [as] counted in the first census." I realize, with Dennis Olson, that this book has led me "to expect some sort of military engagement," especially now, with the people stationed at the southern border of the so-called promised land (1996, 78, 75).

Land and military engagement is a coupling that lies at the very heart of colonialism. Judith Binney nods. "From the government's perspective, the 'sanctuary' of the Urewera had to be broken open. Therefore, the people had to be broken; the most direct way to break them was to take their land" (2009, 99).[8] This was what the government wanted. She quotes a finding from a Waitangi Tribunal Report in 1999: "it therefore becomes obvious that, for the Governor [or the government], the existence of any rebellion was secondary to the confiscation of land" (2009, 93–94).[9]

"Of course," interrupts the storyteller, "Caleb immediately contests the spies' report, calling, in doubly-weighted verbs, 'Let's go! We can easily do this' (Num 13:30)." He directs me to the stem of the opening verb in verse 30: the people are so stirred up, Caleb has trouble quieting them before he can begin urging and encouraging them to cross over into this land not yet theirs. But even before the people can respond, his call is countered by the rest of the spies, saying, "No—we're not able. The people are too strong for us."

At this point the Priestly scribe makes a move forward, holding in his hand his annotated version. I look and realize that in his careful scribal interweaving he has the spies bringing the Israelites an even more unfavorable report, of a land of giants, a devourer of its inhabitants. "Why?" I ask. He seems surprised. Haven't I remembered that the whole of this section of the Torah looks to the taking of Israel's promised land? Not to do so is a sin. He is simply reinforcing the fact that this is a sinful, even evil, report (v. 32)—which needed to be more strongly worded. Not only were the inhabitants too strong, the land itself was "geared for battle" (Coats 1968, 141); the land itself would devour them. Could I not appreciate the irony here? Not to enter would also result in death, the immediate death of the spies, and, finally, of all that generation, apart from Caleb and Joshua (Num 14:29–30). The spies' account of the land did indeed lead to a devouring! Admittedly, he was writing this as if he was the spies'

---

8. Binney is writing in the context of a further confiscation of lands in January 1866.

9. Author's brackets. The Waitangi Tribunal quote refers to the Ngati Awa Report of 1999, 64.

spin doctor, but, he reminds me, he countered all of this by repeating the favorable report in even stronger terms in the next chapter (14:7), drawing in Joshua as extra authority. It was, he says, quite a masterly turn to have Joshua and Caleb declaring that far from the land devouring people, its inhabitants would be as food for their conquerors. But, of course, the whole point is that the *dibbâ* of the spies had already persuaded the crowd. Sin had won the day.

Reading with an Eye for Spin and Counterspin

I reread Num 13:33, which claims the land is inhabited by Nephilim, recalling Gen 6's fallen angels, who showed no sense or even awareness of human/divine boundaries and whose very existence led to the destruction of the flood.[10] "Which of you is responsible for this?" I ask. The Priestly writer is quick in insisting that it is not his writing but that of some glossator or other (see Levine 1993, 359). The early storyteller quietly reminds me that his earlier spy report anticipated this, referring to the "descendants of Anak" (Num 13:28) and naming three of them (v. 22), though, he asserts, the Anakim *were* historical. I remember that they do appear in other conquest accounts, so were clearly there, at least in Israel's sacred memory (Josh 11:21–22; 15:14; Judg 1:10, 20). But, interrupts the Deuteronomist, not only were they giants, they were Rephaim, deathly, wraithlike giants (Deut 2:11).

I turn again to the writers. I am not sure whether to believe the Priestly scribe's protest, but even if he did not write this, I am wondering why, when he was supposedly both writing and editing a history, he allowed such a resonance of unreality to remain in the final version. Why this turn to "mythologizing"? Nor, as I remind them, talking in purely narrative terms, and quoting Olson, does it "correspond to what the spies had actually seen. Nowhere does the narrator report any basis for these claims" (Olson 1996, 79). Both gently remind me they put this into the mouths of the spies, who use every ploy they can find to dissuade Caleb.

I sense Judith Binney nodding, recognizing the ploy. "A recurring European construct imagined the Urewera as … the home of 'wild men,'" which, in itself, justified taking land. "With the onset of war in the North

---

10. See Levine (1993, 359): "The Hebrew plural form *nepilim* represents the *qatil*, active participle, predicated as singular, *napil*, meaning 'the fallen, one who fell.' One thinks of fallen gods, who had been ejected from the celestial realm."

Island from the early 1860s, the movements of people in the Urewera would be watched closely. They would be interpreted with suspicion—and suspicion too often finds its own proof" (Binney 2009, 68). There were telling examples of this: in 1866 two informants were murdered, and, as she explains, the court ordered that land "be confiscated from the tribal groups to whom the men charged with these murders belonged, and from Tuhoe, to whom *none* of those who were charged belonged." It was, she declares, "punitive ... without lawful cause." Such confiscation "was a policy designed to 'tame' 'wild men' by dispossessing them. The people of the Urewera were seen to need 'taming'" (2009, 93–94).

The wildness charge is, of course, a little different in the Numbers narrative, with its echoes of Gen 6:1–4. The Priestly scribe is now justifying his work, seemingly quoting Kyle McCarter:

> The ancient Israelites looked back at the aboriginal inhabitants of Canaan with a mixture of awe and fascination—and perhaps a bit of fantasy.... [But] the memory of the expulsion of these aboriginal peoples at the time of the arrival of the Israelites was central to the theological idea of the promised Land with all of its corollary implications for Israel's self-understanding as a chosen people. (McCarter 1995, x)

As for "mythologizing," am I not aware of scholars' findings that cultural memory often has "links to a vague mythological antiquity" (Van Dyke and Alcock 2003, 3)? I hesitate and recall that these so-called memories "are not ready-made reflections of the past, but eclectic, selective, reconstructions" (Lowenthal 1985, 210, cited by Van Dyke and Alcock 2003, 1). It is not just that people remember or forget "according to the needs of the present"; the salient point is that these so-called memories are "often used to naturalize or legitimate authority" (Van Dyke and Alcock 2003, 3). The Priestly scribe is nodding. That is how the Nephilim serve his purpose. There is now no question: the Nephilim alone justify seizing Others' land, since these Others are clearly inherently sinful.

But, he stresses, there is even more involved here. It is a matter of self-identity, of belonging, and "cultural memory" is an important part of this. I turn again to the scholars in the field, who note that such memory typically includes the "heretical, subversive, and disowned," encompassing "a quantity of bonding memories and group identities," both "diverse and timeless," which are "remembered" even though the usual understanding of memory no longer applies (Assmann 2005, 27, 29). Verse 29 has already addressed the matter of self-identity: Israelites were Other to Amalekites, Hittites, Amorites, or Canaanites. Enter the Nephilim, however, and the Israelites are the people who, through the divine promise, eventually even overcome "fallen" semi-divine giants.[11] "Yes," I say, "whoever decided to dredge up these prehistoric giants, there are shrewd purposes in including them here."

I pause to reflect. While both the early storyteller and Priestly scribe have contributed to this two-layered narrative, the full force lies with the final version, with the spy report now described as a *dibbâ*. That this is, at heart, a theological spy story becomes all the more apparent when read with Num 14, where it is brought into the murmuring tradition of rebellion. It is in this chapter that Joshua and Caleb, chapter 14's "good" spies, "get to the theological heart of what is at stake," which is "trusting in the power of Israel's God" (Olson 1996, 80). The Israelites are significantly failing to do this. The people reject Moses's leadership and the promised-land mission: they look backward and decide for Egypt (14:4). The consequences, heightened in YHWH's word in 14:26–38, come as no surprise. In a tragic attempt to put their failure right, after YHWH's verdict against them has been delivered, the people now set out to take the land, despite Moses's warning that YHWH will not be with them (vv. 39–44). The result is predictable: a routing defeat (v. 45). Despite continuing source differences in both time sequence and location, in the final version the result is that journeying is to continue for forty years—that significant generation span—before the goal is reached and conquest achieved. This has merely been a hitch on the way.

Fearful Political Considerations

But as I keep pondering these Others, not only the Nephilim and the descendents of Anak, but the Amalekites, Hittites, Jebusites, Amorites, and Canaanites, I wonder more about the politics of this writing. For the Israelites addressed by this narrative are also the exiled people who, after another generation span, cross back over the borders from Babylon, after

---

11. Since the Nephilim are mythically associated with the dead, as the Deuteronomist insists with his Rephaim connection, there is no questioning their annihilation: "the fact that they do not exist demonstrates the fact that they have been exterminated!" (Liverani 2006, 277).

Cyrus's decree. This is a narrative finally edited in Persian Yehud.[12] I turn again to the Priestly writer and ask of the political gains to be made by writing such a narrative of failure. As he explains, admittedly helped here by Gale Yee, "Israel's failure to abide by Torah accomplishes several things from a Persian perspective." It now "'explains' why Israel no longer possesses the land, ... why it is no longer an autonomous nation, and why it now exists as a colony subservient to a foreign imperial order" (Yee 2010, 229). "That is what the Persian colonizers will hear if they come to vet my work," he says. "But as one of the educated class, the so-called Jewish élite, I also have an interest in a narrative that clearly marks the divide between those of us who returned to claim the land that was legitimately ours and the riff-raff who were working on land that was not rightly theirs at all, claiming to be Jewish, but no better than the Amalekites, Hittites, Amorites, or Canaanites."

"That's all very fine," I say, "but you are openly employing a propaganda of fear. In fact, both of you are employing a fear strategy. Your texts are as overtly political as they are theological." This fear strategy, I tell them, is well recognized and documented by our contemporary political theorists, noting that while it is frequently used for quite "specific political goal(s)," it "seldom, if ever, is created out of nothing"; it always and inevitably "arrives ... wrapped in layers of intellectual assumption" (Robin 2004, 16, 28). "Your assumptions are theological," I say, "but your strategy certainly has a political goal."

I turn again to the Priestly scribe, recognizing once again that whatever the situation before the earlier tellings of the tale, this final interwoven "fearful" narrative, set in Israel's story world of wilderness experience but now carefully rewritten and reinterpreted to address his people back in the land in Yehud, is finally the work of a member of the scribal élite, presumably acting as the voice of the religious leadership, who, to apply Robin's words,

> identify a threat to the population's well being, who interpret the nature and origin of that threat, and who propose a method for meeting that threat. It is they who make particular fears items of civic discussion and public motivation. ... In choosing, interpreting, and responding to these

---

12. Note, among many others, Ben Zvi (2009), arguing that it was the Persian period that was responsible for the production of the Pentateuch, the prophetic corpus, and the Deuteronomistic historical collection.

objects of fear, leaders are influenced by their ideological assumptions and strategic goals. They view danger through a prism of ideas, which shapes whether they see a particular danger as threatening or not, and a lens of political opportunity, which shapes whether they see that danger as helpful or not. (2004, 16)

So here in the context of Yehud, where self-identity and belonging was a particular issue for the returnees from Babylon, you were deliberately using fear as a political tool, in the desperate attempt to maintain the belief that you yourselves were the true Israel. Those who currently study identity write that "[m]uch of our theory asserts that we exist as social beings in the midst of process. We don't 'have' or own an 'identity', but rather, identity emerges and is acknowledged in situations"; "we live in the identity process" (Altheide 2002, 8). You are manipulating that process and making it one of fear. For rewritten and edited for Yehud, your tale has now become a means of persuading your intended audience that the *people of the land*, despite being ethnically related, are to be viewed as external, "foreign" enemies. And, of course, once written down, such ancient constructed memory, bolstered by its divine warrant, is seen and understood as "secure and reliable" (Dyke and Alcock 2003, 3–4). You have done your work well!

It is also, of course, as I have been noting, grounded in a theology. Your narrative is not only driven by fear of Others but fear of sin before God. In fact, I say, turning to the early storyteller as well, the whole of chapter 13 with its fearful conclusion is a very clever piece of propaganda. On the one hand, to quote Baruch Levine, its "overall objective ... is to explain why it was that the Israelites failed to penetrate southern Canaan soon after the Exodus," but you, of course, interpret that "theologically, so that it was Israel's lack of faith in God." True faith in YHWH meant penetrating the land, no matter how superhumanly strong the opposition. You conclude that by failing to cross the border "the Israelites were sorely lacking in heroism and faith" (Levine 1993, 349). You use the fear of the spies and the people ironically, to carry the threat that not following the divine plan, which is no less than conquest, itself leads to death. And, I say to the priestly scribe, all this is underpinned most significantly and effectively by the appearance of the awesome kabod *kābôd* YHWH, which you introduce in 14:10.

I end the conversation, still wondering what I am hearing through this text. Is there another memory preserved here? Was there a different view of the so-called conquest? Is there a hint in the spies' report in 13:29 that some hesitated to enter land occupied by others? Was it simply a matter of fear, or was there a sense of hesitation about taking what wasn't theirs? If so, any such suggestion of moral opposition is overridden in the final version by the theology undergirding the dominant conquest theme. The colonial history, with its recorded correspondence, does include countervoices, such as that of the British secretary of state for colonies, writing in a letter dated 1864 to express "'grave objections' to the policy of land confiscation" (Binney 2009, 102). But to little or no avail. I note, too, the lack of women in the Numbers narrative and remember Miriam, who questioned Moses's leadership and was silenced in the previous chapter, and sense her "haunting" here (see Donaldson 2005, 97–113). This, of course, is beside that other haunting silence, of the peoples about to lose their land. Laments do, however, survive from the Urewera:

> Lamenting for their land,
> Taken away at the hand of the Governor,
> The sobbing and crying resounds.[13]

That was written in 1891. History, however, never ends. I turn again to Judith Binney to explain.

> The northern border of the Urewera today is the 1866 confiscation line. … It was at this boundary also, on 15 October 2007, that the police placed an armed defence squad, the Special Tactics Group, which searched everyone who entered or left Ruatoki. Positioning themselves on that boundary, as they looked for 'terrorists' and their weapons.

Once again, there are colonial ironies, as Binney notes (2009, 604–605): the police have, in fact, "endorsed the existence of the Rohe Potae," and the boundary line "is a frontier again."

Once again, fear lies at the heart of the incident. Gatherings in remote areas were misinterpreted as terrorist training camps, planning civil insurrection and assassinations. Once again, there is the use of the "wild man" strategy, which one Tuhoe activist, in particular, with his full-face *moko* (Maori term for "tattoo"), was made to fit. Descriptions

---

13. Translation of a waiata composed for Tuhoe by Te Kooti in 1891, quoted by Binney (2009, 319).

of the raid read like a film script: the police arrived "in full riot gear. ... Cars were stopped, occupants were instructed at gunpoint to leave their vehicles" (Keenan 2008a, 19). Not only did "the police action ... put fear into the hearts of many New Zealanders by raising the spectre of terrorism," but, as the Maori commentator, Derek Fox, wrote at the time, this was a twofold fear: fear of terrorism felt by "many New Zealanders" and fear of state force experienced by local Maori.[14] Although the charges that were initially laid under the Suppression of Terrorism Act of 2002 were dismissed by the ruling of the solicitor general, criminal charges were eventually laid against four of the people arrested. In the trial held, a full five years later, in February–March 2012, the jury was unable to reach a verdict on the more serious charges of participating in an organized criminal group but found the four accused guilty of the much lesser charge of the misuse of firearms. The two Tuhoe have now been given prison sentences of two and a half years. Many Tuhoe see this as another case of history repeating itself, for "in 1916 a jury found Tuhoe prophet Rua Kenana not guilty of treason but the verdict was ignored by the judge who sentenced him to 2 and a half years imprisonment" (Edwards 2012). An appeal is anticipated. As one Maori lawyer writes, "the most nagging question is why the authorities were prepared to permit the police to unleash a dreadful and unwarranted fear in the hearts and minds of innocent people." But then, he states, "the colonisation of Maori, as of most other indigenous nations over the last five hundred years, has always been about the dispossession and indeed the terrorizing of innocent peoples" (Jackson 2008, 1–2).

Why Such a Bricolage?

This in 2007! Does it answer the question why I have engaged in such a contrapuntal bricolage, mixing an ancient Israelite narrative with both colonial and postcolonial events in Aotearoa New Zealand? As already noted, Sugirtharajah, writing in 2002, lamented the "failure" of postcolonial biblical study "to relate it to the society in which its work is done," stating that "by and large, the world of biblical interpretation is detached from the problems of the contemporary world" (2002, 16). Detachment is not quite so easy when narratives that draw upon a *Realpolitik* justify-

---

14. Fox 2007 (9), quoted with comments by Abel 2008 (118).

ing intrusion across borders, disregard of boundaries, and the taking of Others' land resonate so clearly with one's own country's past and present. Fernando Segovia also calls for taking our critical readings "out of the academic realm and into the social-cultural arena" and asks "to what extent should any discursive, theoretical analysis do without the historical, the concrete, social-cultural context," adding "that the academy is also part of this arena and demands action in its own right" (2008, 499, 501).

Yet I note that there has of late been some critical backlash against so-called local readings. Moore and Sherwood in their recent manifesto, linking this rather loosely with "identity readings," suggest that "paradoxically, though such readings are typically motivated by a passion for social justice and human rights, their insistent situatedness and principled distrust of 'universals' seems to preclude, or at least complicate and not sit quite comfortably with appeals to such universal notions as 'human rights,' which, by definition, are the very antithesis of the ethnic, the cultural, and the local." Yet, they conclude, "one can not write off the writing of the local … least of all when such writing is intent on the righting of wrongs" (2011, 121–22).

As I finally consider what it is that I have been doing as I have woven these two narratives together, far apart in time, place, and genre, I am very aware of Tat-siong Benny Liew's observation that "at the end one cannot be sure if race/ethnicity and/or postcolonialism is a lens through which one interprets the Bible, or whether the Bible is a lens through which one investigates race/ethnicity and/or postcolonialism" (Liew 2005, 146). Certainly, the sharpened focus of the postcolonial lens is invaluable in probing the ideological manipulating that lies behind such carefully crafted narratives as Numbers, in ancient Israel's so-called remembered history. To help in teasing out the issues involved in relating biblical texts to present history, which, for me, lies at the heart of the postcolonial project, I have been reading others' comments, although I recognize that, as with all biblical criticisms, there are many ways of "doing" postcolonial study. Jon Berquist, for example, writes, of the "postcolonial canon" in general, as "a place for interpreters' ideologies to work themselves out in textual strategies and in the present world, where colonialisms and decolonizing are still at work" (1996, 33). I find Todd Penner and Lilian Cates's term "the dual colonial edge" helpful, where "the ancient colonized (and colonizing) text meets our own forms of colonization." As they explain, it "is not a question of interpretative strategy but instead of translation," where we graft ourselves and, I would add, our histories "onto and unto a text, creating a bricolage of self and text" (Penner and Cates 2007, 37.14). It is a matter of doing one's postcolonial work @home, to use Gerald West's term (West 2008).

This is neither an easy nor comfortable task, for, as Penner writes elsewhere, "unveiling the oppressive structures of the Bible is easy—unmasking those in our culture is much less so—revealing our own is perhaps the most difficult" (2010, 76). This certainly applies to those of us who are the descendants of colonizers and settlers, who live in supposedly postcolonial countries, where history has a way of appearing yet again in the guise of present reality. As the twofold Tuhoe narrative indicates, the past travels with us and refuses to be forgotten. So in response to the question posed some years ago by Daniel Patte, "why did I choose this interpretation rather than another one?" (1998, 22), for me, as the daughter of settlers, embedded and complicit as I am in the ongoing politics of a postcolonial society, it has, quite simply, been a personal matter of ethics. For some years, I worked alongside a Tuhoe *kaumatua*,[15] Te Hiko o te Rangi Ngatai Riini, and dedicate this paper to his memory.

Works Consulted

Abel, Sue. 2008. Tuhoe and "Terrorism" on Television News. Pages 113–28 in *Terror in Our Midst? Searching for Terror in Aotearoa New Zealand*. Edited by Danny Keenan. Wellington, N.Z.: Huia.

Altheide, David L. 2002. *Creating Fear: News and the Construction of Crisis*. New York: de Gruyter.

Anderson, Benedict. 1991. *Imagined Communities: Reflections on the Origin and Spread of Nationalism*. New York: Verso.

Assmann, Jan. 2005. *Religion and Cultural Memory: Ten Studies*. Translated by Rodney Livingstone. Stanford: Stanford University Press.

Ben Zvi, Ehud. 2009. Towards an Integrative Study of the Production of Authoritative Books in Ancient Israel. Pages 15–28 in *The Production of Prophecy: Constructing Prophecy and Prophets in Yehud*. Edited by Diana V. Edelman and Ehud Ben Zvi. London: Equinox.

Berquist, Jon L. 1996. Postcolonialism and Imperial Motives for Canonization. *Semeia* 75:15–35.

---

15. An elder, held in high regard.

Binney, Judith. 2009. *Encircled Lands: Te Urewera, 1820–1921*. Wellington, N.Z.: Bridget Williams.

Coats, George W. 1968. *Rebellion in the Wilderness: The Murmuring Motif in the Wilderness Traditions of the Old Testament*. Nashville: Abingdon.

Donaldson, Laura. 2005. Gospel Hauntings: The Postcolonial Demons of New Testament Criticism. Pages 97–113 in *Postcolonial Biblical Criticism: Interdisciplinary Intersections*. Edited by Stephen D. Moore and Fernando F. Segovia. London: T&T Clark International.

Dube, Musa W. 2000. *Postcolonial Feminist Interpretation of the Bible*. St. Louis: Chalice.

Dubovsky, Peter. 2009. *Hezekiah and the Assyrian Spies: Reconstruction of the Neo-Assyrian Intelligence Services and Its Significance for 2 Kings 18–19*. Biblica et Orientalia 49. Rome: Editrice Pontificio Instituto Biblico.

Edwards, Bryce. 2012. NZ Politics Daily: Does NZ Now Hold Political Prisoners in Its Jails? *The National Business Review*, May 28. Online: http://www.nbr.co.nz/article/nz-politics-daily-does-nz-now-hold-political-prisoners-its-jails-ck-119821.

Fox, Derek. 2007. Into the Heart of Tuhoe. *Mana Magazine*, December, 9.

Jackson, Moana. 2008. Preface: The Constancy of Terror. Pages 1–10 in *Terror in Our Midst? Searching for Terror in Aotearoa New Zealand*. Edited by Danny Keenan. Wellington, N.Z.: Huia.

Keenan, Danny. 2008a. Introduction: Searching for Terror. Pages 17–33 in *Terror in Our Midst? Searching for Terror in Aotearoa New Zealand*. Edited by Danny Keenan. Wellington, N.Z.: Huia.

———. 2008b. Autonomy as Fiction: The Urewera Native District Reserve Act 1896. Pages 79–92 in *Terror in Our Midst? Searching for Terror in Aotearoa New Zealand*. Edited by Danny Keenan. Wellington, N.Z.: Huia.

Knierim, Rolf P., and George W. Coats. 2005. *Numbers*. Grand Rapids: Eerdmans.

Lee, Won W. 2003. *Punishment and Forgiveness in Israel's Migratory Campaign*. Grand Rapids: Eerdmans.

Levine, Baruch A. 1993. *Numbers 1–20*. Anchor Bible 4A. New York: Doubleday.

Liew, Tat-siong Benny. 2005. Margins and (Cutting-)Edges: On the (Il)Legitimacy and Intersections of Race, Ethnicity, and (Post)Colonialism. Pages 114–65 in *Postcolonial Biblical Criticism: Interdisciplinary*

Intersections. Edited by Stephen D. Moore and Fernando F. Segovia. London: T&T Clark International.
Liverani, Mario. 2006. *Israel's History and the History of Israel*. Translated by Chiara Peri and Philip R. Davies. Oakville, Conn.: Equinox.
Lowenthal, David. 1985. *The Past Is a Foreign Country*. Cambridge: Cambridge University Press.
McCarter, P. Kyle, Jr. 1995. Foreword. Pages ix–xii in *Nations Mightier and More Numerous: The Biblical View of Palestine's Pre-Israelite Peoples*. Edited by Edwin C. Hostetter. Bibal Dissertation Series 3. North Richmond Hills, Tex.: Bibal.
Milgrom, Jacob. 1990. *Numbers*. Philadelphia: Jewish Publication Society.
Moore, Stephen D., and Yvonne Sherwood. 2011. *The Invention of the Biblical Scholar: A Critical Manifesto*. Minneapolis: Fortress.
Olson, Dennis T. 1996. *Numbers*. Louisville: John Knox.
Patte, Daniel. 1998. Critical Biblical Studies from a Semiotics Perspective. *Semeia* 81:3–26.
Penner, Todd. 2010. Is Boer among the Prophets? Transforming the Legacy of Marxian Critique. Pages 67–81 in *Secularism and Biblical Studies*. Edited by Roland Boer. London: Equinox.
Penner, Todd, and Lilian Cates. 2007. Textually Violating Dinah: Literary Readings, Colonizing Interpretations, and the Pleasure of the Text. *Bible and Critical Theory* 3 (3):37.1–37.18.
Robin, Corey. 2004. *Fear: The History of a Political Idea*. Oxford: Oxford University Press.
Sakenfeld, Katharine Doob. 2008. Whose Text Is It? *Journal of Biblical Literature* 127:5–18
Segovia, Fernando F. 2008. Postcolonial Biblical Criticism: Taking Stock and Looking Ahead. *Journal for the Study of the New Testament* 30:489–502.
Sharp, Carolyn J. 2009. *Irony and Meaning in the Hebrew Bible*. Bloomington: Indiana University Press.
Styers, Randall. 2009. Postcolonial Theory and the Study of Christian History. *Church History* 78:849–54.
Sugirtharajah, R. S. 2002. *Postcolonial Criticism and Biblical Interpretation*. Oxford: Oxford University Press.
Van Dyke, Ruth M., and Susan E. Alcock. 2003. Archaeologies of Memory: An Introduction. Pages 1–13 in *Archaeologies of Memory*. Edited by Ruth M. Van Dyke and Susan E. Alcock. Oxford: Blackwell.

West, Gerald O. 2008. Doing Postcolonial Biblical Interpretation@Home: Ten Years of (South) African Ambivalence. *Neotestamentica* 42:147–64.

Yee, Gale A. 2010. Postcolonial Biblical Criticism. Pages 193–233 in *Methods for Exodus*. Edited by Thomas B. Dozeman. Cambridge: Cambridge University Press.

Border Crossing/Body Whoring:
Rereading Rahab of Jericho with Native Women

Nāsili Vaka'uta

> The abject ... is racially excluded and draws me toward the place where meaning collapses ... from its place of banishment, the abject does not cease challenging its master. ... The abject is perverse because it neither gives up nor assumes a prohibition, a rule or a law; but turns them aside, misleads, corrupts; uses them, takes advantage of them, the better to deny them. It kills in the name of life ... it lives at the behest of death. (Kristeva 1982, 15)

Border Issue

This chapter crosses several borders. First, it crosses into Josh 2 to read Rahab of Jericho from a native woman's standpoint. Second, it crosses the border of biblical interpretation to negotiate an alternative lens for rereading Rahab of Jericho. The first crossing requires a shift in perspective. This shift begins with departing from imperialist readings of the text (which privilege Joshua, the spies, and the advancing Israelites) and seriously takes the interests of natives, especially women, into account. The second crossing is interventive in orientation. Its goal is to rehabilitate (read: rahab-ilitate) the construction of "native women" in biblical and imperial border crossing accounts. This is in response to the colonial construction of native women in Oceania. There is a third crossing: I as a native man offer a reading that favors native women.

Throughout the Hebrew Bible, Israel's journey toward their "promised land" sees them crossing many borders. The narration of most, if not all, of these border-crossing events stigmatizes native women as harlots and/or potential seductresses. These women are exposed to danger and sexual abuse. In these narratives, the women are situated on the border as boundary markers. The upshot is that when borders are crossed, female bodies are whored.

This whoring tendency operates upon a claim resembled by this syllogism:

Premise 1: Harlotry pollutes both people and land. For that reason, Israel is warned against playing the harlot. Leviticus 19:29 enjoins, "Do not profane your daughter by making her a prostitute, that the land not become prostituted and full of depravity."[1]

Premise 2: Foreign[2] women are "harlots," and by implication, foreign people are unclean. Exodus 34:15 reads, "You shall not make a covenant with the inhabitants of the land, for they prostitute themselves to their gods and sacrifice to their gods."

Conclusion: Foreign people must therefore be "cleansed" to purify the land. This is clearly outlined in Deut 7:1–6:

> When the LORD your God brings you into the land that you are about to enter and occupy … you must utterly destroy them. Make no covenant with them and show them no mercy. Do not intermarry with them, giving your daughters to their sons or taking their daughters for your sons, for that would turn away your children from following me, to serve other gods. … But this is how you must deal with them: break down their altars, smash their pillars, hew down their sacred poles, and burn their idols with fire. For you are a people holy to the LORD your God; the LORD your God has chosen you out of all the peoples on earth to be his people, his treasured possession.

This Deuteronomic claim echoes throughout the Hebrew Bible and resonates with colonial border-crossing narratives.

I will argue that the depiction of "native women" as harlots is a trope employed to justify the *invasion/occupation* of their lands and the *dispossession* of their peoples. "Harlotry" serves as the ultimate pretext for violent negotiations of identity, belonging, and land claims. Joshua 2 is a case in point, and I will reread Rahab of Jericho with native women—in the

---

1. All biblical references are from the NRSV unless otherwise indicated.

2. The use of the term "foreign" in imperial literature is largely ironic, because it is with reference to native peoples in their own lands. It is a misrepresentation of the "other." When one speaks of "others" as "foreigners" it exposes an alienating attitude.

Bible and in Oceania—whose "borders"/"bodies" had been, and still are, "crossed"/"whored."

Body Matter

Why read with native women? I read with native women not because I want to rescue or speak on their behalf. Nor do I believe that female subjects depend on their male counterparts for "salvation." I read with native women for the following reasons. First, I have a wife, daughters, a mother, and sisters, who are natives of Oceania, and whom I adore and love. They are natives of a region with experiences of border crossings, where islanders are victims of the colonial illusions of discovery, exploration, invasion, and occupation. Our people are required in many situations to display the colonizer's "scarlet cord" (values, language, knowledge, fashion, manners, and so forth) in order to be "saved" and to belong. We have to conform in order to survive. In many islands, the natives (like Maoris, Hawaiians, Aborigines, Maohi, Kanaks, to name a few) are strangers at home.

Second, the visual depictions of Oceania are preoccupied too much with island women's bodies. This is evident in Paul Gauguin's (1978, 2009, 2011) visual portrayal of Tahitian women in nude and semi-nude states. These are examples of the colonial feminization of Oceania.

Third, native women of Oceania are portrayed in writings of colonial border crossers as promiscuous figures who offer themselves voluntarily to be penetrated by male (mostly imperial, white) intruders. This (mis)representation is found in Margaret Mead's assumption of so-called sexual freedom in the case of Samoan women: "Sex is a natural, pleasurable thing; the freedom with which it may be indulged in is limited by just one consideration, social status" (Mead 1928, 201).

Kathryn Rountree brings to the fore the missionary perception of Maori women's bodies in "Re-making the Maori Female Body" (2000, 49–66). When missionaries arrived at the Bay of Islands in New Zealand, one of the first and major concerns, especially among missionary wives, was Maori women. Rountree remarks on the view of Marianne Williams (a missionary wife),

> To this early 19th century English missionary woman, the Maori woman symbolised complete absence of control: she was unclothed or scantily dressed, her hair hung loose, she cared little for housework, was free with her affections, moved freely about the countryside, slept or swam as the

mood took her. ... Everything about her contravened Marianne's sense of propriety, particularly with respect to sexuality. Maori women's apparent absence of control contrasted sharply with the numerous controls and restrictions placed on 19th century, middle-class English women with respect to dress, conduct and their freedom to move outside the domestic sphere. The latter's sexuality was covered and controlled according to strict and narrow prescriptions. She was idealised as the embodiment of purity and piety. Potentially, we might guess, Maori women's relative sexual freedom posed a threat not only to English notions of propriety and Maori's speedy acceptance of Christian morality, but also to the missionary woman's feelings about her own sexuality and the security of her exclusive sexual relationship with her husband. There was the latent fear that the *other* woman would become "the other woman." (2000, 58)

The solution to this problem, according to Marianne, is to remake the female Maori body, to transform and domesticate it. She worked on the premise that "to colonise the soul, one must first colonise the body" (2000, 64).

In Australia, Aboriginal women found themselves in a similar situation. In her article "Disciplining the Female Aboriginal Body" Hannah Robert describes sexual relations between colonizers and colonized as occupying an unstable place in the colonizing process. "On the one hand, they play out the metaphors of conquest, penetration and violation so that racism and sexism reinforce each other as tools of colonisation. Yet on the other hand, inter-racial sexual relations also hold the possibility of personal interaction, negotiation and partnership" (2010, 69; see also Buckman 1995). She also speaks of the link between the colonization of Aboriginal land and Aboriginal bodies, the measuring of white Australian "Self" against an Aboriginal "Other," and the designation of Aboriginal women's bodies as sexual rather than reproductive (Robert 2010, 70).

Robert refers to the discourse of miscegenation as a powerful tool that aimed at the subjugation of bodies and the control of populations. In this discourse, Aboriginal women's bodies are there for the purposes of the white men's sexual access (Robert 2010, 71). She further remarks,

Aboriginal women's bodies were inscribed with sexuality to the extent that their consent was often treated as irrelevant or presumed to be ever present in non-Aboriginal discourses. ... The sexualisation of Aboriginal women meant that much of their resistance against the controlling mechanisms of reserves and missions was construed as evidence of their immorality. (2010, 75)

This whoring of native female bodies represents a common perception that our region is a paradise, a place of sexual freedom with women readily available to be viewed, entered, and crossed. This is colonial *sexualization* of Oceania.

The perversions of native women's bodies shattered their sense of belonging and turned them into what Julia Kristeva refers to as "the abject." The abject is banished, yet manages to resist; perverted, yet fails not to challenge any master. Oceanic women may have faced forces of domination and exclusion on the border, yet they rose up to the occasion and exerted their female *mana* (power, magic) as a mode of resistance. The border in this case becomes an intersection of force and resistance.

These features of colonial feminization and sexualization resemble what Anne McClintock calls the *porno-tropics* of the *imperial imagination*. McClintock coined and defined the term "porno-tropics" to explain the European tendency to *sexualize* foreign (non-European) women as "a fantastic magic lantern of the mind onto which Europe projected its forbidden sexual desires and fears" (1995, 22).[3] The hallmarks of the porno-tropic tradition are its obsession with *feminization* of foreign lands and *sexualization* of foreign women.

Embedded in these two inseparable processes are the following. First, foreign lands are viewed to be *spatially spread for male exploration*, then reassembled and deployed in the interests of imperial power. Feminizing *terra incognita* is an imperial strategy of violent containment.

Second, in the feminization process, the erotics of imperial male *conquest* become also erotics of *engulfment*. Feminizing foreign lands serves as a compensatory gesture, disavowing male loss of boundary by reinscribing a ritual excess of boundary accompanied by an excess of violence.

Third, in foreign lands, *women serve as boundary markers*, and female figures are *situated like fetishes at the ambiguous points of contact*. At the contact zone, on the border, women serve as mediating figures by means of which men orient themselves in space, as agents of power and agents of knowledge.

---

3. She also speaks of a porno-tropic tradition that goes back to European explorers such as Christopher Columbus. In 1492, Columbus feminizes the earth as a cosmic breast to which the epic male hero is a tiny, lost infant, yearning for the Edenic nipple. That image, according to McClintock, is invested with an uneasy sense of male anxiety, infantilization, and longing for the female body.

Fourth, when travelers sail beyond their charted seas, they enter a *liminal condition*: they *become marginal figures on the border between the known and unknown*; they become *creatures of transition and threshold*—there they are in danger and emanate danger to others. Men at the margins usually resort to violence. There male anxiety and crisis of identity are exposed. The *fear of engulfment* by the unknown is projected onto colonized peoples, leading to imperial violence to ward off being engulfed.

Fifth, at the margins, the feminized land and sexualized female bodies are usually renamed. *Naming*, according to McClintock, is a means of staking one's claim to a place or a person.

Rahab Named

Joshua 2 displays features of a porno-tropic narrative. According to YHWH, the land promised is there for Joshua and the chosen people to possess and occupy. The only requirement is for them to walk in and take it. Instead, Joshua sends spies *to view* the land. If the land is a divine gift, why would he demand a reconnaissance mission? Does Joshua finally realize that the gifted land is not empty after all? Or is he simply threatened by the uncertainty of an unknown place?

Since it is a covert operation, the spies are supposed to conceal their identity and the reason for being there. But as soon as they *cross* the *border* and enter the land, they lodge at the house of a woman, whom the narrative *names* as Rahab the *harlot*. The naming of Rahab, and tagging her as a harlot, is both intriguing and suspicious. The Hebrew *rāḥāb* and its cognate *rĕḥôb* refer to a broad and open place (BDB, 932).[4] The NRSV and other translations render the word as "the square," and one can find several references to such a place in the Hebrew Bible. The square is a preferred place for the unhomed and the displaced (such as outsiders, strangers, prostitutes), despite it being portrayed by the homed and the well placed as a place of danger. In Gen 19, the square is where the two angels who visit Sodom prefer to spend the night. After Lot invites them into his house, they respond: לא כי ברחוב נלין ("No, for in the square [*rĕḥôb*] we will spend the night," v. 2 [my translation]). Upon Lot's insistence, they comply. What would have happened had they spent the night in the square? There

---

4. J. A. Emerton criticized E. R. Leach for wrongly making this association, since the two Hebrew words have different middle consonants. Emerton clearly was wrong (see the discussion of Emerton's critique of Leach in Noble 2002, 223).

are two possibilities: (1) the people of Sodom would have had the chance to "know" them, and (2) Sodom may not have been destroyed, because the people would not have had to force their way into the bounded space of Lot's house.[5]

In Judg 19, the story of the Levite and his concubine, the square is identified as the "town square" (ברחוב העיר, "in the square of the city" [my translation]), and that is the place where the Levite, his attendant, and his concubine intend to spend the night. As strangers in the place (Gibeah), they are invited by a man into his house, where he provides for all their needs. Their host, the one with a house, warns them about being in the square in the night. Here again, the guests are bounded inside. Like the portrayal of the people of Sodom, the men of Gibeah challenge this by demanding that the guests be let out of the house that they may know them. Like Lot, the host negotiates with the men on behalf of his guests by offering them his virgin daughter and the Levite's concubine (v. 24). Unlike the Sodom episode, here one of the guests, the concubine (a female), is pushed out by her own man to be raped and abused, to save himself and other men "inside the house."

The square is depicted in other texts as a "red light district," where prostitutes lie in wait for young men (Prov 7:12). Ezekiel refers to the square in his prophecy against Israel's faithlessness:

> After all your wickedness (woe, woe to you! says the Lord GOD), you built yourself a platform and made yourself a lofty place in every square; at the head of every street you built your lofty place and prostituted your beauty, offering yourself to every passer-by, and multiplying your whoring. You played the whore with the Egyptians, your lustful

---

5. The narrative is woven in favor of Lot, making the people act and speak in a way that portrays them negatively as homosexuals, the very stuff of alienation. Traditional readings of the text identified the men of Sodom with homosexuality and inhospitality and sentenced them accordingly. But if we read the narrative with the people in the open, not the one in the house, new insights come to light. The people are portrayed as being angry with Lot, yet one might ask: Were they really after the visitors or after Lot's egotistic attempt to confine the visitors, in his house, for himself? This is a plausible view, given that Lot prefers to give up his daughters but not the two men. He prefers to close himself and the two men in the house without giving those in the open a chance. The best Lot could have done is to "come out" into the open with his men, rather than "eloping" with them at the cost of his fellowmen and his wife. No wonder that his daughters had to make him drunk in order to preserve his line.

neighbors, multiplying your whoring, to provoke me to anger. (Ezek 16:23–26)

Here the square is the place where Israel adulterates herself with foreign nations. The issue is not the square itself but what Israel does in the square. Warning against the square is an attempt to prevent Israel from "mingling" with others and exposes the insecurity of the one uttering the warning.

Isaiah speaks of the square as the place where honesty stumbles: "Justice is turned back, and righteousness stands at a distance; for truth stumbles in the public square, and uprightness cannot enter" (Isa 59:14). This negative perception is largely from those whose interests are not served nor taken into account in the square. Any claim of domination is decimated and buried in the square (2 Sam 21:12). In the square, the honor of the displaced is restored (Esth 4:6, 6:9, 11). From these references to the square, it is clear that its boundary cannot be marked, simply because it has no boundary. It is an open place where people from all walks of life have the liberty to socialize and express themselves without the interference of those in authority or those who seek to control.[6]

These references to the square raise the following questions: Was Rahab a real woman at Jericho, or was it a naming game by the Deuteronomists with intention to portray the land of Canaan as an open and dangerous place? Was Rahab really a harlot? If so, why did the spies enter straight to her house and abandon their mission to view the land? Or was viewing Rahab itself viewing the land?

I do not have the space to address all these questions, but a glance at existing scholarship will indicate that Rahab has been a subject of diverse interpretations (see Aubin 2001; Gillmayr-Bucher 2007; Mansfield 2000; Pardes 1994; Seeman 2004; Sharp 2012; Thelle 2007; Wu 2001). Rabbinic tradition celebrates Rahab as "a pre-eminent model of the righteous proselyte, one who goes beyond all others in her recognition of God's true powers" (Baskin 1979, 142). Rahab's harlotry, to the Rabbis, is considered redeemed because of her good work and conversion. Josephus acknowledges that Rahab became the wife of Joshua and refers to her not as a harlot but as an innkeeper. The main reason for this is to save Joshua's image (Feldman 1989, 353).

---

6. Information on the "square" is adapted from Vaka'uta 2011, 139–41.

The Greek Church fathers praise Rahab as an example of faith and hospitality, a model of repentance, a prophetess, a representative of foreigners and women. With regards to Rahab's portrayal as a harlot, H. F. Stander writes, "Rahab never managed to shake off this epithet. It was not because the Church Fathers doubted her conversion or righteousness. It was rather a technique to emphasize the wonder of her repentance" (2006, 39).

Many readers follow the flow of the narrative in celebrating what became of Rahab the harlot. D. J. Wiseman speaks of Rahab as "an example of the Divine grace working through sinful people" (1964, 11). Bernhard Robinson refers to Rahab as "a resourceful and trusting woman ... who is converted to belief in the sovereignty of YHWH. To such a person the harsh law of חרם does not apply" (2009, 257). From a queer perspective, Erin Runions describes Rahab as a trickster and a queer, especially in regards to her treatment of the spies and her own people (2011, 41–69). Rahab's harlotry appears to have been forgiven and ignored because she saved the spies, acknowledged Israel and YHWH (Josh 2:11), and above all abandoned her own people. Here lies the danger that Judith McKinlay points out in her reading of Rahab. She states,

> The Deuteronomists used Others against whom their community could assert and define themselves, even if those Others, like Rahab, were in reality their own ethnic grouping, now set apart and stigmatized. Different readers will continue to hear this text differently, but those whose own cultural experiences bring to the fore a jangling recognition of this co-opting but polarizing strategy may be moved to ask to what extent our readings and our narratives contribute to this silent bleeding in our own contexts. The conflict narratives of the conquest are indeed dangerous tales. If Rahab is a hero/ine, then let the reader read again. (McKinlay 1999, 57)

From these readings, Rahab remains a harlot. After all, that is what the Bible says! But I am troubled by the lack of attempt to release Rahab from the whoring orientation she has been subjected to in the text. That demands *rahab-ilitation*!

Rahab Released

"Rahab-ilitation" is coined herein to indicate the need, first, to *release* Rahab (and her native sisters) from the violent gaze of the Deuteronomists' porno-tropic texts, and second, to *rehabilitate* the way we read in order to resist buying into the illusions of imperial imaginations inscribed in the text, and thereby avoid becoming porno-tropic readers.

Let me further scrutinize the narrative using the *porno-tropic* categories outlined above. First, Canaan is characterized as a female body in the person of Rahab. Rahab's body is positioned on the border, so that crossing the border is at once crossing Rahab's body. Likewise, the depiction of Rahab as a harlot is at once the depiction of Canaan. Feminizing the land goes hand in hand with the sexualization of the female body. Canaan, like Rahab, is portrayed as an open space, broad and *readily spread to be penetrated and explored in the interests of YHWH's chosen.*

Second, Rahab is sexualized and whored. She serves as the advancing Israelite's boundary marker; she is positioned by the narrator at the point of contact, at the border, on the wall. There she serves as a mediating figure between the spies (outsiders) and the king (insiders). The narrator also gives the impression that the easy entry of the spies into Rahab's house symbolizes conquest that is to come. They can enter and lodge. Ironically, they find themselves *engulfed, contained, hidden,* and *sent back.*

Third, the story mentions no men on the border. The spies would rather pick on a woman than face men of the land. The story talks up the spies as if they are security concerns to the natives. Even the king of the land sends orders to Rahab asking for them. Who would know they are in the land? Why would the king of the land waste his time looking for unknown and displaced men? When the king's men come looking for the spies, they are hidden in the secrecy of Rahab's roof, under stalks of flax. The spies seem "not man enough" to face the king's men and negotiate on behalf of Joshua and Israel. They entered Canaan to view, but they are afraid to be viewed. They are there to provide intelligence back to the camp, but instead they have sought refuge under the roof of a woman. The female space and body here provide the safety that they need and thus expose male anxiety and fear on the border.

Fourth, the spies find themselves in unknown territory. They enter a liminal condition, where they become creatures of transition and threshold. There they are in danger and pose danger to others. They resort to violence, and that is what YHWH commands in Josh 1 and executes in Josh 6, to invade and annihilate. At the margins, however, male anxiety and male crisis of identity are exposed. Violence, such as the events that follow after Josh 2, becomes the means to avoid *being engulfed.*

A close reading of Josh 2 opens up insights neglected by dominant scholarship. First, Rahab is a native woman who knows her *turangawaiwai*, where she stands. That is evident from her knowledge of the area and the king's knowledge of her. She also knows how to deal with the spies/strangers. She sends them back without a chance to "view" the land.

Second, Rahab does not speak the language of the spies. Unless there was a common language at the time, there is no reason to assume the spies and Rahab would understand each other. But the majority of interpreters go along with the story as if Rahab speaks Hebrew or the spies speak Canaanite. To speak the language of one's master is an imperial expectation, and a lot of island natives in Oceania are unable to speak their native languages due to the impact of colonization.

Third, there is a claim of religious superiority. The story describes Rahab and the Canaanites as knowing YHWH, and they melt. Again, this is a common imperial nonsense, that the colonizer's deity and belief system is superior to those of the natives. The native inhabitants are therefore made to acknowledge the deity of the colonizers.

Fourth, Rahab and the spies make a covenant, and as the story reveals, both parties keep their part of the deal, but to the detriment of the Canaanites. Who needs a covenant? Covenant with strangers is not a good idea. New Zealand Maoris have firsthand experience from the Treaty of Waitangi. The treaty was agreed upon and signed by colonial officials, missionaries, and native leaders for the purpose of protection. As a result, native lands and rights of native Maoris have been compromised.

Fifth, and finally, Rahab as a native needs no "scarlet rope," but she is given one as an *imperial mark of belonging*. In order to be saved, she has to display it clearly from the window of her house. This is an all too familiar aspect of imperialism. On the one hand, there is the demonization of native values, cultures, beliefs, and knowledge. According to colonizers, anything native is an impediment to growth and development. On the other hand, the natives are given the *colonial cord of belonging* (i.e., values, cultures, language, treaty, etc.)—natives have to display them in order to belong and be accepted.

'A ENA IA!

In Tonga, when a person wants to respond to negative remarks by someone else, one says, *'a ena ia!* As discussed above, there is a dark side to border crossing due to the feminization of lands and sexualization of women. Women are placed on the border as boundary markers and to serve the interests of colonizers. Men tend to be violent on the border. Sense of belonging is threatened on the border. The story of Rahab is a good example of these. She is named and labeled a harlot. But as I have argued, "harlotry" is a Deuteronomic ploy to justify land acquisition and dispossession of native peoples in their lands. Portraying Rahab as a harlot has no substance. To conclude, I would respond together with Rahab to her story and readers: *'a ena ia!*

Works Consulted

Aubin, Melissa. 2001. "She Is the Beginning of All the Ways of Perversity": Femininity and Metaphor in 4Q184. *Women in Judaism: A Multidisciplinary Journal* 2.2:1–23.

Baskin, Judith Reesa. 1979. The Rabbinic Transformations of Rahab the Harlot. *Notre Dame English Journal* 11:141–57.

Bauckham, Richard. 1995. Tamar's Ancestry and Rahab's Marriage: Two Problems in the Matthean Genealogy. *Novum Testamentum* 37:313–29.

Buckman, Alyson R. 1995. The Body as a Site of Colonization: Alice Walker's *Possessing the Secret of Joy*. *Journal of American Culture* 18 (2):89–94.

Feldman, Louis H. 1989. Josephus's Portrait of Joshua. *Harvard Theological Review* 82:351–76.

Gauguin, Paul. 1978. *Writings of a Savage*. New York: Viking.

———. 2009. *Noa Noa: The Tahitian Journal*. New York: Classic Books.

———. 2011. *Gauguin's Tahiti*. Boston: MFA.

Gillmayr-Bucher, Susanne. 2007. "She Came to Test Him with Hard Questions": Foreign Women and Their View on Israel. *Biblical Interpretation* 15:135–50.

Hawkins, Peter S. 2010. Dante's Rahab. *MLN* 124 (5) Supplement:S70–S80.

Kristeva, Julia. 1982. *Powers of Horror: An Essay on Abjection*. Translated by Leon S. Roudiez. New York: Columbia University Press.

Mansfield, Ken. 2000. Rahab and the Spies: An Exegetical Evaluation of Joshua 2. *IIIM Magazine Online* 2 (26):1–20.

McClintock, Anne. 1995. *Imperial Leather: Race, Gender, and Sexuality in the Colonial Contest*. London: Routledge.

McKinlay, Judith E. 1999. Rahab: A Hero/ine? *Biblical Interpretation* 7:44–57.

Mead, Margaret. 1928. *Coming of Age in Samoa*. New York: Morrow.
Noble, Paul R. 2002. Esau, Tamar, and Joseph: Criteria for Identifying Inner-Biblical Allusions. *Vetus Testamentum* 52:219–52.
Pardes, Ilana. 1994. Imagining the Promised Land: The Spies in the Land of the Giants. *History and Memory* 6 (2):5–23.
Prior, John Mansford. 2006. "Power" and "the Other" in Joshua: The Brutal Birthing of a Group Identity. *Mission Studies* 23:27–43.
Robert, Hannah. 2010. Disciplining the Female Aboriginal Body: Interracial Sex and the Pretence of Separation. *Australian Feminist Studies* 16 (34):69–81.
Robinson, Bernard P. 2009. Rahab of Canaan—and Israel. *Scandinavian Journal of the Old Testament* 23:257–73.
Rountree, Kathryn. 2000. Re-making the Maori Female Body: Marianne Williams's Mission in the Bay of Islands. *Journal of Pacific History* 35:49–66.
Runions, Erin. 2011. From Disgust to Humor: Rahab's Queer Affect. Pages 41–69 in *Bible Trouble: Queer Reading at the Boundaries of Biblical Scholarship*. Edited by Teresa J. Hornsby and Ken Stone. Atlanta: Society of Biblical Literature.
Seeman, Don. 2004. The Watcher at the Window: Cultural Poetics of a Biblical Motif. *Prooftexts* 24:1–50.
Sharp, Carolyn J. 2012. "Are You for Us, or for Our Adversaries?": A Feminist and Postcolonial Interrogation of Joshua 2–12 for the Contemporary Church. *Interpretation* 66:141–52.
Stander, H. F. 2006. The Greek Church Fathers and Rahab. *Acta Patristica et Byzantina* 17:37–49.
Thelle, Rannfrid I. 2007. The Biblical Conquest Account and Its Modern Hermeneutical Challenges. *Studia Theologica* 61:61–81.
Vaka'uta, Nāsili. 2011. *Reading Ezra 9–10 Tu'a-wise: Rethinking Biblical Interpretation in Oceania*. International Voices in Biblical Studies 3. Atlanta: Society of Biblical Literature.
Wiseman, D. J. 1964. Rahab of Jericho. *Tyndale Bulletin* 14:8–11.
Wu, Rose. 2001. Women on the Boundary: Prostitution, Contemporary and in the Bible. *Feminist Theology* 28:69–81.

Deuteronomy 30: Faithfulness in the Refugee Camps of Moab, Babylonia, and Beyond*

Jeanette Mathews

In the mid-1980s, emerging from a conservative evangelical upbringing that valued Christian otherworldliness above the concrete reality of lived experience, I wrote a small treatise defending the importance of the land for the people of the Hebrew Bible. It focused specifically on the community addressed by Deuteronomy whose land was their *naḥălâ*, their "inheritance," terminology that evoked the idea of the divine giver as a loving father. Even at that time, I was not insensible to the irony of a people receiving with gratitude a land that was already occupied by others, but my analysis nevertheless paid attention to the tangible and material in the relationship between Israel and YHWH.

Today I find my view is back at the other end of the spectrum, informed largely by an understanding that the composition and compilation of the majority of the Hebrew Bible traditions took place during exile or later, that is, from a perspective that was outside of (or out of control of) the land. Further, such a claim recognizes that the "exilic" or even "postcolonial" perspective is the most creative in the history of the Israelite people and arguably the situation in which biblical faith is most fully expressed. If the editors of the biblical material shaped their answers to the questions "who are we" and "how are we to live" while *outside* the land, this perspective gains a normative status that becomes a measuring stick by

---

* A word is warranted regarding terminology. While I recognize a semantic difference between "exiles" and "refugees," both result from removal from one's home country that is not by choice, in contrast to émigrés and expatriates. I will therefore use the terms "exile" and "refugee" interchangeably in this essay. See Said (2000, 181) and Groody (2009, 642–43 n. 15) for detailed comments on the subtle distinctions between these categories.

which also to judge their time *within* the land. Indeed, the short period of independent control over the land was seemingly the most problematic for Israel, with its temptations to be like others, worshiping a multitude of gods and embracing stratified social structures that led to exploitation of their own kin.

In an essay responding to Yoder's critique of Christianity's embrace of Constantinianism, Gerald Schlabach suggests that the greatest challenge for the people of the Hebrew Bible was that warned of in Deut 8, that they would settle in the good and fulsome land and forget the one who had given it:

> God *does* want to free, heal, and bless even if, in blessing, God risks the possibility that God's people will abuse God's gift. Our most basic problem, then, is the Deuteronomic challenge of receiving and celebrating God's gift without oppressing, violating, and hoarding in new ways. (Schlabach 1999, 454, emphasis original)

This recognition has given rise to several attempts to formulate an "exilic theology" (for example, Yoder 1973; Smith-Christopher 2002; Ellis 2002). But it is not only theology that claims the importance of this motif. Edward Said says that the exilic condition has become "a potent, even enriching, motif of modern culture" (2000, 173), impacting academic, aesthetic, and intellectual thought. Said warns of the danger of forgetting the real experience underlying this motif—there is a tendency to romanticize an experience that is at heart "truly horrendous" (2000, 174). But he is critical, too, of "making a fetish of exile" (2000, 183), arguing that it is only the experience of detachment that can offer meaning.

Clearly a delicate balance is needed: a way of talking about an exilic experience that retains a hope for return to the homeland but with enough detachment from place so as not to slip into rampant nationalism that hoards and excludes, and forgets that all life is a gift.[1]

---

1. Links between Deut 30 and an exilic community were inspired, as will be discussed later in this essay, by my own experience of teaching at a refugee camp in Thailand. Theological reflection and an introduction to the work of Edward Said has been aided by an essay by Alain Epp Weaver (2003).

The Fictional Setting of Deuteronomy 30 in Moab

The fictional setting of the book of Deuteronomy provides this subtle balance in its ostensive placement in the land of Moab on the edge of Canaan. Canaan, of course, is designated the "promised land" by the biblical writers. In the story, the community of Israel is camped on the river that separates them from the land promised to their ancestors. At the end of the book, although he will be prevented from entering, Moses himself is led by YHWH up a mountain to view the extent of the land. Deuteronomy preserves three sermons of Moses addressed to the community, creating a lengthy interlude between the wilderness wanderings recorded in Exodus, Leviticus, and Numbers and entry into the land as recounted in Joshua. Yet there are obvious clues that the recipients of the sermons are, in reality, a community who have already experienced life in the land and expulsion from it. According to Schlabach, at least six historical settings for the Israelite community can be discerned behind the text of Deuteronomy: the house of slavery in the land of Egypt; the great and terrible wilderness where they have been tested and humbled; "today" on the banks of the Jordan; the time of prosperity in the good land; the time of growing complacency when they have forgotten YHWH; and the experience of exile (Schlabach 1999, 457).

Other scholars add later historical settings again, such as Mark Biddle, who points out specific details in Deut 29–30 that suggest a *postexilic* consciousness: the declarative tone of the text that assumes Israel has already suffered invasion and exile (29:22–29 [21–28 in MT]); the use of "when" and not "if" at 30:1; the prediction of a future restoration in 30:1–10; reference to "this book of the law" (30:10) that presupposes the writer already knew of the existence of Deuteronomy as a book. The nation's situation as a colony under imperial Persia is thus envisaged as a seventh context for the recipients of the speeches across the Jordan (Biddle 2003, 436–43).[2]

The sermons of Deuteronomy, therefore, are addressed to the community in a variety of contexts, both inside and outside the land, and in various sociopolitical circumstances; but the same message is presented with its urgent exhortation to "choose life" and to love and obey YHWH. Deuteronomy "telescopes" the generations of audiences so that what applied

---

2. See also Ben Zvi (2009, 15–28), who presents a case for the production of several biblical corpi including the Pentateuch in the Persian period.

in the past continues to apply in the hearer's "today" (Biddle 2003, 437). The call to covenant with YHWH and right living with one's neighbor is relevant both within and outside the land.

Deuteronomy as an Exilic Document

The exhortation that includes Deut 30 is primarily heard by a landless people. The community portrayed in Deuteronomy could be described as a refugee camp on the River Jordan, which formed the border between Moab and Canaan, made up of the second generation of a people whose flight from oppression landed them in a no-man's land for forty years in spite of their hopes for a better future. If the Babylonian exile was the impetus for a re-presentation of the tradition, then the audience was again landless, further removed from the land of promise but again camped by a river, at the mercy of their captors, although the biblical traditions give differing pictures of their plight (2 Chr 36:20 states they became servants to the king of the Chaldeans and his sons; 2 Kgs 25 suggests they were prisoners in Babylon but also records the release of King Jehoiachin of Judah to "sit in the king's presence"; Jer 29 indicates a relative freedom for the captors in its exhortation to build houses and plant gardens in Babylon). The urgency of Deut 30 with its focus on "today" (*hayyôm* in vv. 2, 8, 11, 15, 16, 18, 19) is a reminder that this text is intended to be reappropriated in each new generation, a point well expressed by Walter Brueggemann:

> The book of Deuteronomy stands as the primal example of the dynamism of the Torah tradition whereby old memories are endlessly re-presented and reinterpreted, rearticulated, and reimagined in ways that keep the main claims of faith pertinent and authoritative in new circumstances. (2003, 93)

Bringing this ancient text into dialogue with a contemporary situation, therefore, is entirely consistent with the intentions of the compilers and canonizers of the Hebrew Bible. As James Sanders states, "tradition that becomes canonical [is] material that bears repeating in a later moment both because of the need of the later moment and because of the value or power of the material repeated" (1987, 21).[3]

---

3. Merilyn Clark (in her essay, above) gives a similar discussion of Sanders's work. Clark's essay also explores issues of identity and belonging in the Hebrew Bible, spe-

An Exilic Community in Thailand—Mae La

In 2006, I had the privilege of spending some time in Mae La, one of several refugee camps in Thailand that run along the border with Burma. The particular community I visited was in Zone C of the camp, comprising residences, a Baptist church, a primary school, an orphanage, and the Kawthoolei Karen Baptist Bible School and College. The Bible school was established in 1983 in traditional Karen land inside Burma but relocated following attacks by the Burmese army troops to Mae La Refugee Camp in 1990. The Reverend Doctor Saw Simon had been newly appointed as principal of the Bible school at that time, so it fell to him to establish what he terms "the school in exile" in 1990. Doctor Simon was born in a Karen village in Burma into a Christian family, studied theology in Burma and the Philippines, and was previously appointed to a theological post in Rangoon, Burma. Following the "People Power Movement" of August 8, 1988, during which education facilities in Rangoon were closed indefinitely, Dr. Simon chose to follow what he understood as God's call to cross the border and live in solidarity with his own people, the oppressed Karen. The Karen people are one of the minority hill tribal groups whose traditional land spanned the Burmese and Thai border. Popular folklore among the Christian Karen lays claim to being the first ethnic group to settle in Burma who trace their lineage back to 739 B.C.E., identifying as one of the lost tribes of Israel (Welch 2007, 131). A long-held desire for a separate state was encouraged by the British colonizers in the Second World War, with promises to support the separatist ideals in return for allegiance with Britain against the Japanese. This fueled tension with the Burmese majority, who had sided with Japan. Britain did not fulfill the promises made to the Karen but instead acceded to a newer alliance with Burmese leader Aung San, whose change of allegiance enabled negotiation for an independent state of Burma. In the aftermath of the assassination of Aung San in 1947, not only were the Karen deprived of their hopes for a separate state, they (along with other ethnic minorities) began to be persecuted by the Burmese state and driven from their traditional lands. This persecution has steadily increased throughout the volatile history of independent Burma, particularly since the military coup of 1988. The recent release of Aung

---

cifically through the story of Jacob. Especially notable is the claim that Israel's identity began to be shaped by the experiences of Jacob (renamed Israel), all of which were marked by transience, landlessness, and boundary dwelling.

San Sui Kyi from house arrest and local elections reflect a degree of compromise on the part of the democratic movement and some softening of the policies of the military regime. Even so, many of the students that I met in the Bible school in 2006 testified to experiences of themselves or family members being imprisoned, raped, tortured, driven from their homes, or forced to flee for their lives across the river border to the refugee camps. In 1949 the Karen National Liberation Army (KNLA) was established and continues to give hope to the Karen that their long struggle will result in an independent state. The Karen support for the guerrilla army results in an uneasy alliance between an armed struggle and Christian identity, evidenced in a hymn sung daily at the Bible school that exhorted troops (among others) to praise God.

Approximately 30–40 percent of Karen people claim a Christian identity, with the majority being Baptist due to the successful impact of the American Baptist Mission Society, led by Adoniram Judson and George Boardman in the early nineteenth century. Oral Karen folklore that spoke of a "Golden Book" of salvation and freedom has been connected to the gold-edged Bible of one of the early missionaries. Such interpretation combined with claims to an ancient heritage result in some Karen perceiving themselves to be legitimate recipients of the promises to Abraham—this was the message conveyed by Doctor Simon as I participated in the Bible school. The main purpose of the college is to equip students for ministry across the world, but a secondary aim is to supplement United Nations–provided basic education by offering higher education opportunities, thus providing much-needed activity to stave off despair and idleness for young people who are so severely restricted. Doctor Simon himself expresses it this way:

> They call us a displaced people, but praise God; we are not misplaced.
> They say they see no hope for our future,
> But praise God, our future is as bright as the promises of God.
> They say the life of our people is a misery,
> But praise God, our life is a mystery.
> For what they say is what they see, and what they see is temporal.
> But ours is eternal.
> All because we put ourselves in the hands of a God we trust. (Welch 2007, 6)[4]

---

4. Although these lines do not express hope in terms of birth or transformation,

The Mae La Camp was established in 1984, and the Bible school has been running now for over twenty years. Although the school is a well-established three-story structure with planted flower and vegetable gardens, equipped with donated computers enabling communication with the rest of the world, its open sides and bush materials epitomize the precariousness of its existence.[5] Frequent raids by Thai authorities, arbitrary restrictions,[6] and risks of arrest taken whenever a member of the community leaves the camp are constant reminders that true settlement is not possible. Moreover, the community lives within earshot of their traditional land. Live mines are a hazard between camp and river, and gunshot can occasionally be heard, often interpreted as skirmishes between the KNLA and Burmese armed forces. The temporary nature of the refugee camp ensures that the focus is always on "home"—the territory across the river that is considered the rightful and traditional homeland—perhaps even the "promised land" from the perspective of those who understand themselves as heirs of Abraham. The expectation of return continues to inspire and sustain residents, as shown in a recent communiqué from Doctor Simon that states, "I am strongly convinced that [in the next] twenty-one years of my life ... the Lord will open the door and enable us to return to our own beautiful land called Kawthoolei (literally 'Land without evil') [to] rebuild our life and live and serve the Lord."[7]

Rereading Deuteronomy 30 in Mae La

My current teaching includes highlighting the compositional aspects of the Pentateuch. As I stress the importance of an exilic perspective in the shaping of biblical traditions and values, and as I recollect teaching ancient

---

they embody a similar resilience and expectation of new life as described by Kathleen Rushton (in her essay, above) in the wake of several natural crises across the globe in recent years.

5. In fact, not long after I completed the first draft of this essay the Bible school was burned to the ground—news of this event was received by email on May 1, 2012, but a month later construction of a new building had already commenced, which was completed by July.

6. For example, during my visit a curfew was imposed that restricted movement around and between the camps, and instructions for the removal of live chickens (a food source) was received due to the threat of bird flu. On other occasions foreign visitors have been banned from staying overnight at the camp.

7. Personal email communication received March 30, 2012.

Israelite history in the Bible school at Mae La, I am struck by the congruence between the refugee community among whom I lived on the Thai-Burmese border and the Israelites who were the original recipients of the traditions found in Deut 30.

This chapter contains words that are particularly relevant to the community I worked with in Mae La:

- a people who are not in their own land;
- a people of great faith who believe in God's promises;
- a people who need to know how to live with each other in close confinement within a refugee camp;
- a people who must prepare for life amongst strangers in a new land; and
- a people who want to remember their history, hold onto their identity, and be reestablished in the land of their ancestors.

Deuteronomy 30 comes among the chapters usually designated "covenant renewal in Moab" (29:1 [28:69 MT]–32:52). The idea of a "new" covenant made at Moab has been viewed as puzzling given the binding nature of the Horeb formulation, but it is entirely consistent with the notion of Scripture reenacted for new settings. The combination of several forms, including poetry, narrative, and hortatory address, is characteristic of preaching. Connections to earlier parts of Deuteronomy underscore an interpretation that reads the chapter as part of a sermon on earlier texts reflecting on the theme of covenant. In good Baptist style the sermon has three main points, focused on past (29:1–8 [28:69–29:7 MT]), present (29:9–15 [29:8–14 MT]), and future (29:16 [29:15 MT]–30:10), and concludes with a rousing appeal for decision (30:11–20).

The sermon begins with a reference to past events in the context of blessings and curses. Mae La residents describe their life's experience in similar terms, acknowledging suffering and pain but also recognizing God's hand in the success of their Bible school, including the support received from other Christian communities around the world. There is less identification with the concept that the Lord has "driven" them into a foreign land and that they need to be brought to repentance, since description of their persecution is usually given from a perspective of innocent suffering. But the NRSV translation of Deut 30:1 ("if you call them to mind") perhaps unduly stresses this petitionary aspect, since the literal translation of *hăšēbōtā 'el-lĕbābekā* is "you will return to your heart." The verb *šûb* ("return") could be considered a *Leitwort* since it is used seven times in the first ten verses of Deut 30.[8] It is unsurprising that "return" would be a dominant theme for an exilic community.

There is a great emphasis on obedience (Deut 30:2) in the Bible school community. One of the specific aims of the Bible school is to occupy young people so that they are not tempted by other dangerous activities (such as prostitution and drugs) resulting from boredom and depression. As well as several of the students from the Bible school, Doctor Simon's family home supports approximately fifty orphans, and all are engaged each dawn and prior to retiring at night in family-based devotional activities. Chores, school activities, and children's choirs in school and church fill their days. This is a community that takes seriously the injunction to "recite [these words] to your children and talk about them when you are at home and when you are away, when you lie down and when you rise" (part of the *Shema* in Deut 6:7, alluded to in Deut 30:2).

The explicit promise of return in Deut 30:3–5, as noted above, is held firmly by Doctor Simon and other Karen refugees. Over and over in written material of the students[9] there is an expressed hope and expectation of eventual return to the homeland. Such expectation forms a contrast with intellectual and aesthetic expressions of exile that tend to give greater value to the existential experience of exile itself than the possibility of return (Said 2000, 173). Yet in all cases there is need to recognize the pragmatic reality that return may not be imminent, despite being held as the sustaining force for existence in exile. Said describes the work of Palestinian poet Mahmoud Darwish as "an epic effort to transform the lyrics of loss into the indefinitely postponed drama of return" (2000, 179). One poem ends with the line "so that our children will remember to return"—a poignant balancing of realism in assessing his own unlikely repatriation with the hope that the next generation will have a different future. Jeremiah's letter to the exiles captures such pragmatism too, encouraging the Israelites to settle down and seek blessing in the place they are (Jer 29:1–9). Despite the appearance of temporary surroundings and the rhetoric of expectation of return, the Bible school in the Mae La Refugee Camp is clearly operating within a framework that understands exile to be an ongoing opportunity

---

[8]. Alexander Rofé describes Deut 30:1–10 as "a majestic fugue on the home of *šûb*" (1993, 270).

[9]. See my article on lament poems from Mae La (Mathews 2013) and also collected writings in Welch 2007.

for mission. The urgency of decision making exhorted in Deut 30:11–20 and the setting aside of possible objections resonates with the single-mindedness focus of the Bible school. Despite the limitations of geography, politics, personnel, and knowledge, the mission is considered to be neither too hard nor too far away. Many people have crossed "from the other side of the sea" (Deut 30:13) to teach in the Bible school or encourage the community, only to find that God's word is already alive and well in that place. The theme of "return" becomes an important one for foreign visitors as well as refugees, who either return home perceiving themselves to be profoundly changed by the experience, or they themselves return often to reexperience the genuineness of a faith community at work. Attempts to align the programs with accredited institutions have not been successful, but the Bible school presses on in the confident assurance that the young people of the camp are being equipped for further study. Indeed, many students I worked with in 2006 have subsequently undertaken tertiary study in other parts of the world. Classes and daily chapel services constantly renew the sense of mission among the students. Obedience to this calling is understood to result in God's blessing: as students are resettled in third countries they are perceived to be fulfilling the "prophecy" of the Karen National Anthem, which reads: "God of our fathers, our hope for the ages, we believe in you. Help us become your disciples and take the Gospel to the whole world."

Contrapuntal Hermeneutics[10]

This study has been especially focused on the Karen refugee community at Mae La, but reflecting on faithfulness while in exile could be just as relevant to other exilic communities. This discussion may also be informed by the experience of internal displacement, such as we see in Palestine or even my own homeland with its poor treatment of indigenous Australians both historically and in the current time.[11]

---

10. Here I am using a term originating with Edward Said in his essay "On Exile" (2000, 186) describing an awareness of simultaneous dimensions. See Judith E. McKinlay's chapter in the present volume for an example of a contrapuntal reading of Num 13.

11. The ongoing Northern Territory Intervention is widely criticized as a misguided process of dealing with difficult issues, and one which contravenes Australia's human rights obligations as embodied in legislation such as the Racial Discrimination

As noted earlier, there is danger in over-romanticizing the exilic condition at the expense of the real experience of dispossession, as stated emphatically by Schlabach:

> But let us be clear: we do no favor to any dispossessed people if we think of land only in a figurative rather than an earthy sense. That European Christians have identified God's cause with their lands, taken others' land, and abused both, means only that we are doubly or triply irresponsible if we now embrace the urbane delusion of those who consume the products of late industrial society while pretending not to be in relationship with the land at all. Those of us who are theological intellectuals may be able to read the Exodus abstractly as a journey into "freedom" or "history" rather than into actual land, but human rights are more basic, less abstract, and most earthy for those who need them most. If Constantinian *ways* of living in the land are what have left us uneasy about speaking to this question, then we should *both* renounce Constantine *and* demonstrate positive models for dwelling in the land without ejecting other inhabitants. (1999, 463–64, emphasis original)

Despite the recognition of a predominantly landless perspective in the latter stages of the editing of the Hebrew Bible, the ideology that informs the surface meaning is quite clearly related directly to the land. Furthermore, it is a land heavy with theological significance, since it is claimed to be a "promised" land, one part of the threefold promise undergirding Israel's identity: of posterity, divine-human relationship, and land. Said argues that exile is "a condition legislated to deny dignity—to deny an identity to people" (2000, 175). If having a land to call one's home is the basis of identity, then landlessness is a terrible threat to the very being of a community. One of the students at Mae La asked poignantly:

> We heard from our forefathers that we are the original people in Burma. And almost every Karen believes it is the truth. Whether it is true or not, is it important to be an original people? Or do we need to concentrate only in the present situation? How do we fight for our own independence without caring about our identity in the past? (Naw Hsar K'Nyaw Htoo, in Welch 2007, 189)

Act of 1975. The Intervention has resulted in loss of land, self-determination, and dignity for many indigenous Australians. See Budden (2009) and Thompson (2010) for theological perspectives on this issue.

Faithfulness Thus Needs a Material Context: A Theology Informed by Land

Yet there is an equal risk of celebrating the landed condition at the expense of the outsider. Zionism is seen by many as a painfully ironic reversal wherein the intention to reclaim land for a people who had been landless for two millennia resulted in the creation of another landless people. Persecuted become persecutors. Becoming settled and "at home" has relegated others to the status of homeless outsiders. In this regard Said comments on the Jewish "symmetry of redemption" (1986, 150), wherein return to the promised land that brings closure for the Jew exiled from their land is nonetheless a return that forsakes the moral insights of exile, a return that reaches back to retrieve a pristine past without concern for the human cost.

The fact that Deuteronomy, which completes the Pentateuch, remains open ended, thus resisting the symmetry of fulfilling the promise of land, is highly suggestive of the importance of maintaining an exilic perspective, including the moral insights inherent in it, for the editors of the Hebrew Bible. Another clue to the importance of this perspective is the recurring legislation that takes the interests of those without land into account, that is, the "Levite and sojourner, widow and orphan." Indeed, that the distribution of land among the tribes in Deuteronomy precludes an inheritance for the Levites, the priestly tribe, suggests land is *not* essential for the divine-human relationship. Continual warnings of the dangers in the land in the book of Deuteronomy add their weight to a perspective that suggests faithfulness in the context of the land is difficult. Deuteronomy 30's emphasis on choosing this day, each day, to be faithful to the covenant, and the assurance that the ultimate responsibility lies with YHWH, who will "circumcise your heart and the hearts of your descendants" (30:6), relocates identity in the divine-human relationship that is not dependent upon physical land.

Faithfulness Thus Needs an Ethical Context: A Theology Informed by Landlessness

A contrapuntal "theology of land" (or, perhaps, a "theology of exile") acknowledges the independent melodies of the experience of landedness and landlessness but recognizes also that they must be related harmonically. Those in the land must hold on to the values of exile. Those in exile must continue to be sustained by the values of land. Deuteronomy holds this tension by addressing itself to its audience both within and outside the land. There is an implication that from each perspective one must hold an awareness of the possibility of finding oneself in the alternative situation. Faithfulness for those in the land includes seeing their own home as a gift to be held lightly, not a possession. It includes a genuine compassion and just treatment for those on the borders, who also need a home. Faithfulness for the refugee includes acting as if one were at home wherever one finds oneself, seeking the shalom of that place, "for in its *šālôm* you will find your *šālôm*" (Jer 29:7). And for both, the emphasis on choosing to live that way "this day" maintains a capacity to live in the moment, freed from being enslaved by the past or captive to the future. Said could have been describing the editors of Deuteronomy in Babylon or Yehud when he states:

> For an exile, habits of life, expression, or activity in the new environment inevitably occur against the memory of these things in another environment. Thus both the new and the old environments are vivid, actual, occurring together contrapuntally. (2000, 186)

For a people in exile, committed to following the God revealed in Judeo-Christian literature and tradition, Deuteronomy has a pivotal place. Its own literary placement at the juncture between the wilderness and the promised land has much to say to a people who are border dwellers. Deuteronomy 30 claims it is YHWH's own actions that will bring about their restoration and the downfall of the forces opposing them (30:6–10). At the same time, Deut 30 is well suited to unsettle those who feel they belong in a place already—those who have achieved the status of homecoming ("When all these things have happened to you…," 30:1)—since it urges that life and blessing come only through "loving the Lord your God, walking in his ways, and observing his commandments, decrees and ordinances" (30:16). Theologies of land and exile thus belong together, each informing the other perspective. And what better place to engage in this interaction than in a refugee camp?

Works Consulted

Ben Zvi, Ehud. 2009. Towards an Integrative Study of the Production of Authoritative Books in Ancient Israel. Pages 15–28 in *The Production* of Prophecy: Constructing Prophecy and Prophets in Yehud*. Edited by Diana V. Edelman and Ehud Ben Zvi. London: Equinox.

Biddle, Mark. 2003. *Deuteronomy*. Smyth & Helwys Bible Commentary. Macon, Ga.: Smyth & Helwys.

Brueggemann, Walter. 2003. *An Introduction to the Old Testament: The Canon and Christian Imagination*. Louisville: Westminster John Knox.

Budden, Chris. 2009. *Following Jesus in Invaded Space: Doing Theology on Aboriginal Land*. Eugene, Ore.: Pickwick.

Ellis, Marc H. 2002. *Practicing Exile: The Religious Odyssey of an American Jew*. Minneapolis: Augsburg Fortress.

Groody, Daniel G. 2009. Crossing the Divide: Foundations of a Theology of Migration and Refugees. *Theological Studies* 70:638–67.

Mathews, Jeanette. 2013. Framing Lament: Providing a Context for the Expression of Pain. Pages 187–204 in *Spiritual Complaint: The Theology and Practice of Lament*. Edited by Miriam J. Bier and Tim Bulkeley. Eugene, Ore.: Pickwick.

Rofé, Alexander. 1993. The Covenant in the Land of Moab (Deuteronomy 28:69–30:20): Historico-Literary, Comparative and Formcritical Observations. Pages 269–80 in *A Song of Power and the Power of Song: Essays on the Book of Deuteronomy*. Edited by Duane L. Christensen. Winona Lake, Ind.: Eisenbrauns.

Said, Edward W. 1986. *After the Last Sky: Palestinian Lives*. London: Vintage.

———. 2000. *Reflections on Exile and Other Essays*. Cambridge: Harvard University Press.

Sanders, James A. 1987. *Sacred Story to Sacred Text*. Philadelphia: Fortress.

Schlabach, Gerald W. 1999. Deuteronomic or Constantinian: What Is the Most Basic Problem for Christian Social Ethics? Pages 449–71 in *The Wisdom of the Cross*. Edited by Stanley Hauerwas et al. Grand Rapids: Eerdmans.

Smith-Christopher, Daniel. 2002. *A Biblical Theology of Exile*. Minneapolis: Augsburg Fortress.

Thompson, Greg. 2010. "White Man's Dreaming"—the Northern Territory Emergency Response: "The Intervention." *St Mark's Review* 214:86–98.

Weaver, Alain Epp. 2003. On Exile: Yoder, Said, and a Theology of Land and Return. *Crosscurrents* 52:439–61.

Welch, Twilla R. 2007. *Creative in Struggle*. Lincoln: iUniverse.

Yoder, J. H. 1973. Exodus and Exile: Two Faces of Liberation. *Crosscurrents* 23:279–309.

Reading Rizpah across Borders, Cultures, Belongings ... to India and Back

Monica Jyotsna Melanchthon

Every morning as the sun came up the whole family would wail. They did that for 32 years until they saw me again. Who can imagine what a mother went through? But you have to learn to forgive. (On a memorial plaque at the Reconciliation Park, Adelaide, South Australia)

The public sphere is the site where struggles are decided by other means than war. (Negt and Kluge 1993, ix)

Priyatama

On the night of August 27, 2008, Abhimanyu Nayak, a marginal farmer from the Barapalli village in the Kandhamal district of Orissa, was asleep on the veranda of his small home. His daughter Ragini was beside him, while his wife, Priyatama, and their son Tukuna were asleep inside.

Close to midnight a mob of masked men woke him, put a sword to his neck, and asked him if he would renounce Christianity and become a Hindu. When he responded in the negative, they dragged him into the nearby forest and beat him. He pleaded for mercy; he was stripped naked, his hands and legs were bound, and he was hung from a mango tree. His still living body was doused in diesel and kerosene, and he was set on fire and left to die. The fire burned the ropes and he fell; he managed to crawl toward his home with his body still aflame. His family, hearing his cries, managed to put out the flames, but not before 80 percent of his body was burned.

Neighbors, not wanting to invite the wrath of the bigots, refused to help, and he eventually died. A complaint was registered in the local police station by Tukuna on the very same day, FIR no. 90 u/s 147/148/436/

506/302/149, dated August 31, 2008 (Subrahmaniam 2010), but no help arrived, and dogs were attempting to feed on the body. The locals went to the police several times complaining that dogs were trying to eat the burned body. For five days, according to one report (Akkara 2009, 33–35), or ten, according to another (Subrahmaniam 2010), the body lay where he died until the police came with a doctor to conduct a postmortem on what was by then a rotting body. "All these days, I had to struggle to keep dogs away from the body. I had virtually gone mad by the time the body was buried," said Priyatama (Akkara 2009, 35; see also Singh 2009; Kendra 2010, 192).

In March 2009, following unceasing threats from those named in the First Information Report (FIR), Priyatama, who also petitioned the chief minister and the governor, took her case to the Orissa Human Rights Commission, which ordered the Kandhamal district magistrate and the superintendent of police to hold an inquiry into the case and take action against the errant policemen. In March 2010 a National People's Tribunal was held in Delhi, and Priyatama appeared before the tribunal to share her story; even by then no action had been taken against the perpetrators.

The Lot of Women

We live in a crises-ridden world, in which external factors (political, social, religious) impinge upon deep-rooted and imagined realities of identity and belonging. Constant recognition of identities, boundaries, borders, and collectivities, the world over, is intensifying distrust of the other. Politics of identity resonate with the notions of borders and boundaries and therefore differ in their histories and in their application. Religion, language, class, race, caste, ethnicity, and gender shape identity, and these are in contestation in any given place. In spite of the globalizing spread of modernity and its avowed values of secularism and humanism, people (re)invest intensely in ethnic and raced identities, and ethnic violence is a prominent part of political life across the world.

The matter is far more complex for women, who are not always free to choose between conflicting allegiances in an open political way. Issues of hegemony and belonging shape the collective and individual belongings of women. Women negotiate the politics of belonging amid the many fractures that characterize the world today, where multiple identities of nation, gender, ethnicity, and religious belief are held together by "imagined communities" (Anderson 1991).

Indian feminists have observed the reality of uneven development that both shapes and draws on gender relations, thereby affecting the nature of women's struggle for change. When dominant groups fail in their attempts at hegemony, namely, "politico-ideological control," they use violence as the chief instrument of control. The resistance of marginalized and oppressed communities, women included, takes place on several levels of response, from nonviolent collective struggle to armed insurgency. The subjectivities of women, their notions of belonging, as victims of violence and agents of resistance, are constituted through negotiations of these situations.

Returning to Rizpah

The Rizpah story caught my attention some years ago, and I have reflected on the action of this woman and perceived it as not being conducive to replication in actuality or within representational structures. It is a historical example—locked within a temporality. I celebrated the success and achievement of this narrative, for Rizpah's vigil and unspoken resilience give the story its power. But like many others, I saw it only as her story, until the news item cited above caught my attention and led me to revisit the Rizpah narrative.

Focusing on the two texts, this chapter examines the relationship between ethnic violence and the questions about belonging that haunt communities and particularly women of those communities. "How do the politics of resistance to entrenched forms of domination enable women to rise out of deeply subjugated positions into more self conscious positions of belonging to histories of oppression, reclaiming that oppressed space as the space of resistance and power?" (Kannabiran 2006, 89). This question will foreground the analysis of Rizpah with the help of Priyatama's experience.

The borders within which Rizpah and Priyatama lived failed to offer them security, or justice. Borders obviously contain fault lines, conflicts, and differences. For most women, justice, change, and security come only through the crossing/blurring of boundaries, transcending or subverting them (with risks, of course!). The emancipatory potential in such crossing needs to be tapped by those involved in the task of effecting justice, and perhaps more so by women (Mohanty 2003, 2). This paper explores the blurring of boundaries and identities in the two narratives and brings into relief select issues—life/death, dead/living bodies; silence/speech; sacrifice/slaughter.

The Kandhamal Pogrom

A "developing country" such as India is characterized by severe inequities in caste, class, ethnicity, language, community, and gender relations, which generate endemic violence characteristic of its social structures. Communalism is a major social and political force that has acquired an "explosive dimension" in the recent past. Despite general aversion to it, communalism persists and is a powerful threat to the life and property of our people and to their struggle for life in all its fullness. The 2008 riots in Kandhamal in Orissa

> signify a vicious political turn that indicates that communalism as a socio-political project has come to stay in our society as an ideology and as a political practice that combines communal terror with mass mobilisation for the capture of power. … A serious consequence of this communal pogrom was the undermining of democratic processes and institutions of a modern secular state by communal forces in the country. (Muricken and Kendra 2010, 1)

On August 23, 2008, Swami Laxananda Saraswati, a prominent Hindu leader, was shot dead along with five other people in his Jalaspeta ashram near Tumudibandha (Kandhamal district, Orissa). Naxalite groups[1] especially prominent in this region have taken credit for the attacks. The Swami was eighty-four years old and was especially known for violently opposing cow slaughter and conversion to Christianity and for initiating a movement for the Hinduization of dalits and tribals in Orissa. In retaliation for the August 23 killings, the *Vishva Hindu Parishad* (VHP)[2] and its allied political families called for a *bandh* (road blockade) on August 25. But in retaliation for the Swami's death, the extremist wing of the VHP also engaged in a series of attacks against Christians. Ajit Muricken and Vikas Adhyayan Kendra write,

> The scale of organised brutal violence in a most macabre of forms that engulfed tribal belt of Kandhamal reveals the prevailing deep religious

---

1. Maoist-oriented and militant insurgent separatist groups that claim to represent the poorest and most marginalized members of Indian society such as Adivasis and Dalits.

2. Founded in 1964, the VHP is a Hindu organization that aims to consolidate the Hindu society under Hindu pride, and to protect Hindu dharma.

divide. Actions of mobs well armed with weapons and explosives for a "search and destroy mission," selectively targeting a particular community cannot be treated as violence from the fringe. The execution of this "search and destroy policy" with precision by the Sangh Parivar ["family of organizations"] under the protection of the ruling party and with the complicity of the State machinery of a democratically elected government makes explicit the fascist character and the modus operandi of the perpetrators of the carnage. (Muricken and Kendra 2010, 1)

It is believed that more than 300 villages were ransacked; 44,000 homes burned; 5000 people rendered homeless; 59 killed; 18,000 dalits and *adivasis* (tribals, indigenes) injured; 151 churches destroyed; many burned alive, and several women gang raped (Kendra 2010, 7).

The David and Gibeonite Pogrom against Saul and Family

Nestled among the final chapters of 2 Samuel is the strange, troubling, and poignant tale of Rizpah (21:10-14). It is lodged within the larger narrative (21:1-14) about the house of Saul,[3] whose name is mentioned thirteen times in the span of fourteen verses, and about the bloodguilt that has come upon his house on account of his having disobeyed the treaty between the Israelites and the Gibeonites. There is a famine in the land, and David waits for three years[4] before seeking a solution to the famine. The oracle reveals that there is bloodguilt on the house of Saul "because he put to death the Gibeonites" (21:1-2). By attempting to annihilate the Gibeonites, Saul has dishonored the alliance Joshua made with them (Josh 9), an alliance forged through deception on the part of the Gibeonites.[5]

---

3. Saul is responsible for the famine; his descendants pay the price; and it is his wife who preserves the integrity of the dead bodies, ensuring them (including the body of Saul) a burial (Pigott 2002, 161).

4. "The famine of 3 years' duration is a sign of divine displeasure and a tangible indication that the land is out of synchrony with the normal cosmic order of seedtime and harvest, life and earth, renewal and destruction" (Exum 1992, 110).

5. When their deception was exposed, the Gibeonites were made hewers of wood and drawers of water for the congregation and for the altar of Yahweh (Josh 9:27). For more on the Gibeonites, see Kearney (1973, 1-19) and Blenkinsopp (1972). Violation and breach of treaty oaths is a serious offense, and the violator is cursed, but "the curse could not negate the treaty; it could only make the obligations heavier" (Fensham 1964, 99). Natural calamities and disasters such as famine and plague were often perceived as direct consequences of such a breach (Malamat 1955, 1-12).

The Gibeonites, seeking to curry favor with David, are perhaps lying, very well aware of the tensions between the House of Saul and the House of David. Saul is therefore damned—ironically, it seems, for attempting to destroy the inhabitants of the land as per the instructions of Deut 7, which stand in contradiction to the subsequent pledge/covenant to spare the Gibeonites (Josh 9).

> The issues of justice and guilt here turn out to be complex. When does one covenant—or promise, or commandment—override another? For how long must bloodguilt haunt a house? If Saul's house has blood guilt on its hands, what of David's? (Fewell and Gunn 1993, 160–61)

David asks the Gibeonites how he can atone for the breach of the covenant by Saul, through a process that is "an elitist, male negotiation" (Ortega 1994, 136). They respond that they do not seek monetary restitution, but they have no power to demand blood. David perhaps could offer money (West 2004, 101), but instead he prods them further, "What do you say that I should do for you?" The Gibeonites understand "the unspoken intent in David's repeated question" (West 2004, 101) and respond, "The man who consumed us and planned to destroy us, so that we should have no place in all the territory of Israel—let seven of his sons be handed over to us, and we will 'impale'[6] them 'before Yahweh in Gibeah of Saul,[7] the chosen of the Lord'[8] on the mountain of Yahweh" (2 Sam 21:5-6). Does Yahweh really approve of this slaughter of innocent men?[9] This response suits David, and

---

6. There are several meanings to this verb: being impaled, being cast off a cliff, being exposed, being crucified, and the like. McCarter (1984, 442) suggests that it should perhaps be understood as "crucifixion and subsequent exposure." Numbers 25:5 uses the same verb, and the context there suggests it is "impalement"; the LXX renders it as "exposure to the sun." In Gen 32:26 the same verb is used for the disjoining of Jacob's hip (de Vaux 1964).

7. Cf. 1 Sam 11:4; 15:34.

8. The LXX reads, "at Gibeon, in the mountain of the Lord" (so NRSV). Gibeon functioned as a Yahwistic sanctuary in the early monarchical period; cf. 1 Kgs 3:4 (Tatlock 2011, 44 n. 27).

9. Based on Josh 9–10 and 2 Sam 4:1-3 and 21:1-14, we can conclude that the Gibeonites worshiped Yahweh. Despite the author's attempt to distinguish them from the Israelites (2 Sam 21:2), the Gibeonites claim a place in the territory of Israel (21:5) and invoke the sanctions of Yahweh (Gottwald 1979, 572).

he comes across as being very democratic—as one who seeks the opinion of the afflicted. David says simply, "I will deliver them."

David spares Mephibosheth, the physically challenged son of Jonathan, on account of a promise made to Jonathan. "An oath leads to the death of an entire household but it is an oath that saves Mephibosheth. … Yet the fact that one descendant of Saul is spared heightens by contrast the sacrifice of seven others" (Exum 1992, 112). David "deliver[s] … into the hands of the Gibeonites," seven[10] men of Saul's family: Armoni and Mephibosheth, sons of Rizpah, the "concubine" of Saul; and the five unnamed sons of Michal,[11] the daughter of Saul. The seven men are impaled on the mountain of Yahweh, and they are "put to death in the first days of harvest, at the beginning of barley harvest" (21:9). The presumed Gibeonite revenge gives David the perfect pretext to put to death the sons of Saul and effectively end any further attempt on their part to usurp the throne. But David, of course, escapes chastisement. The text does not ascribe any ulterior motive to David. He is cautious and never admits his compliance in what happens. The Divine points to Saul as the cause of the famine, and the Gibeonites, the offended party, request the sons of Saul to be offered as sacrifice. All that David does, he does in order to appease the Divine and atone for the misdeeds of Saul, which have brought the curse of famine on the entire land and suffering to its people.[12] The men are impaled and left exposed; burial is denied to them as punishment for breach of the oath (Fensham 1964, 100). The executions happen at the beginning of the harvest, perhaps in anticipation of the end of the famine. But it does not bring rain as expected.

---

10. Seven was a number that signified completeness, and the word "seven" bears affinity with the verb meaning "to swear" or "to take an oath."

11. Many translations read "Merab" in place of MT's "Michal." Michal had no children (2 Sam 6:23), and it was Merab who was wife to Adriel (1 Sam 18:19). The Targum explains that Merab bore these five boys but Michal raised them (cf. Walters 2008, 462). Glück argues that the text says she had no children by David (2 Sam 6:23) but does not say that she was barren. Glück thus emends the text to read "Michal … whom she bore to Phaltiel, the son of Laish." It is nonetheless important to remember that with the death of these five children, Saul is left with no descendants (Glück 1965, 72–81).

12. All rivals are removed, but David himself does not bring about their deaths (Saul, Abner, Ishbaal, Absalom, Amasa, Sheba). Cf. Stone 2006, 216. The Chronicler omits 2 Sam 9 and 21 and erases any memory of the affair.

The story therefore "depicts in excruciating detail the annihilation of Saul's remaining descendants" to confirm that David's claim to kingship is still legitimate (Pigott 2002, 162). Mephibosheth will continue the line of Saul (McCarter 1984, 128), but David destroys all potential contenders from the house of Saul who might vie for the throne, and he conveys an unambiguous message to any Saul sympathizers or others who might aspire to the throne and to those who have doubts regarding his leadership (cf. 2 Sam 21).

Rizpah's Vigil

The action of Rizpah is pivotal to the story and critical for the resolution of the crisis. Rizpah, meaning "daughter of a falcon" or "glowing coal" (Fewell and Gunn 1993, 161), is the daughter of Aiah,[13] the secondary wife of Saul[14] and mother of Armoni and Mephibosheth, whom she bore to Saul. Rizpah is first mentioned in 2 Sam 3:6–11. Saul has been killed by the Philistines. Ishbosheth, the successor to the throne of Saul, questions Abner, his uncle and general of the army, as to why he took the "concubine" (Rizpah)? It remains unclear why Ishbosheth makes this accusation and whether there is any truth attached to this.[15] It "was customary for kings and aspiring kings to consolidate their political authority by symbolically appropriating their predecessor's women publicly" (Brenner 2005, 123). Ishbosheth/Ishbaal accuses Abner of trying to usurp the throne when he asks, "Why have you gone in to my father's concubine?" (2 Sam 3:7). The silent Rizpah

---

13. Most scholars assume that Aiah is the name of her father (Gen 36:24; 1 Chr 1:40), making her a foreigner. Brenner argues that the name Aiah is a feminine form and a semantic word for "falcon," "vulture," or "kite," in line with other women named after animals, such as Deborah (bee), Jael (mountain goat), and Huldah (mole). If Dinah is called "daughter of Leah" and men were similarly identified by their mothers (Joab son of Zeruiah), then there is no reason to doubt that Aiah is the name of Rizpah's mother (Brenner 2005, 121–22).

14. Note that she is not referred to as the "concubine" of Saul until two verses later. Exum maintains that the English "concubine" would perhaps mislead one to assume that she was an illegitimate wife and suggests that the "legal wife of secondary rank," is a better translation (1997, 261).

15. Two Greek manuscripts indicate that Abner did have sexual intercourse with Rizpah, but McCarter dismisses them as exegetical expansions (McCarter 1984, 105–6).

therefore becomes the cause or excuse for an open rift between the two and gives Abner the pretext to desert Ishbosheth and go to David's side.

After the impalement and death of her children, Rizpah takes sackcloth,[16] and she "stretches out" for herself "to the rock." Could she have pitched a tent for herself (Walters 2008, 461 n. 17)? Most have seen her as one who sits out in the rain and the sun and "joins her body to theirs in their exposure and faces out the months" (Fewell and Gunn 1993, 161). I am drawn to the Hebrew phrase "to the rock." The phrase "to the rock" is also used in Isa 30:29 and Isa 51:1–3a. Walters observes that in Isa 30 the "rock" is a symbol for God and in Isa 51:3, the rock refers to the "founding parents of Israel, … a metaphor expressing pristine source and origin" (Walters 2008, 455). Walters concludes in the light of these two passages that Rizpah is figurative for Zion, the mother who has lost her children, the barren mother of Isa 54, the penitent Israel who longs for restoration and blessing (2008, 460). I would like to use Walter's findings and suggest that what Rizpah is doing is calling for help to God, "the Rock" (2 Sam 22:2, 3, 32, 47), and to "the ancestors," demanding their intervention (cf. Levenson 2006; van der Toorn 1996). Radford Ruether argues that women are subordinated within the religious tradition by silence being enforced upon them (1983, 74). But praying and prayer is an obvious contradiction to this expectation. Rizpah's silent and contemplative prayer to the "rock" speaks loudly in the oral and praying tradition of Israelite women.

Rizpah sits "from the beginning of the harvest until rain [falls] on them" (several months), to prevent the desecration of the bodies of her sons and her nephews by animals and birds. When David is informed of Rizpah's silent vigil, he takes the bones of Jonathan and Saul (whose bodies were desecrated by the Philistines; 1 Sam 31:8–13)[17] and buries them in the tomb of Saul's father, Kish, in the territory of their tribe, Benjamin (1 Sam 21:14).[18] After that, we are told, "God heeded supplications for the

---

16. Cf. 2 Sam 16:22. It reminds me of Hamida Banu Begum, wife of Humayun the Mughal ruler, who is said to have pitched a tent beside the grave of her husband and lived in it until a tomb was built for him.

17. Later the men of Jabesh Gilead recover the bodies, burn them, and bury the bones. This act is described as an act of covenant loyalty by David in 2 Sam 2:5. They bury them not in the family tomb in Benjamin but under a Tamarisk tree in Jabesh (1 Sam 31:3), with due honor.

18. The MT does not explicitly mention that the seven were buried. It only speaks of the bones of Saul and Jonathan. If their bones were also collected (by someone else) we can safely assume that it was for burial. The LXX states that they were buried. Per-

land" (v. 15). According to Exum, God is appeased only after the burial of the bones that Rizpah has made possible through her vigil (1992, 162). But Ortega contends that the rains come only when the leaders acknowledge her action: "Only at the moment when they recognized what she was doing did God heed their supplication for the land" (Ortega 1994, 138).

Blurring of Borders/Lines …
Crossing Over and Forging New Belongings

Rizpah and Priyatama are women without official power. A mob arrived at Abhimanyu's house in the middle of the night, and they whisked him off into the nearby forest. How many did David send to pick up the seven boys/men from Saul's home? The text does not describe how these men were captured and "delivered" to the Gibeonites or whether they resisted, cried out, or fought back. I am certain they would not have gone passively and quietly. They must have resisted, cried, assured their mothers, and comforted them with promises to return but pretty much certain that they would not. Nor does it tell us how the members of the family, the women, may have responded. Exum maintains that Rizpah "is silent and does not interfere with the decreed execution" (1997, 264). I am not sure about this. Could she have remained stoic in these circumstances? She may not have been able to stop the execution, but I imagine that she and Michal held on to their children as they were dragged away. They must have implored and pleaded, beat their chests and cried aloud, begged around for help, beat the ground as they lay on it and watched their children being taken away. They perhaps cursed David and the soldiers, questioned God, and cursed their own lives. Did the neighbors come out to help? Could they have helped? Were they perhaps also afraid? Did they comfort them after the men were taken away? What could or did they say? Was there a neighborhood meeting to discuss this? Did they follow the group? Did they watch them being impaled? They probably did, for the men were impaled in a public space.

When did the crying stop, and the beating of the chest? When did the silence descend? The silence in my opinion came after the slaughter, when there was nothing more she could do to keep them physically alive—when it was all finished. Rizpah was a silent pawn in quarrels between men

---

haps the author was trying to redeem David by portraying him as the one who buried Saul in the tomb of his ancestors (Olyan 2005, 601–16).

(2 Sam 3:7), until now. But her silent determination and devotion here have stirred the king. Perhaps she could shame the very king who brought about the deaths of her two sons so that he would change his course of action and treat the bodies of his enemies with honor (Stone 2006, 221). Priyatama persevered and continued to do so for the sake of justice for her murdered husband. How did they do it? Priyatama was supported by her family and neighbors. In situations such as the one she was in, the police are often in collusion with the perpetrators or are just too afraid to take action. But she was relentless, and eventually some of her formerly reluctant neighbors joined her in her pursuit of justice.

Although the biblical text presents Rizpah's vigil as a solitary one, it has been suggested that Rizpah was perhaps supported and sustained by members in the community, mostly women, but surely by some men as well, all of whom were affected by the untimely death of these young men. They perhaps brought her food, water, and clothing and joined her in prayer. It was mostly a women's vigil that challenged the logic of men that was more concerned with "maintaining national security and keeping an alliance of death" (Ortega 1994, 137). The deaths and the subsequent vigil of Rizpah gave rise to a public space and a civil discourse. Her act was a political one and one of deep spirituality, a spirituality of resistance (Welch 1985, 39). It is possible that the number of those who sympathized with her grew day by day, and it was in David's best interest to take note and act. In fact, David may have benefited by an immediate burial of the dead men. The longer he opposed their burial, the bigger and stronger grew the group in support of her. It led to debate, conversation, and a spread of ideas. It forced David to respond, and he arranged for the bones of the dead men to be collected and the bones of Saul and Jonathan as well, for good measure, to be brought and buried in the family tomb. Her attitude and actions illustrate the power that can flow from those who have a real commitment to others. She wanted to expose and call attention to David's inequity. She wanted justice for herself and her family. The seven were dead, but it is in the context of death that people shape forms of community and difference along lines of ethnicity, class, gender, religion, and kinship through the mutuality of their emotions, their pain and tears. Her vigil brought her into the presence of a community that was created and forged around the bodies of her dead children and her grief and her efforts to seek justice for them.

Their initial helplessness/powerlessness was transformed; it was active, driven, goal oriented; a force that was obsessed by the need and the yearning for justice, for dignity, for humanhood. While they addressed a specific issue through their vigils—the burial of their loved ones—they convey a deeper and larger message to those who read their stories. Their acts were performed within the confines of the limited resources available to them, and yet the result was explosive!

Sacrifice or Slaughter?

A horrific death! Scholars suggest that what is being described here is a fertility ritual performed with the aim to bring rain, a sacrifice performed in concession to Canaanite beliefs shared by a section of the Israelite population (Arvid S. Kapelrud, cited by Bodi 2005, 54). They were "put to death"—sacrificed—"for the sake of eradicating the contamination brought on by shedding innocent blood; in this instance to restore land's fertility" (Tatlock 2011, 42). That blood sacrifice brings rain and fertility is a common belief in many traditional cultures, and this reproductive function of sacrifice is upheld also by most socio-anthropologically based theories of sacrifice (Good 2009, 383).

There might be another possible function of sacrifice as evident in this narrative: its capacity to engender a social identity that is both domestic and political. Cazelles claims that David sought ways to assimilate the Canaanites and their sacred cities (1955, 171). For example, special status was given to the queen mother, or the *gebirâh*, for she was the mother of kings. Similarly, royal concubines, by virtue of their maternity, according to Cazelles, provided for the sacral character of the king in the eyes of the community. The sacrifice is perhaps connected with this maternity of the royal concubine and the fertility beliefs among the Canaanites (Cazelles 1955, 173). The specific influence of this sacrificial ritual is toward homogenization and to overcome differentiation across tribal boundaries, in this case between the Gibeonites/Canaanites and Israelites/David. David's choice was therefore driven by political expediency. "It primarily functioned, especially for the Deuteronomists, as a means of capital punishment through which the land and nation were cleansed" (Tatlock 2011, 47).

But I see this "sacrifice" as a manifestation of repressive institutional violence generative of patriarchal domination, a violent instrument of a political and ideological mechanism. But was this a sacrifice, or was it slaughter? It was beneficial for the powers that be to render it a "sacrifice" so as to absolve themselves of the guilt of murder. If Yahweh sanctions this sacrifice for his own appeasement and in return for rain (Exum 1992, 261), has God been co-opted? Is this not the politicization of religion? To use religion to justify violence and provide cover for the carnage was a clever ploy on the part of the authorities. For the victims, however, especially since they were not sacrificed out of their own volition, it was slaughter, unwelcomed death. The issue is significant, because the rain that was to come upon the death of these men did not come. The drought continued until the community reacted to their deaths and until the powers that be allowed for honor to be restored to them. By being allowed the burial, the family was given the opportunity to memorialize the dead and observe other ancestral rites.

Silence That Speaks, a Silence That Is Remembered!

The narrative begins with much speech that wanes in the latter half of the unit. The dialogue is replaced by a narrative report, which Exum suggests is intentional in order "to create a distance" between the reader and the character, to hinder us from witnessing directly Rizpah's personal anguish (1997, 262). Several scholars have commented on this deafening sound of Rizpah's silence. Her action blurs the lines between speech and silence. The understanding of women's silences and speech has grown to be an area of crucial theoretical as well as political consequence for contemporary feminism. The conversion of women's speech and silence into the categories of testimony is a specific attribute of feminist politics. Since speech is identified as self-expression, and silence as self-extinction, they are closely tied into the project of subject constitution. But there are limits and ambiguities that surround both silence and speech in the project of subject constitution.

Silence and speech are not absolutely distinct categories; speech is never transparent, and silence is not always an imposition. Silence is a rich social space that can operate as a vehicle for either memory or forgetting and can be used for various purposes (Vinitzsky-Seroussi and Teeger 2010, 1104). The silence of Rizpah is overt with the absence of narrative and speech;[19] but it is pregnant with meaning, with protest, resilience. It is a silence that is not easily forgotten or ignored; it enhances memory. It

---

19. Vered Vinitzsky-Seroussi and Chana Teeger make a distinction between overt and covert silence. The former is characterized by the literal absence of speech and narrative. Covert silence is a little harder to recognize or identify and, hence, critique.

is apparent and easily discernible. She wants to remember, and she wants to make others remember, and hence she turns to total silence. It is intentional, purposeful, and planned; the reason is to commemorate the incident and her children. She chooses silence, for it provides her the opportunity to be introspective and reflect, to commemorate, and it speaks louder than words.[20] I am also wondering whether she has taken an oath of silence,[21] to pressure God and David to provide for the burial of her children. Her silence inscribes itself on her body. Her silence is ritualistic—internalized so that she can discipline herself in the act of memory.

The silence is powerful also because of the location. Rizpah does not sit behind closed doors to mourn over her children. The killing of the men is a public action, brutal and ruthless, intended to be a warning and an example to others. Rizpah grieves in silence and *in* public. She sees not a political spectacle but a human tragedy. The death of these men is not a display of indignity and shame; it is an assault upon the dignity and worthiness of God (Boesak 2010); she is there for months, visible to passersby and at the mercy of the elements. How can anyone who knows her sleep in comfort knowing that there is a solitary woman holding vigil, day and night, over dead bodies? No words are needed. Her silence accompanied by her posture of resistance is effective enough to broker a response from others in the community, from David and ultimately even from God. "Her act of love and solidarity releases us from the power and the grip of the palace into the freedom of sacrificial resistance. She draws our attention away from the centers of power to the margins of suffering and righteousness" (Boesak 2010).

The counter to silence in the politics of representing subaltern resistance cannot be only speech. Action, too, needs to be recognized as a significant alternative image in the textual representation produced by the cultural unconscious and, consequently, as an exploitable political resource (Sunder Rajan 1993, 88ff.). This is what Priyatama chose. Her response was interspersed with words and action (frequent visits to the

---

It is covered and veiled by mnemonic talk; it is not about the complete absence of talk, ritual, or practice but about the absence of content (2010, 1104).

20. "Perhaps silence is simply the space to hear the echo of a deeper voice or a place apart to grieve or a way to deny bullets the last word—or all of these. Breathing Space" (Neumark 2003, 58).

21. In Hinduism this is called a *mouna vratha* ("ritual or vow of silence"), which helps calm one's mind.

police station; filing an FIR; petitioning the government; appearing before a tribunal).

Death and Life; Dead Bodies and Agency

The Rizpah narrative "verges on a world of elemental terror, the point of contact between the realm of the living and the realm of the dead, a place where human actions are undertaken in response both to perceived supernatural demands and to a sense of primal obligation of the living to the dead" (Exum 1992, 110). In ancient Israel, women performed religious roles outside the male-defined rituals, and one such role was providing for the ancestors by tending to their graves, consulting the ancestors as the mediator between the generations (Bird 1990, 12–13, 19–20). That Rizpah takes on this task on behalf of her dead children and nephews comes as no surprise. She takes sackcloth and stretches out for herself "to the rock"—to God; she mediates on behalf of her children and calls upon the ancestors. She is aware of the assumption that nonburial or improper burial is shameful and perhaps indicative of divine punishment (Jer 7:33; 8:1–2; 9:21; 16:6; 22:18–19; 36:30).[22] There are several reasons why she would do so:

- She needs to restore the humanity of the seven, who have been dehumanized (Ortega 1994, 137).
- She needs to memorialize them, for the children and their father, since loss of memory is always accompanied by loss of identity.
- She needs to bury them, because leaving them on the field is the ultimate form of dishonor to the dead and to the living (Olyan 2005, 601–16; Bloch-Smith 1992, 213–24).
  a. Lack of burial is an impediment to the spirit's rest in the afterlife; it causes inability to share physical proximity with deceased kin.

---

22. In the movie/documentary "The Stoning of Soraya M." a 2008 American Persian-language drama film adapted from French journalist Freidoune Sahebjam's 1990 book *La Femme Lapidée,* based on a true story, the Iranian woman accused of adultery is stoned to death and not allowed burial. Her body is cast by the river to be consumed by birds and dogs.

b. Burial is needed for the purposes of feeding and memorializing rites (ancestral rites) and to perpetuate the relationship of the deceased with the living and the dead.
   c. To erect a tomb reinforces family claims to the patrimony, to the inheritance (Josh 24:30; Judg 2:9). The existence of the tomb constitutes a physical, perpetual witness to ownership of the land and in some cases serves as boundary marker (1 Sam 10:2; Josh 24:30).

Through her mourning Rizpah mitigates some of the damage caused, and yet it is imperative that they be buried.

It strikes me that so much of our attention thus far has been on Rizpah and others still living in the text that we fail to recognize the impact of the seven dead men in the narrative. Death is a taboo for some of us. Fear is associated with it. A dead body is polluting, unwanted, disruptive and a manifestation of absence, of no life. Most would want to dispose of a dead body soon, for these many reasons and more, mostly for the convenience of the living. I am reminded of the couple of times I conducted worship using the Judg 19 text and having the body of a young woman playing dead in the midst of the worship space. People were not comfortable. The woman's body, stiff and unmoving, was speaking to them and sending very discomforting messages.

Rizpah could not bury her sons even if she wanted to. Priyatama could have taken the risk of burying her husband before the police and the coroner came. She could have explained and used her neighbors to give witness, and yet she didn't. She waited, watching the body rot. Rizpah also watches as bodies rot. My sensibilities make me recoil at the thought. The dead bodies that constitute the material reality of death, their sight, their smell, will evoke a response from any human being. Death studies remind us that the dead body, when displayed in the public sphere, is symbolically effective. It becomes an active social agent, a reminder and a site of information, contested, evoking a variety of responses. The dead body is more than an "it," an object. It is a social agent that functions in ways similar to that of an art object, blurring the line between subject and object (Harper 2010, 309). Those who view the body that is dead experience an inner agency, and hence, even though they are "dead," they are alive as agents in their own transformation. Both Rizpah and Priyatama perhaps were cognizant of the power of the message that is conveyed via the medium of the visible dead body. By physically positioning themselves beside the dead person(s), they enabled it/them to speak powerfully to those around, to the authorities and even also to God.

In Conclusion

Rizpah and Priyatama are reminders of the mothers and wives who go to extraordinary lengths for the sake of their spouses and their children. They mourn and lament over every child, every life that is prematurely extinguished, and by doing so they redeem the conscience and the soul of their communities and their people. Their experiences and efforts bring to mind the tears of mothers and wives the world over, who wait for years on end for news of their missing children and spouses, children who have been forcefully taken away by oppressive regimes, by legitimate armed forces in the name of national security, and those that have been kidnapped and sold into the flesh trade.

These stories forcefully reminded me of the mothers of the "stolen generation" in Australia. These mothers keep the memory of their children alive through their paintings, their poems, and their songs. The protest, resilience, and courage of Rizpah live on in these women, and in the many mothers organizations—the Meira Paibi ("torch bearers," also known as "Mother's Union") of Manipur, India, fighting against the Assam Rifles and Armed Forces Special Powers Act, which gives special powers to the armed forces and has led to many human rights violations; the Madres de la Plaza de Mayo, seeking "the disappeared" in the political repression in Argentina; the Women in Black movement in Palestine and Israel; to name just a few. They are powerless, marginalized victims of abuse, and yet they have become champions of justice. They resist with their voices, with their tears, with their prayers—silent and spoken, with their bodies, with their energy and their love, with dignity and courage, protecting, preserving, uplifting, redeeming. They question all existing and dominant notions of survival and national security that are secured by injustice and oppression (Boesak 2010).

Rizpah and Priyatama join these women across racial, religious, and other borders to form new belongings, community, and identity. Articulating community with other minoritized and marginalized individuals/groups—this is a transnational practice of identity forming, rooted in the recognition of historical and current violence and shared humanness. At the same time it is also an inscription of the violence of the unbelonging experienced by the marginalized in systems of nation states. Women, by transcending and crossing the private sphere and bringing their concerns to the public sphere, have generated new political discourses, thereby impinging upon those with power, effecting life, change, and transformation.

WORKS CONSULTED

Akkara, Anto. 2009. *Shining Faith in Kandhamal*. Bangalore: Asia Trading Corporation.

Anderson, Benedict. 1991. *Imagined Communities: Reflection on the Origin and Spread of Nationalism*. London: Verso.

Bird, Phyllis. 1990. Gender and Religious Definition: The Case of Ancient Israel. *Harvard Divinity Bulletin* 20:12-13, 19-20.

Blenkinsopp, J. 1972. *Gibeon and Israel: The Role of Gibeon and the Gibeonites in the Political and Religious History of Early Israel*. Cambridge: Cambridge University Press.

Bloch-Smith, Elizabeth M. 1992. The Cult of the Dead in Judah: Interpreting the Material Remains. *Journal of Biblical Literature* 111:213-24.

Bodi, Daniel. 2005. *The Michal Affair: From Zimri-Lim to the Rabbis*. In Collaboration with Brigitte Donnet-Guez. Sheffield: Sheffield Phoenix.

Boesak, Allan. 2011. The Dignity of Resistance in Solidarity: The Story of Rizpah. *Kairos Southern Africa* (blog), May 8. Online: http://kairossouthernafrica.wordpress.com/2011/05/08/biblical-reflections-on-2-samuel-211-14-by-dr-allan-boesak/.

Brenner, Athalya. 2005. *I Am...: Biblical Women Tell Their Stories*. Minneapolis: Augsburg.

Cazelles, H. 1955. David's Monarchy and the Gibeonite Claim (2 Samuel 21:1-14). *Palestine Exploration Quarterly* 87:165-75.

de Vaux, Roland. 1964. *Studies in Old Testament Sacrifice*. Cardiff: University of Wales Press.

Exum, J. Cheryl. 1992. *Tragedy and Biblical Narrative: Arrows of the Almighty*. Cambridge: Cambridge University Press.

———. 1997. Rizpah. *Word & World* 17:260-68.

Fensham, F. Charles. 1964. The Treaty between Israel and the Gibeonites. *Biblical Archaeologist* 3:96-100.

Fewell, Danna N., and David M. Gunn. 1993. *Gender, Power and Promise: The Subject of the Bible's First Story*. Nashville: Abingdon.

Glück, J. J. 1965. Merab or Michal? *Zeitschrift für die Alttestamentliche Wissenschaft* 77:72–81.
Good, Leslie. 2009. "Creating Descent" after Nancy Jay: A Reappraisal of Sacrifice and Social Reproduction. *Method and Theory in the Study of Religion* 21:383–401.
Gottwald, Norman. 1979. *The Tribes of Yahweh: A Sociology of the Religion of Liberated Israel 1250–1050 B.C.E.* Maryknoll: Orbis.
Harper, Sheila. 2010. The Social Agency of Dead Bodies. *Mortality* 15:308–22.
Kannabiran, Kalpana, et al. 2006. Introduction. *Patterns of Prejudice* 40:189–95.
Kearney, P. J. 1973. The Role of the Gibeonites in the Deuteronomistic History. *Catholic Biblical Quarterly* 35:1–19.
Kendra, Vikas Adhyayan. 2010. Definitive Dossier on Kandhamal Communal Violence. Countercurrents.org, August 15. Online: http://www.countercurrents.org/vak.pdf.
Levenson, Jon D. 2006. *Restoration of Israel: The Ultimate Victory of the God of Life*. New Haven: Yale University Press.
Malamat, A. 1955. Doctrines of Causality in Hittite and Biblical Historiography: A Parallel. *Vetus Testamentum* 5:1–12.
McCarter, P. Kyle. 1984. *II Samuel*. Anchor Bible 9. New York: Doubleday.
Mohanty, Chandra Talpade. 2003. *Feminism without Borders: Decolonizing Theory, Practicing Solidarity*. Durham, N.C.: Duke University Press.
Muricken, Ajit, and Vikas Adhyayan Kendra. 2010. Introduction: Lessons from Kandhamal. Pages 1–4 in Definitive Dossier on Kandhamal Communal Violence. Countercurrents.org, August 15. Online: http://www.countercurrents.org/vak.pdf.
Negt, Oskar, and Alexander Kluge. 1993. *Public Sphere and Experience: Toward an Analysis of the Bourgeois and Proletarian Public Sphere*. Foreword by Miriam Hansen. Translated by P. Labanyi et al. Minneapolis: University of Minnesota Press.
Neumark, Heidi. 2003. *Breathing Space: A Spiritual Journey in the South Bronx*. Boston: Beacon.
Olyan, Saul M. 2005. Some Neglected Aspects of Israelite Interment Ideology. *Journal of Biblical Literature* 124:601–16.
Ortega, Ofelia. 1994. The Gospel of Solidarity. *Ecumenical Review* 46:135–41.
Pigott, Susan M. 2002. Wives, Witches, and Wise Women: Prophetic Heralds of Kingship in 1 and 2 Samuel. *Review and Expositor* 99:145–73.

Radford Ruether, Rosemary. 1983. *Sexism and God-Talk: Toward a Feminist Theology*. Boston: Beacon.

Sayer, Duncan. 2010. Who's Afraid of the Dead? Archaeology, Modernity and the Death Taboo. *World Archaeology* 42:481–91.

Singh, Ajay Kumar. 2009. Stories of Faith from the Persecuted of Orissa. AsiaNews, September 4. Online: http://www.asianews.it/news-en/Stories-of-faith-from-the-persecuted-of-Orissa-16233.html.

Stavrakopoulou, Francesca. 2010. *Land of Our Fathers: The Roles of Ancestor Veneration in Biblical Land Claim*. New York: T&T Clark.

Stone, Ken. 2006. 1 and 2 Samuel. Pages 195–221 in *The Queer Bible Commentary*. Edited by Deryn Guest et al. London: SCM.

Subrahmaniam, Vidya. 2010. Three Pogroms Held Together by a Common Thread. *The Hindu*, September 4. Online: http://www.thehindu.com/opinion/op-ed/article611933.ece.

Sunder Rajan, Rajeswari. 1993. *Real and Imagined Women: Gender, Culture and Postcolonialism*. New York: Routledge.

Tatlock, Jason. 2011. The Place of Human Sacrifice in the Israelite Cult. Pages 33–48 in *Ritual and Metaphor: Sacrifice in the Bible*. Edited by Christian A. Eberhart. Atlanta: Society of Biblical Literature.

Toorn, Karel van der. 1996. *Family Religion in Babylonia, Syria and Israel*. Leiden: Brill.

Vinitzsky-Seroussi, Vered, and Chana Teeger. 2010. Unpacking the Unspoken: Silence in Collective Memory and Forgetting. *Social Forces* 88:1103–22.

Walters, Stanley D. 2008. To the Rock: 2 Samuel 21:10. *Catholic Biblical Quarterly* 70:453–64.

Welch, Sharon D. 1985. *Communities of Resistance: A Feminist Theology of Liberation*. Maryknoll: Orbis.

West, Gerald. 2004. 1 and 2 Samuel. Pages 92–104 in *The Global Bible Commentary*. Edited by Daniel Patte. Nashville: Abingdon.

Whybray, R. N. 1968. *The Succession Narrative: A Study of II Sam. 9–20 and I Kings 1 and 2*. Naperville, Ill.: Allenson.

Borderless Discipleship: The Syrophoenician Woman as a Christ-Follower in Mark 7:24–30

Jeffrey W. Aernie

Evaluations of the Markan theme of discipleship frequently revolve around certain rhetorical dualities that are understood to be an outworking of Mark's specific redaction of the material and his particular theological framework. The narrative function of persons deemed followers of Jesus within the Gospel is consequently characterized along certain lines, such as major versus minor, positive versus negative, or pastoral versus polemical. This type of dualistic characterization, however, seemingly neglects the variegated portrait of disciples and discipleship developed throughout Mark's narrative. Mark's portrayal of both the successes and failures of Christ-followers emphasizes the need for a more nuanced understanding of Markan discipleship that overcomes the rhetorical boundaries set up around certain persons within the Gospel. The specific intent of the present essay is to provide an analysis of Mark 7:24–30 that highlights the position of the Syrophoenician woman as an exemplar of the Markan theme of discipleship.[1] The argument will focus primarily on the woman's culturally audacious interaction with Jesus as an example of the bold faith that Mark's narrative requires of its audience. The woman's persistent interaction with Jesus despite the presence of explicit ethnic, geographic, and gender-oriented divides develops a portrait of discipleship that exists irrespective of those boundaries. Her discipleship, therefore, crosses both physical and

---

1. The present essay is focused specifically on Mark 7:24–30, and so the synoptic parallel in Matt 15:21–28 remains out of the narrative purview at this stage. For readings of Matt 15:21–28 that stress the borderless nature of the text, see Wainwright 1995 and Guardiola-Sáenz 1997.

rhetorical borders and helps to define the theme of Markan discipleship as existing on a borderless plane. An attempt will then be made to cross the temporal border between ancient and present contexts in order to offer some introductory insights into how the borderless nature of this Markan narrative might continue to define Christian discipleship.

1. Narrative Analysis of Mark 7:24–30

The well-known narrative of the interaction between Jesus and the Syrophoenician woman in Mark 7:24–30 has, like many of the so-called hard sayings of Jesus, received a significant amount of scholarly attention. Questions revolve primarily around the central narrative dialogue, with attempts to explain both the apparently harsh nature of Jesus's parabolic statement and the intriguing speech-act of the woman herself, who, by her response, attains the healing for her daughter that she originally sought. In light of the transparently harsh and enigmatic nature of the dialogue, the theological sum of the narrative is often left behind in favor of a focus upon its constituent parts, with efforts either to soften the negative import of Jesus's statement or to praise the woman for her extraordinary persistence and wit. Inasmuch as these individual foci aid in understanding the significance of the present passage, they serve to illuminate its function within the broader scope of Mark's narrative. There is an exegetical risk, however, in focusing so intently on the dialogue that its narrative function is lost in the forest of interpretation. The import of the passage is dependent not only on the sum of its parts but also on its place within the larger context of the Gospel (France 2002, 96).

1.1. Crossing Borders

The narrative begins with Jesus crossing into the Gentile region of Tyre on his own initiative. No specific reason is outlined for the journey, and the intended result is relatively enigmatic, with Jesus apparently seeking privacy upon his entrance into the house. However, in both Mark 2:1 and 3:20 news of Jesus's entrance into a house is met with a gathering of a crowd. In the present scene his desire for anonymity is met with a parallel result, as even in this non-Jewish region his presence cannot be kept secret, and an individual woman from the area quickly comes to request healing for her demon-possessed daughter. Interestingly, in the following scene, Mark 7:31–37, Jesus unsuccessfully attempts to prevent those who witness his healing of the deaf mute in the Decapolis from disclosing information about the activity. Both of these scenes, then, revolve in some way around the attempt to prevent disclosure of Jesus's identity and action. Marcus argues that both themes developed in these narratives, Jesus's position in a Gentile setting and the motif of secrecy, are intentional developments in Mark that emphasize the "boundary-effacing power of the God who reveals himself in Jesus" (2000, 467; cf. Donahue and Harrington 2002, 232). Even if this theological appropriation of these two narratives is considered an overemphasis, there is little to dissuade from the reality that knowledge about Jesus has spread rapidly in Mark's narrative (Stein 2008, 350).

Once the woman comes to Jesus with her request, however, their subsequent dialogue becomes the central topic for many interpretations of the passage, and the geographic position of the narrative is often left in the contextual background. It would be a mistake, however, to diminish the geographical and cultural setting of what follows. Due to the influential sociohistorical analysis of Theissen it is now relatively common knowledge among Markan commentators that the socioeconomic and political relationship between Tyre and Galilee was significantly strained (1991, 61–80). The agricultural relationship between the two areas was often particularly tenuous, with the result that there was a sharp economic divide between urban Tyre and rural Galilee (Theissen 1991, 72–75). Josephus notes that the political relationship between the two areas was equally acrimonious due to past injustices related to both economics and geographical expansion (*Ant.* 14.313–321), some of which came to fruition in the circumstances surrounding the Jewish War (66–73 C.E.), during which the Tyrians killed and imprisoned a significant number of Jews (*J.W.* 2.478; cf. Marcus 2000, 471; Theissen 1991, 75–77). The economic and political divisions that existed between the two geographic areas were severe enough for Josephus to refer to the residents of Tyre as hostile enemies to the Jews (*Ag. Ap.* 1.71; cf. Marcus 2000, 462; Theissen 1991, 77; Witherington 1984, 168). In light of this situation, Mark's specific identification of the location of the narrative provides a dramatic backdrop to the subsequent dialogue. Indeed, the abusive distinction developed between the children and the dogs with respect to the appropriate distribution of bread in Jesus's statement in Mark 7:27 may stem at least in part from the inherent socioeconomic and political situation that plagued the region (Marcus 2000, 462). In other words, the geographical boundaries of the narrative provide a key lens through which to view the subsequent material.

That the geographic context outlined in Mark 7:24 is crucial to the narrative is confirmed by the double identification of the woman in Mark 7:26, which emphasizes both her cultural (*hellēnis*) and national identity (*syrophoinikissa tō genei*). The initial description of the woman as a "Greek" may simply signify that she was a Gentile (cf. Rom 1:16; 1 Cor 1:22–24), but it may also function to insinuate a more nuanced understanding of her background in terms of language, cultural integration, and socioeconomic and political status. In light of the cultural progress of Hellenization and later novel interpretations of the Syrophoenician woman's biography (e.g., Ps.-Clem. *Hom.* 13.7), Theissen argues that the term suggests the likelihood that the woman belonged to a relatively high social class (1991, 68–72; cf. Bengston 1965, 252; Donahue and Harrington 2002, 223). That the woman is a "Syrophoenician by birth" highlights her regional affiliation and confirms her relation to the hostile area in which the narrative unfolds. The description of the woman as both "Greek" and "Syrophoenician by birth" brings the geographical setting of the story into focus and highlights the dramatic ethnic distinction between the woman and Jesus (Miller 2004, 91–94). The remarkable part of the narrative in the first instance is not that she is a woman but that she is a *cultured Greek Syrophoenician* woman (Hurtado 1983, 115; Beavis 1988, 6; Rhoads 1994, 367). This is not to say that the woman's gender is unimportant either in the present narrative or in the larger framework of Mark's Gospel. The primary point here is that the geographical setting and the geopolitical identification of the woman form the frame in which the dialogue between Jesus and this woman takes shape. The contrast between children and dogs, which both Jesus and the Syrophoenician woman take up, revolves in the first instance around ethnic and geographic categories, not those of gender.[2]

---

2. Contra, for example, Cadwallader (2008, 66), who argues that the "primary dyad" of the narrative is that of the women's (both mother and daughter) gender. Cadwallader's study is enlightening at a number of points, but his apparent dismissal of the geographic situation as the lens through which to interpret the narrative leads him to denounce the sociopolitical analysis of Theissen and others too readily. For the way in which the geographic background of the narrative can reshape one's reading of the material, see the analysis of Ringe 1985, and her later reassessment of the text in Ringe 2001.

1.2. Crossing Narratives

The introduction of this Greek Syrophoenician *woman*, however, draws parallels to the earlier narrative of the woman with the hemorrhage in Mark 5:25–34. Apart from the basic connection with respect to gender, the description of both the Syrophoenician woman's recognition of Jesus (*akousasa gynē peri autou*; cf. 5:27: *akousasa peri tou Iēsou*) and the position in which she approaches him (*elthousa prosepesen pros tous podas*; cf. 5:33: *ēlthen kai prosepesen autō*) evokes the narrative in Mark 5 (Marcus 2000, 466–67). Furthermore, despite the drastic circumstances surrounding each woman, their interaction with Jesus is marked by a significant amount of persistence, the unnamed woman in Mark 5 enduring a remarkable amount of suffering prior to engaging Jesus, and the Syrophoenician woman moving past the immense cultural divide that would have separated her (and her daughter) from Jesus. This parallel development of persistence in both women is evocative of the type of "active faith" that is a defining characteristic for disciples in Mark's Gospel (e.g., 2:1–5; 5:24–29, 35–36; 9:14–27; 10:52; see especially Malbon 2000, 53; cf. Marshall 1989, 237). The thematic parallels between the two women, however, also serve to emphasize the stark difference in the way that Jesus initially responds to both parties. In spite of presumed assumptions about how a man would have been expected to respond to a woman supplicant in the first century, Jesus's positive interaction with the woman in Mark 5:25–34 creates a certain amount of contextual dissonance for the reader when Jesus then responds negatively to the Syrophoenician woman's request in Mark 7:27 (contra Donahue and Harrington 2002, 437).

This same type of contextual dissonance arises from the relationship between the Syrophoenician woman and Jairus, whose narrative is intertwined with that of the woman suffering from persistent bleeding (Mark 5:21–24, 35–43). Although these two figures are ostensibly different in terms of their ethnicity, gender, and social position, their narrative situations are developed along similar lines, with each approaching Jesus in a position of humility (5:22; 7:25) with the hope of receiving healing for a suffering daughter (5:23; 7:26) from a source outside their normal context (Iverson 2007, 92–93). Jairus's narrative then becomes another contextual foil for the Syrophoenician woman's situation, and the distinction in Jesus's initial response to both individuals serves to underline the differences between them. The framing of the Syrophoenician woman's situation along the lines of both of these preceding figures highlights the cultural complexity of her situation and stresses her persistent determination to care for her daughter.

1.3. Crossing Cultural Borders

Jesus's stark response to the woman's request, "Permit the children to be satisfied first, for it is not right to take the bread from the children and throw it to the dogs" (Mark 7:27), does not directly address her concern. Rather, it consists of a parable developed with metaphorical language, and the subsequent dialogue has nothing to do with literal children, bread, or dogs, but it has to do with the distinction between Jews and Gentiles manifest by the contextual placement of the narrative (Iverson 2007, 45). The reference to dogs arises in the present context not from the cultural identity of the woman but from the household matrix of the parable itself. Thus, while Nanos (2009, esp. 469–74) has helpfully disputed the notion that the reference to dogs should automatically draw attention to a cultural divide between Jews and Gentiles, it seems relatively clear that the parable itself is meant to evoke a cultural contrast in light of its contextual placement in Mark's Gospel. Indeed, the apparent force of the statement is that it is inappropriate for this cultural outsider "to impose on the 'bread' (i.e., blessings of the kingdom) that rightfully belongs to the 'children' of Israel" (Iverson 2007, 48). Furthermore, there is no question that the reference to dogs is negative in the present context. In the New Testament alone dogs are associated with both unclean swine (Matt 7:6) and heretics (Phil 3:2; 2 Pet 2:22; Rev 22:15), and the broader biblical tradition uses language about dogs in similarly negative ways (e.g., Exod 22:31; 1 Sam 17:43; 1 Kgs 21:23; 22:38; 2 Kgs 8:13; 9:36; Prov 26:11; Isa 56:10–11).[3] Thus, in spite of confusion about why Jesus utters this particular saying, there is little mystery surrounding its contextual referents. The parabolic form of Jesus's words does not detract from the notion that the statement is a clear rejection of the woman's request due primarily to her ethnic and cultural identity. Consequently, the statement focuses on the division between children and dogs as a means of relating the perceived contrast between (cultural) insiders and outsiders.[4] The statement functions, then, as an overtly nega-

---

3. See especially the survey in Feldmeier 1994, 218–19.

4. The notion that the diminutive form of *kynaria* somehow makes the statement more palatable, creating a scene involving the interaction with children and "little puppies" in a household, is untenable (contra, most recently, Edwards 2002,

tive rejection of the woman's request because of her identity as a Greek Syrophoenician.

Apart from the negative associations tied up with Jesus's use of the pejorative term "dogs," a significant amount of weight has been heaped upon the adverbial adjective *prōton* ("first") as a guide to understanding Jesus's statement as a broad description of the salvation-historical dimension of the in-breaking of God's kingdom, in which Israel has priority and the Gentiles enter into God's reign only secondarily. Jesus's statement then is seen to reflect the same idea inherent in Paul's assertion in Rom 1:16 that the gospel brings about salvation first to the Jew and then to the Gentile (cf. Boring 2006, 211–12). Mark has indeed used this term in contexts pertaining to historical timelines (e.g., Mark 3:27; 4:28; 9:11–12; 13:10), but the difficulty with emphasizing the temporal scheme in the present context is that the woman's reply does not suggest that she finds some measure of hope in the possibility of a *later* feeding of the dogs (contra Stein 2008, 352). She apparently understands the parable as a rejection of her request and seeks to create a revised (cf. 7:28) parabolic matrix in which her daughter can receive the benefits of Jesus's ministry along with the children ("even the dogs under the table eat the crumbs from the children"). Her immediate focus then centers on the notion of *exclusivity*, not *temporality* (Guelich 1989, 387; cf. Marcus 2000, 466). This framework comports well with the contextual setting that Mark has established for his readers by emphasizing the geopolitical identity of the woman. The question the narrative raises is not "*When* will these women receive the benefits of the kingdom?" but rather "*Can* they receive them?"

The parabolic framework that the woman creates for Jesus to work within is actually a more representative description of Jesus's ministry to this point of the Gospel than Jesus's own negative statement in Mark 7:27. Although Israel has indeed been the primary focus of Jesus's ministry, the Gentiles have not been systematically excluded (see Iverson 2007). Jesus has already healed people from Gentile regions (including Tyre) suffering from unclean spirits (Mark 3:7–12) and has traveled into the region of the

---

219–20). In the New Testament, diminutives frequently reflect no apparent distinction in meaning from their regular forms, and the presence of a number of diminutives within the present context (i.e., *thygatrion, kynaria, psichiōn, paidion*) is a reminder of the fact that Mark uses these particular forms more frequently than any other New Testament writer (BDF, 60). For the notion that the diminutive form itself has negative connotations in the present context, see Cadwallader 2008, 74–81.

Gerasenes (5:1–20), healing a man described as having an unclean spirit (*en pneumati akathartō*) and being demon possessed (*ton daimonizomenon*), and instructing him to relate the act of mercy to his own people. Likewise, the narrative context of Mark 6–8 highlights the inclusion of the Gentiles into Jesus's messianic program. The initial portion of Jesus's statement in Mark 7:27, "Permit the children to be satisfied first," seemingly alludes to the broader narrative, in which Jesus feeds and satisfies both Jews (6:30–44) and Gentiles (8:1–9). The apparent import of both feeding narratives is that Jesus's concern is not limited by ethnic boundaries; both Jews and Gentiles are satisfied (*chortazō*) by his miraculous provision of bread (6:42; 8:8). If the term *prōton* carries any salvation-historical significance (for Mark's readers), it is that the time for the inclusion of Gentiles into the kingdom is *already present* in Jesus's ministry.

The preceding context, therefore, develops precisely the opposite idea of that inherent in Jesus's statement in Mark 7:27. The bread of the kingdom is already being offered to both Jews and Gentiles. Apart from the actual feeding narratives, bread (*artos*) plays an important role in Mark 7:1–23, the material directly preceding the present pericope. In this section of the narrative, questions concerning the disciples' consumption of bread with unclean hands (7:1–5) result in a stark confrontation between Jesus and the Jewish leaders concerning God's commands and human traditions (7:6–13), which leads Jesus to instruct both the crowd (7:14–15) and the disciples (7:17–13) about the way in which a person is defiled, emphasizing that the product of one's heart is the only measure by which one is defined as clean or unclean (Iverson 2007, 51). The notion that neither food nor people are defiled by external factors paves the way for the introduction of the Syrophoenician woman, who becomes in effect a living illustration of the redefinition of cleanliness, while her daughter's miraculous healing becomes the catalyst for Jesus's continued ministry among the Gentiles (Mark 7:31–8:10; cf. Aquino and McLemore 1993, 412; Miller 2004, 99; Rhoads 1994, 348, 362). That is, the resolution of her situation is a further example of Jesus's positive interaction with Gentiles and an expression of the theological import of declaring all foods clean, both of which signify that it is indeed right for the bread to be distributed across cultural borders.

1.4. Crossing Parables

Given this contextual analysis we are forced to return to Jesus's apparent rejection of the woman. If it is the woman's parabolic framework that more readily coordinates with preceding descriptions of Jesus's ministry, what do we make of his harsh statement concerning the children and the dogs? Given both the contextual acceptance of Gentiles outlined in earlier portions of the Gospel and the parabolic form of Jesus's words in the present narrative, it seems most likely that the statement functions as an ironic representation of the preconception manifest in the preceding narrative, to which the woman responds appropriately with a parabolic reassessment of the situation. The two key elements upon which this reading is constructed, the notions of Jesus's irony and the woman's parabolic reassessment, require more detailed explanation. In his seminal work on the function of irony in Mark, Camery-Hoggatt argues that Jesus's statement should be defined as a piece of peirastic irony, which functions to challenge one's response to a statement that may not represent the speaker's own attitude (1992, 149–51). As a way of enhancing Camery-Hoggatt's thesis it may be helpful to develop the notion of irony along the lines manifest in relevance theory, a branch of pragmatic linguistics in which irony is defined as the event in which a statement or thought of another is represented by the speaker as a means of reflecting a "dissociative attitude" toward the idea inherent in the statement (see especially Noh 2000, 94–98). Jesus's statement, then, would represent not his own perception of the situation but the implied assumption inherent in the preceding narrative pertaining to the distinction between clean and unclean foods.

Reading the statement as an ironic representation is not intended to mitigate its confrontational nature within the pericope but is an attempt to coordinate the dialogue with the preceding narrative and the positive outcome of the present situation. The immediately preceding pericope in Mark 7:1–23 has illustrated the misconception that ritual practice prevents defilement by eliminating the consumption of unclean foods. As a Gentile outsider the Syrophoenician woman functions as a living representation of these unclean foods, and Jesus's initial statement functions as an *ironic representation* of that same attitude of exclusion. Jesus's preceding response with regard to unclean foods highlights for the reader that this form of exclusion is not representative of his own assessment of the situation. The particular form of irony in the present case is not that Jesus is pretending to affirm something that he does not but that his representation of the expected state of affairs is meant to distance him from that conceptual framework (contra Williams 2006, 347). Consequently, the explicit removal of the categories of clean and unclean in relation to food (Mark 7:17–23) is applied in the present narrative to the relationship between people groups, so that the external boundaries that would have defined the woman as a "gospel-outsider" are removed (Edwards 2002, 218–19). For the sake of clarity, it is important to note that the irony of the statement lies primarily on the contextual level of the narrative and that the Syrophoenician woman would not have had access to the narrative developments available to Mark's readers.[5] In light of the contrast inherent in the woman's reply and her reassessment of the parable, it seems most likely that she understands the statement as an explicit rejection of her request. The description of Jesus's speech-act as an ironic representation, then, is not meant as a way to rationalize the statement so that Jesus appears less harsh. In contrast, it is precisely the confrontational nature of the statement that creates such a dramatic distinction with the eventual outcome of the narrative as it emphasizes so clearly the inclusion of the Gentiles in God's salvific program.

The woman's parabolic reassessment clearly suggests that she understands the negative implications of Jesus's statement but persists within the context of the original parable in order to reformulate the situation so that she and her daughter are included within the blessings of the kingdom (Williams 1994, 120). An important dimension in the determination of the import of both Jesus's statement and the woman's response is in understanding the significance of their parabolic form. Mark has already established that parables are particularly associated with outsiders (*tois exō*; Mark 4:11), a reality portrayed as a representation of the Isaianic (Isa 6:9–10) situation in which those with hardened hearts remain unchanged because of their lack of perception (Mark 4:11–12). The idea developed in Mark 4:11–12 is not that parables are a means to exclude outsiders but rather that their inability to understand Jesus's parabolic language is evocative of their position with respect to the kingdom.[6] For Mark, the conjunction of belief and disbelief surrounding Jesus echoes the situation represented in Isa 6:9–13, which presents a summary of the (eventual) mixed response that Isaiah's ministry receives. It is important to note, however, that irony is at play in both the Isaianic and Markan narratives. That the prophet is commissioned to callous the hearts of his hearers to prevent repentance is ironic in that it represents the opposite of the prophet's contextual mission to bring the people back to the Lord (Isa 6:13). Mark draws

---

5. On the presence of multiple discourse levels in irony, see Muecke 1969, 19–20; cf. Iverson 2007, 56.

6. On the function of *hina* in Mark 4:12, see especially Sim 2010, 144–48.

on this irony by establishing that the disparate responses to parables are representative of the hardened hearts of the people (cf. Matt 13:15) despite the fact that this is not the desired outcome of the parables themselves, which, as seen in Mark 4:26–32, are meant to elucidate the nature of the kingdom (Sim 2010, 144–48). One's ability to understand parables then becomes evidence of the status of one's heart, forging another contextual link between the Syrophoenician woman's parabolic reconstruction and the preceding narrative, in which the internal quality of the heart was positioned as the defining characteristic of cleanliness (Mark 7:18–23).

It is certainly significant, then, that those expected to be insiders, particularly the disciples, often fail to understand the significance of several of Jesus's parables (e.g., Mark 4:13; 7:18), while this Gentile woman responds to Jesus's statement with a parable that establishes her position as insider with ears to hear (cf. 4:9, 23; Iverson 2007, 52–53; Miller 2004, 98). Indeed, the Syrophoenician woman is the only person in the Markan narrative to manifest an immediate understanding of Jesus's parabolic framework, entering into the world of the parable and developing a parabolic expression that accurately illustrates the truly inclusive reality of the gospel in which the blessings of the kingdom are available to both Jew and Gentile (Edwards 2002, 221–22). The notion that the woman enters into the parabolic framework created by Jesus is not meant to suggest, however, that the woman's portrayal of both herself and her daughter as dogs under the table somehow reflects her humility, as if she appropriately accepts a lower or secondary status for both herself and her daughter because of their cultural identity (contra France 2002, 299; Iverson 2007, 54; Williams 1994, 12). That she represents herself and her daughter as dogs is merely an extension of the parable, not an acceptance of the ethnic distinction originally created by Jesus's ironic representation. That the dogs receive the children's crumbs in the woman's parable is, likewise, an expression of neither temporal sequence nor some sort of hierarchy of blessing. The purpose of her parabolic reconstruction is to reflect a situation in which Jews and Gentiles *equally* receive the benefits of the kingdom *now*.

2. The Syrophoenician Woman as Christ-Follower

The intent of the focus on the relationship between Jew and Gentile in the preceding narrative analysis is not meant to result in the Syrophoenician woman and her daughter becoming merely inconsequential pieces that form part of a larger literary puzzle. In contrast, their joint presence in the narrative functions as precisely the main emphasis of the passage, which is to define the identity of those who compose the kingdom of God. The expectation inherent in Jesus's ironic statement (as well as in the preceding passage) is that there is a clear distinction between clean and unclean. The crucial *logos* spoken by the woman further reflects the destruction of the application of the clean/unclean divide with respect to ethnicity. The definition of kingdom insiders is marked not by geopolitical identity but by an association with the *logos* of Jesus. Mark's frequent use of the term *logos* to refer to Jesus's activity and message points to a close textual association between the term and Mark's larger understanding of Jesus's gospel program.[7] Jesus's present characterization of the woman's statement as "this word" (*touton ton logon*) positions her restructured parable within the context of the gospel message (Cadwallader 2008, 208–9; Miller 2004, 110). In other words, the destruction of boundaries between Jew and Gentile developed in the woman's speech-act helps to create a framework for understanding the borderless nature of the kingdom. Her word reflects the inclusivity of the gospel, and Jesus confirms its reality through the miraculous healing of her daughter, an event that for Mark highlights the in-breaking of God's kingdom into the world (Miller 2004, 94). The woman's statement, then, functions not to change Jesus's mind concerning the situation but to enter into the narrative thought world developed in Mark in order to disassociate the ministry of the kingdom from the strict exclusivity inherent in the ironic representation that Jesus formulates in Mark 7:27.

That a key element in the narrative is the notion of crossing boundaries is not a novel concept (see, e.g., Rhoads 1994, 363–65). Indeed, the

---

7. Out of the twenty-three occurrences of the noun in Mark twenty-one have their referent in Jesus's own activity or refer broadly to the gospel message. Both of the apparent exceptions (5:26 and 11:29) may actually revolve around the same general principle. In Mark 5:35 some people from Jairus's house inform him of his daughter's death and encourage him to abandon his endeavor with Jesus. In Mark 5:36 Jesus then rejects their word (*ton logon*) and exhorts Jairus to believe. There is, therefore, an implicit distinction in the narrative between the other's *logos* and the *logos* Jesus speaks to Jairus (*monon pisteue*) and his daughter (*talitha koum*; 5:41), both of which provide clarity about his mission. In Mark 11:27–28 a group of Jewish leaders questions the authority of Jesus, and he in return asks them to answer "one question" (*hena logon*; 11:29) that will "indicate [whether or not] his opponents have caught something of his gospel" (Cadwallader 2008, 208). Their inability to answer (11:31–33) is an implicit rejection of Jesus's own *logos*.

central distinction in the story revolves around the identification of who may or may not receive the benefits of the kingdom. That Jesus heals the daughter of this acute outsider reverses the expectation of what defines followers of Jesus. Their relationship to him is measured not by ethnic or cultural identity but by entrance into kingdom activity, defined in the present context as the woman herself taking up the gospel message (*touton ton logon*). The kingdom develops not through a defense of borders that seeks to maintain a perception of holiness but through an overt expansion *across* borders to all those who enter into the reality inherent in the gospel of Jesus Christ, which has been at the forefront of Mark's narrative since the outset (Mark 1:1; cf. Rhoads 1994, 363–64). Expectations concerning the identity of outsiders and insiders are then reversed, as this Greek Syrophoenician becomes an embodiment of the inclusive nature of the kingdom. The contrast between the woman and the twelve disciples then becomes contextually transparent. In the previous narrative the disciples fail to unravel the significance of Jesus's teaching concerning purity regulations (Mark 7:18; cf. 6:52; 8:14–21), while the woman enters into the parabolic framework and relates an accurate assessment of the situation: the benefits of the kingdom are not constricted by external factors such as ethnicity, geography, and gender (Collins 2007, 365; Edwards 2002, 217; Guelich 1989, 389; Rhoads 1994, 347). Further, the position of the narrative of the Syrophoenician woman between two miraculous feedings (Mark 6:30–44; 8:1–10) turns her narrative into a type of hermeneutical lens through which the significance of the feeding narratives takes shape, showing that one of their imports is to reflect the lack of distinction between Israel and the Gentiles: the boundaries between the two groups have *already* been abolished in the course of Jesus's ministry (Donahue and Harrington 2002, 238).

It would be a mistake, however, to suggest that the woman's gender is the sole catalyst for her positive portrayal in the narrative. Malbon has argued persuasively that the portrait of discipleship in Mark involves more than a simple distinction between the genders of particular figures (2000, 47, 66–67). In contrast, the Syrophoenician woman as a so-called minor character supplements Mark's complex portrait of discipleship. She is indeed an antithesis to the disciples in certain respects, but she is also an antithesis to Herodias and her daughter (Mark 6:14–29). Her importance for the narrative rests in her ability to move across external boundaries such as ethnicity and gender. Her *logos* emphasizes that discipleship is defined in the first instance by an ability to stand in relationship with the two foci of Mark's narrative: Jesus and his gospel (cf. 1:1; Malbon 2000, 67). Returning to the results of Theissen's influential sociohistorical analysis, it is helpful to note that the present narrative revolves around a potentially high-class Gentile prostrating herself before Jesus in order to obtain healing for another. The woman's posture of humility and concern for her daughter suggest that she understands the self-sacrifice required of Markan disciples (8:34–35) and are also illustrative of the Markan reality that discipleship is defined by insignificance and service (9:35; cf. Betsworth 2010, 142; Miller 2004, 105). Thus, although the position of the woman and the daughter as unclean Gentiles would seemingly suggest to the reader that they are outsiders with respect to the kingdom, the outcome of the narrative creates a reversal of those expectations, reshaping the borders of discipleship from distinctions of ethnicity to the parameters outlined in the Gospel itself. Thus, the movement of the gospel (*logos*) in Mark's narrative in defining the identity of Christ-followers cannot be hindered by the existence of the external borders of ethnicity, geography, or gender.

3. Reflections on Borderless Discipleship

If this Markan pericope does indeed develop an idea of Christian discipleship that exists on a borderless plane, then readers of Mark's narrative will consequently be forced to return to their understanding and embodiment of discipleship in their present circumstances vis-à-vis their surrounding community. The most immediate concern that arises in light of the geographic genesis of the present volume seems to revolve around questions of identity and relationship. To frame the import of the Syrophoenician woman's dialogue with Jesus in Lukan terms leads one to again ask the question of the expert of the law in Luke 10—who is my neighbor?—and to respond to Jesus's subsequent instruction, given after relaying the well-known parable of the Good Samaritan, to go and do likewise. The initial question and the subsequent imperative stand dramatically in the immediate forefront of life in Australia, New Zealand, and the surrounding Oceania, in which peoples from various cultures live side by side in light of sheer geographical proximity. The narrative of the Syrophoenician woman requires a line of thought that moves in an outward direction, toward the geographic, cultural, and social other. This movement requires interaction on numerous fronts, including, but not limited to, ethnic dialogue between first and second peoples, socioeconomic dialogue between carbon consumers and asylum seekers, and geographic dialogue between "land owners" and those whose land is being drowned by continually rising waters. The variety of borders that the Syrophoenician woman crosses points to the reality that discipleship for the Markan reader will exist fruitfully only when those deemed outsiders are understood as potential participants in the kingdom and seen as capable of speaking its *logos*.

Works Consulted

Aquino, Frederick D., and A. Brian McLemore. 1993. Markan Characterization of Women. Pages 393–424 in *Essays on Women in Earliest Christianity*. Edited by Carroll D. Osburn. Eugene, Ore.: Wipf & Stock.

Beavis, Mary Ann. 1988. Women as Models of Faith in Mark. *Biblical Theology Bulletin* 18:3–9.

Bengston, H. 1965. Syrien in der hellenistischen Zeit. Pages 244–54 in *Der Hellenismus und der Aufstieg Roms: Die Mittelmeerwelt im Altertum 2*. Edited by Pierre Grimal. Fischer Weltgeschichte 6. Frankfurt: Fischer.

Betsworth, Sharon. 2010. *The Reign of God Is Such as These: A Socio-Literary Analysis of Daughters in the Gospel of Mark*. Library of New Testament Studies 422. London: T&T Clark.

Boring, M. Eugene. 2006. *Mark*. New Testament Library. Louisville: Westminster John Knox.

Cadwallader, Alan H. 2008. *Beyond the Word of a Woman: Recovering the Bodies of the Syrophoenician Women*. Adelaide: ATF.

Camery-Hoggatt, Jerry. 1992. *Irony in Mark's Gospel: Text and Subtext*. Society for New Testament Studies Monograph Studies 72. Cambridge: Cambridge University Press.

Collins, Adela Yarbo. 2007. *Mark*. Hermeneia. Minneapolis: Fortress.

Donahue, John R., and Daniel J. Harrington. 2002. *The Gospel of Mark*. Sacra Pagina 2. Collegeville, Minn.: Liturgical Press.

Edwards, James R. 2002. *The Gospel according to Mark*. Pillar New Testament Commentary. Grand Rapids: Eerdmans.

Feldmeier, Reinhard. 1994. Die Syrophönizierin (Mk 7,24–30)—Jesu, verlorenes' Streitgespräch? Pages 211–27 in *Die Heiden: Juden, Christen und das Problem des Fremden*. Edited by Reinhard Feldmeier and Ulrich Heckel. Wissenschaftliche Untersuchungen zum Neuen Testament 70. Tübingen: Mohr Siebeck.

France, R. T. 2002. *The Gospel of Mark*. New International Greek Testament Commentary. Grand Rapids: Eerdmans.

Guardiola-Sáenz, Leticia A. 1997. Borderless Women and Borderless Texts: A Cultural Reading of Matthew 15:21-28. *Semeia* 78:69-81.

Guelich, Robert A. 1989. *Mark 1-8:26*. Word Biblical Commentary 34A. Dallas: Word.

Hurtado, Larry W. 1983. *Mark*. New International Bible Commentary on the New Testament 2. Peabody, Mass.: Hendrickson.

Iverson, Kelly R. 2007. *Gentiles in the Gospel of Mark: 'Even the Dogs under the Table Eat the Children's Crumbs.'* Library of New Testament Studies 339. London: T&T Clark.

Malbon, Elizabeth Struthers. 2000. *In the Company of Jesus: Characters in Mark's Gospel*. Louisville: Westminster John Knox.

Marcus, Joel. 2000. *Mark 1-8*. Anchor Bible 27. New York: Doubleday.

Marshall, Christopher D. 1989. *Faith as a Theme in Mark's Narrative*. Society for New Testament Studies Monograph Series 64. Cambridge: Cambridge University Press.

Miller, Susan. 2004. *Women in Mark's Gospel*. Journal for the Study of the New Testament Supplement Series 259. London: T&T Clark.

Muecke, D. C. 1969. *The Compass of Irony*. London: Methuen.

Nanos, Mark D. 2009. Paul's Reversal of Jews Calling Gentiles "Dogs" (Philippians 3:2): 1600 Years of an Ideological Tale Wagging an Exegetical Dog? *Biblical Interpretation* 17:448-82.

Noh, Eun-Ju. 2000. *Metarepresentation: A Relevance-Theory Approach*. Amsterdam: John Benjamins.

Rhoads, David. 1994. Jesus and the Syrophoenician Woman in Mark: A Narrative-Critical Study. *Journal of the American Academy of Religion* 62:343-75.

Ringe, Sharon H. 1985. A Gentile Woman's Story. Pages 65-72, 154-56 in *Feminist Interpretation of the Bible*. Edited by Letty M. Russell. Philadelphia: Westminster.

———. 2001. A Gentile Woman's Story, Revisited: Rereading Mark 7.24-31A. Pages 79-100 in *A Feminist Companion to Mark*. Edited by Amy-Jill Levine with Marianne Blickenstaff. Sheffield: Sheffield Academic Press.

Sim, Margaret G. 2010. *Marking Thought and Talk in New Testament Greek: New Light from Linguistics on the Particles ἵνα and ὅτι*. Cambridge: James Clarke & Co.

Stein, Robert H. 2008. *Mark*. Baker Exegetical Commentary on the New Testament. Grand Rapids: Baker Academic.

Theissen, Gerd. 1991. *The Gospels in Context: Social and Political History in the Synoptic Tradition.* Translated by Linda M. Maloney. Minneapolis: Fortress.

Wainwright, Elaine M. 1995. A Voice from the Margin: Reading Matthew 15:21–28 in an Australian Feminist Key. Pages 132–53 in *Reading from This Place.* Edited by Fernando F. Segovia and Mary Ann Tolbert. Minneapolis: Fortress.

Williams, Joel F. 1994. *Other Followers of Jesus: Minor Characters as Major Figures in Mark's Gospel.* Journal for the Study of the New Testament Supplement Series 102. Sheffield: JSOT Press.

———. 2006. Mark 7:27: Jesus' Puzzling Statement. Pages 341–50 in *Interpreting the New Testament: Introduction to the Art and Science of Exegesis.* Edited by Darrell L. Bock and Buist M. Fanning. Wheaton, Ill.: Crossway.

Witherington, Ben, III. 1984. *Women in the Ministry of Jesus: A Study of Jesus' Attitudes to Women and Their Roles as Reflected in His Early Life.* Society for New Testament Studies Monograph Series 51. Cambridge: Cambridge University Press.

Bare Feet Welcome: Redeemer Xs Moses @ Enaim*

Jione Havea

> Emancipate yourselves from mental slavery;
> None but ourselves can free our minds.
> (Bob Marley, "Redemption Song")[1]

This chapter is a song, but not a song in the expected sense, nor in the way of reggae, which is what hops and hips in my neighborhood, and my generation of islanders, but in the way that it is *talanoa* (see below) on ancient texts that function in ways similar to how songlines (dreaming, legends) serve Australia's First People. Scriptures, talanoa, and songlines are boundaries that make me belong, most of the time, especially when i[2] sing those as "myths of belongings." This chapter is a song also in the sense that it challenges those who, as Bob Marley puts it, strive to "fulfill the book":

> How long shall they kill our prophets,
> While we stand aside and look? Ooh!
> Some say it's just a part of it:
> We've got to fulfill the book.

I seek not to "fulfill the book" but to find a "song of freedom" out of the crossing of some of the stories in that book. This chapter is in talanoa mode, spiraling from rescuing toward bothering, troubling, scriptures.

---

* I am grateful for David Neville's careful reading and helpful comments on an earlier draft of this chapter.

1. Lyrics taken from Sing365.com (http://www.sing365.com/music/lyric.nsf/Redemption-song-lyrics-Bob-Marley/326F5783C5461A6048256945000E6461).

2. As mentioned in my previous essay in this volume, i use lowercase "i" because i use the lowercase with "you," "she," "they," and "others." I do not see the point in capitalizing the first person when s/he *is* in relation to everyone/everything else.

Redeeming Talanoa

Talanoa is the confluence of three things: story, telling, and conversation. Talanoa is not story without telling and conversation, telling without story and conversation, or conversation without telling and story. Talanoa is all three—story, telling, conversation—as one. Talanoa draws one out of one's lived worlds so that one moves and engages, departs and drifts, in manners close to what the Samoan novelist Sia Figiel imagines:

> A story [*talanoa*] is like a river. And like a river it trickles from the source until it flows flows flows. Down the mountains of the mountains. Branching onto the land the land the land. Flowing. Spiralling. Flowing towards the sea. Spiralling towards the sky. Where it grows wings and flies towards the universe of the unknown. (Figiel 1999, 3–4)

Talanoa spirals, and transits, but does not exile people. The latter needs to be stated, seeing that the experience of exile applies more broadly, and it is coming to be understood as a state of mind in which return is not required:

> Exile now signified not only forced migration and living in a foreign land under foreign domination, but also a variety of alienations: political disenfranchisement within Yehud, deep dissatisfaction with the status quo, and a feeling of separation from God. In this new interpretation of exile, which was not limited to its geographic dimension, exile persisted despite repatriation; it was a condition that could not be resolved simply by returning to the land. (Halvorson-Taylor 2011, 1)

The ones who submit to, and revel in, talanoa are emancipated (redeemed) from mental slavery, in their telling of and conversing over stories, so that they too flow, whirl, and fly. And in return, they emancipate (redeem) talanoa (story, telling, conversation). Talanoa in this regard is one of Oceania's "songs of freedom."

A biblical story is talanoa as well, drifting in a sea of stories (Havea 2010). It thus makes sense to nudge a biblical story out of its textual borders, the context in which it moors and belongs, and that gives it meanings, so that it flows into other stories and other shores. Such is the gifting of talanoa, which will not be too strange to some midrashic (Boyarin 1990), intertextual (Fewell 1992), and/or contrapuntal (see esp. the essays by Rushton, McKinlay, and Mathews, above) readers of biblical stories. I call upon these modes of reading not in order to canonize, or scripturalize, talanoa cultures, or vice versa, but in honor of the rhythms that free me to be native. Talanoa, favored by my migrating ancestors and even in latter-day island communities in diaspora (Havea 2012), is neither empty nor innocent. Talanoa moves, links, and grabs, as well as cuts, and releases. It is telling, and interchanging.

I attempt in this chapter, in the spirit of talanoa, to *roam*[3] a biblical story involving the baring of the feet of one Redeemer (in Ruth 4), so that it flows into another story, involving the baring of the feet of one prospective Deliverer (in Exod 3). I will nudge these two stories to meet, to cross, in other words, to X, at another story, involving the baring of the "feet" of another kind, at a place where an alternative route occurs, where the road to Timnah branches off toward Enaim (in Gen 38). This talanoa reading will welcome the unwanted Redeemer at Bethlehem (Ruth 4), sympathize with the burned Deliverer at Horeb (Exod 3), and affirm the veiled widow on the side of the road (Gen 38) as one who sings a redemption song. This chapter is therefore acceptance of Bob Marley's request for "help to sing / These songs of freedom."

I choose to read these texts together, because stories that *border belonging* interest me, and i hold together two senses of "border belonging" here: to *protect* belonging and to *prevent* belonging. According to the first sense, stories enable people to belong, to feel at home. They are protected, harbored, rooted. But according to the second sense, stories make people not belong, indicating that they are unwelcomed, exposed, uprooted, routed.

I am drawn to these stories because i have seen too many "No shoes, no service" signs in the islands of Oceania. To local people, such signs also say, "No natives allowed here." This is because natives are imagined as barefoot people, as uncivilized people who are poor and have no class. The "No shoes, no service" signs motivate me to engage stories in which characters remove their footwear, as if they have arrived and bared their feet, which is what natives do when they enter homes. In other words, for me as a native, no shoes is a sign that one belongs. This is my song, and i am sticking to it!

There are no historical or literary connections between the three biblical stories around which i talanoa, and there is no evidence that they were

---

3. I have in mind the Tongan word "fakataka," which refers to letting pigs out so that they enjoy the greeneries of the land, the rubbing of one's skin in order to remove dirt, and the process of rolling coconut and *fau* (a type of tree) fiber in the process of making ropes. To roam/fakataka is freeing, cleansing, and useful.

written to be read with each other. But since they belong in the same sea of talanoa (read: Hebrew Bible), nothing bars them from spiraling toward each other. Their crossing in this chapter, i admit, is due to my expectation that biblical stories drift in a sea of stories also. I imagine that at some point in the past these stories (talanoa) were remembered and told (talanoa) in relation to other stories, and this would have sparked a conversation (talanoa). Nonetheless, i weave this talanoa reading, not because others somewhere thought that intertexting these stories was viable, but because i honor the power of remembering (compare "power of story" in Amit 2001, 1–10) and the spiraling flow of talanoa. Talanoa *likes* and *pokes* other stories.

Whether my talanoa mode of reading frees the chosen stories from their textual frames, or exiles these stories from their literary homes, is for my critics to ponder. No matter what they say, i am still convinced that reading, like talanoa, is a political act that can free stories, texts, and meanings and/or confine and undermine those. Reading can border, fence off, prevent, and/or locate and enable belonging.

Baring So-and-So

Ruth and Naomi are the main characters in the book of Ruth, and a shift in focalization suggests that this is a book about women. Elimelech is the point of focalization in 1:1 and 1:2, with Naomi and "his two sons" identified as his possessions. The shift comes in 1:3 with the announcement of the death of Elimelech, "Naomi's husband," leaving her with "her two sons." Naomi becomes the register of identity. The sons, Mahlon and Chilion, also die off, leaving behind three widows: Naomi, Orpah, and Ruth. At that point, the book of Ruth becomes the story of these women. One is from Judah, and two are locals of Moab. But the story (talanoa) continues to tell (talanoa) of interactions with and of other male characters. The narrator spirals, roams, the story back to the world of men, and back to Judah.

Across the gender divide, Boaz is the character with the most words and seeds—as well as needs, but he was not needy. His interchange with Ruth takes up most of Ruth 2–3. Another male character enters in Ruth 4, but he is not named. He is identified as Goʼel (גאל), which indicates that he was "the nearest male kin, who was responsible for the economic survival of his relatives if they became insolvent" (Halvorson-Taylor 2011, 112). Boaz pulls the nameless Goʼel into the story because Elimelech, *their* dead relation, needs redemption. The Goʼel belongs in the story for the sake of Elimelech, the remnants of whose household are Naomi and Ruth. Boaz addresses him as *pĕlōnî* (פְּלֹנִי), as So-and-so (NJPS), which could be very affirming and respectful, something like "friend" (NRSV). *Pĕlōnî*, in this regard, is the biblical equivalent of "buddy" or "mate." On the other hand, *pĕlōnî* can also belittle, similar to how some people use "buddy" and "mate" to patronize and vilify others. There seems to be a bit of both aspects in Boaz's usage.

Boaz is the "well-to-do" (2:1 JB) kin of Elimelech, but So-and-so is a closer relation. A curious twist in the story (talanoa) makes Boaz admit that he too is Go'el, leading him to take over the redeeming function from, the "redemption song" of, So-and-so. To get to that twist, we need to rewind. Naomi tells Ruth to prepare and go to Boaz's threshing floor, with instructions on what to do (3:1–4), and Naomi refers to Boaz as their kinsman (מֹדָע). Later that evening, when Boaz is stirred from sleep, Ruth addresses him as kinsman (גֹאֵל; 3:9). Ruth nudges Boaz from one kind of kinship (מֹדָע) to another (גֹאֵל), and i imagine that she knows the difference between the two (מֹדָע and גֹאֵל). Rewind further. In 2:20, Naomi tells Ruth that Boaz is their redeemer (גֹאֵל) but opts to speak of him as מֹדָע in 3:2. So i imagine that Ruth is intentional in the slide from מֹדָע to גֹאֵל in 3:9, and not just because she is a Moabitess who has not grown up speaking Hebrew. I do not make light of the crossing of language borders when one crosses cultural borders, or deny that the tongue slips and slides across borders. But i honor the Moabitess. Ruth knows what she is saying, and she is as stealthy with her mouth as she is with her body (3:7).

Ruth is a different kind of foreigner compared to Moses in Midian. It is not clear if Moses confronts the bullying shepherds who drive Reuel's daughters away from the well, but he has courage to come to their rescue (Exod 2:16–22). Yet, he does not say much to his in-laws except to explain the name of his son Gershom, because he is "a stranger in a foreign land" (2:22), and to seek permission for his return to Egypt (4:18). His failure to change G-d's mind at the burning bush portrays him as one who does not have the gift of persuasion. He is not a native speaker of the mountain, even if the narrator wants readers to think that Hebrew was the common language of the region. In multilingual Oceania, such an expectation is ridiculous.

Compared to Moses, Ruth is very smooth with Boaz. In Ruth 2:13, she butters Boaz up by addressing him as *ădōnî*, "my lord," and Boaz becomes generous with her in return (2:14). I imagine a similar impact in 3:10–13. In response to Ruth calling him גֹאֵל Boaz praises her for not going after younger men, rich or poor. In both instances, Ruth knows how to click Boaz on. I therefore read the slide from מֹדַע (3:2) to גֹּאֵל (3:9) as one of her clicks on Boaz. She makes Boaz want to be her redeemer. Boaz accepts that he is a Goʾel but admits that there is another Goʾel closer than he (3:12). That late evening at the threshing floor, Boaz tells Ruth to lie with him until morning, and he will see if the rightful Goʾel will redeem her. If he won't, Boaz himself will redeem her.

Before the closer Goʾel appears on the scene, he is introduced and then discounted, made dispensable. He is needed but not necessary, and definitely not wanted. He is the redeemer that is expected to be redeemed, as if he was in exile, the state at which one needs redemption (Halvorson-Taylor 2011, 112). He is, after all, *pĕlōnî*, So-and-so. Without a proper name, he enters the story as nobody, anybody, and everybody.

When the Goʾel appears, Boaz calls him to the side and tells him to sit down. In talanoa circles, this could be a voice of welcome and hospitality or expression of power, of telling off. Boaz also calls ten men of the city over, and he tells them to sit down also. Then he informs So-and-so that the field belonging to their deceased relative Elimelech is available from Naomi. So-and-so may redeem the field in the presence of the witnesses. If he won't, Boaz will redeem it himself (as he committed to Ruth the previous night). When Boaz pauses, as if to bait a response, So-and-so sounds sincere: "I will redeem it" (4:4b). He sounds eager.

Boaz then adds that So-and-so will also need to take Ruth the Moabite widow, in order to "raise up the name of the dead upon his inheritance" (4:5). So-and-so quickly changes his mind, because being Goʾel to Elimelech will mar his own inheritance, but he does not clarify whether his problem is with the Moabite woman or with the dead relative. His decision is clear, and firm. He wants to hand over his Goʾel-ship. Bringing to mind Esau handing over his birthright to Isaac for some bread and a bowl of lentil stew (Gen 25:29–34), So-and-so gives Boaz the right to redeem. To confirm the transaction, So-and-so follows the custom of removing his shoe and giving it to the beneficiary. So-and-so bares his feet, in the presence of the silent men who are seated there.

The baring of feet implies several things in this story, inviting different conversations (talanoa). First, it presents So-and-so as someone who may be unnamed but who is firm. He knows what will damage his inheritance, and he has enough grace to give up some of his responsibilities in order to protect his interests. He is not greedy. He is protective of his household, and he may not be as "well-to-do" as Boaz is.

Second, to the contrary, So-and-so comes across as being discriminatory, but it is not clear what his issue is when he changes his mind in 4:6. Fewell and Gunn (1990) suggest that he may have issues with Ruth being a Moabite and a widow. Ruth comes from a people who were not welcomed by the descendants of Jacob. And like Tamar (Gen 38), she is used property. It is also possible that word has spread about what happened the night before at the threshing floor. There is something about oral cultures and secrets, which tend to seep through the seams, because everyone is looking and listening. I can therefore understand, but i do not approve, if So-and-so is discriminating against Ruth.

Third, after the threshing floor, Ruth is in "exile," and Boaz is the right one to redeem her. So-and-so was the Go'el for Elimelech, but Boaz is the one proper redemption song for Ruth. It makes sense therefore that So-and-so steps aside to let Boaz do the right thing, to take Ruth as his wife in the presence of witnesses. Unfortunately for So-and-so, borrowing the words of Judah, no one sees how he is more in the right than Boaz (cf. Gen 38:26). But fortunately for Boaz, Ruth redeems him, together with Elimelech, Mahlon, Naomi, and many others.

Burning Moses

Moses is a literary character with multiple roots that entangle and pull him across several borders, leaving him buried in quagmires of unresolved issues. His nameless father disappears soon after his conception, and at the end of his days, his followers move on, leaving his body for Yhwh to bury at an unnamed grave somewhere in Moab. I can't be sure if and how Yhwh buries Moses, but i am certain that in talanoa circles, what the people do is dishonoring. This is, of course, suggestive of how they feel about their leader. They could carry his remains for proper burial with the ancestors in Canaan, but they leave him as if he belongs nowhere. In spite of how biblical theologians read the story of Moses (e.g., Sweeney 2008, 42–63), i give more weight to the action of the people. They must know that it is disrespectful to walk away from his dead body, seeing that they are carrying the remains of Joseph for burial in Canaan, but they are not troubled (cf. Freud 1955). I, on the other hand, am troubled,[4] but not burdened.

---

4. This is mainly because a dead body is a sacred object in Pacific island cultures (cf. Havea 2013).

Moses is born into a household under intense stress because of highly organized and tightly enforced labor (Exod 1:8–2:3). A son of Hebrew slaves whose hungry ancestors migrated to Egypt several generations past, he is born into a settler community made up of outsiders in the inside, people who are not fully accepted as locals. Being born in Egypt does not make Moses Egyptian. An Egyptian princess takes him into her house and feeds him the privileges of being her son, but Moses does not let go of his Hebrew roots when he kills for the sake of his kin (2:11–12). His kinsmen, however, do not welcome his charity (2:13–14). So he runs away as a fugitive to Midian, where the Midianite priest Jethro gives him his daughter. Boaz maneuvers to redeem Ruth; Moses is given Zipporah as a wife, and they begin a family (2:15–22). But they do not live happily ever after.

Boaz has a field and a place on the threshing floor; Moses used to have a place in a nation but now moves around the wilderness, attending to the flock of his father-in-law. It is in the wilderness, at Horeb, once upon a time, that Moses sees the burning bush and decides to check it out, because the fire does not consume the bush (3:1–3). The biblical account presents the burning bush as a site of divine revelation. Yhwh speaks from the bush, telling Moses to go back and confront Pharaoh to release Yhwh's people (3:7–10). But it appears as if Moses has taken a wrong step when he turned to inspect the appearance, for the voice from the bush stops him:

> "Come no nearer," he said. "Take off your shoes, for the place on which you stand is holy ground. I am the God of your father," he said, "the God of Abraham, the God of Isaac and the God of Jacob." At this Moses covered his face, afraid to look at God. (3:5–6 JB)

In cultures where people remove their shoes or sandals when they enter homes, the command to Moses suggests that he has arrived and is welcomed. In this regard, "holy ground" does not necessarily mean that that is the space of G-d or that G-d is present (e.g., McConville 2006, 65–66) but that it is a point of arrival, not necessarily permanent, but it is homely. It is holy because it is welcoming, home. Put another way, "Take off your shoes, for you will be here a little while." The holy ground is a place to pause, before transiting somewhere else. To fail to remove one's shoes in such places is to disrespect.

Boaz tells So-and-so to sit, and he later takes his shoes off to seal an agreement. Yhwh tells Moses to stop, and to immediately take his shoes off, because he is on holy ground. In this story (talanoa), holiness is not just an attribute of G-d but the reality of the ground also. The removing of shoes has different meanings in these two stories. So-and-so knows when to take his shoes off; Moses has to be told, and this portrays him as someone who is not aware of simple cultural protocols. How was he to know that the place is holy ground? If only he had met Ruth prior to hearing G-d!

I cannot be sure if So-and-so and/or Moses knows that shame is associated with people with bare feet (cf. Chinitz 2007), but i suspect that this would not be as big a problem for So-and-so as it would be for Moses. I make this claim on the basis that So-and-so knows what to do, and he willingly does so, whereas Moses does not know what to do, and it is interesting in this regard that the narrator does not report whether Moses actually removes his shoes, only that he covers his face, for he is afraid to look at G-d. He would rather not see, thus putting him in the shadows of Judah, who does not see that he is sleeping with Tamar his daughter-in-law and who is quick to order that she be burned before examining her (Gen 38:15–19, 24–26).

In this talanoa, So-and-so is not so bad when seen alongside Moses. This is not to say that Moses is therefore bad. He is pushed into a situation not of his own making, but because G-d finally hears the groans of the people and suddenly remembers the covenant with their ancestors (Exod 2:23–25). It is a coincidence that Moses is curious about the burning bush at the time when G-d needs to make up for many generations of having forgotten the people of Israel. This prompts me to return and rethink the happenings at the holy ground.

In approaching the burning bush, Moses steps over an invisible boundary that he should have respected. Moses does not know the "songline" of the mountain. What happens at Horeb is not like someone stepping through a threshold or the gates of a town, which would be visible. Rather, it is more like breaking the hymen, that barrier whose existence is known only in its breakage. As the virginity of a female is known at the moment when she is no longer a virgin, so is the holiness of the ground known when it is transgressed. In this connection, it would be impossible for Moses to know that he is approaching holy ground. Moses turns to look at the burning bush and fails to realize that the bush is a bait. Moses in the end gets burned.

Moses turns to look at the burning bush because he is curious, and this brings Judah to mind. He too turns to the side of the road, to look, take, and lay with a veiled woman, when he goes through Enaim. The difference between the two is that Judah is, so to speak, burning, whereas Moses is roaming his flock.

Eye-Opening Roadside

Tamar the widow hears that her father-in-law is coming through for sheep-shearing at Timnah (Gen 38:14), so she goes and sits down around the place where the road to Timnah branches off to Enaim. It is a place where diversion might happen. Translators imagine this place as a crossroad or an open place (NJPS), but the name Enaim also means "opening of eyes." I favor this sense, because this part of Tamar's story, helped by the foregoing talanoa reading, involves elements of concealment and revelation.

Tamar has removed the signs that she is a widow, has put a veil on her face, and is "heavily swathed" (JB). She is so well wrapped with clothes that she becomes So-and-so on the side of the road. She does not look like a widow, but there is nothing seductive about her outfit. Just how Judah sees her as a prostitute (38:15) is hard to explain. A veil on the face of woman, flirting in my native mind, signifies r-e-s-p-e-c-t in other cultures. Though disguised, Tamar is still the main character. Like Ruth, the story revolves around her. She is the agent that drives the plot. Compared to Zipporah, who is the sideshow to the burning bush spectacular, Tamar is a round character.

Having been comforted after the death of his wife, Judah would be looking for a redemption song of the bodily kind. His wanting to sleep with Tamar is therefore more about his urges than about what she looks like. He does not even realize that he is approaching the proverbial "burned bush" from his own household.

When Judah sees Tamar at the side of the road, i imagine a situation like when a thirsty person sees a waterhole after a long and tiring journey. Eyes pop, mouth drops, brains rush, desire rises. These are probably true of the shepherds who drive Reuel's daughters away from the well (Exod 2:16–18). Tamar is more desired than desiring, but that is not to say that she is undesiring or completely passive.

Like Ruth, Tamar is wise and calculating. She too dresses up, determined that she will be ignored no longer. She is stealthy and courageous, appearing to cross a boundary without transgressing it. She veils herself, but that is not necessarily about seduction in a context where a woman who wears a veil would be seen as a respectful woman. Her veil would be similar to the traditional tattoos of a titled Samoan woman, except that Tamar could easily remove her veil. Tamar takes a place, and she sits before anyone tells her to sit down. She appears to be one who would know how to operate on holy grounds and on threshing floors. She comes to the roadside, not because she is desperate, but because "Shelah had now grown up, as she saw, and yet she had not been given to him as his wife" (38:14b JB). She comes so that she may be given away, not necessarily for the sake of being given away or because she lives in a culture where women are given away, as Zipporah is, but because this is owed to her. In other words, she comes to redeem herself. Tamar's redemption song is similar to Ruth's, and it helps that Boaz and Judah are burning. In the case of both women, their redemption is in their songs (Boaz, Judah), who are not the rightful songs (So-and-so, Shelah).

Tamar was burned previously when Judah sent her back to her father's house (38:12), and she is not going to be burned this time. Judah asks her to sleep with him, and she asks for payment. He does not have a kid with him, but he can leave a pledge and send payment later. She consents. He gives her the pledge and then bares his feet (read: has sex) with Tamar. In transit. Then Judah and his friend Hirah continue on to Timnah. The "stop, come no closer" in this story comes later, when Judah hears that Tamar is pregnant. He orders that she be taken out and burned, and this begins the revelation process that exposes him as the one who has fathered Tamar's twin sons. Judah earlier blamed Tamar for the death of his first two sons (Gen 38:11b), and in the end, she gives him two more sons.

Hirah is the only named Adullamite character in the biblical narrative. He accompanies Judah and witnesses his affairs, and he is the one who returns with a kid to settle Judah's debt to Tamar (38:20–22). He could redeem Judah, as David does for the desperate people who gather at the cave of Adullam (1 Sam 22:1–2), but he does not find Tamar. Hirah is the companion and assistant who cannot redeem his friend, and this comes back to trouble Judah later. Hirah is not identified as Judah's kin, so he is not obliged by the usual duties expected of a kinsperson, an expectation that runs very deep in the story of Tamar. Notwithstanding, the consequence of Hirah's failure is the kind of outcome that Elimelech's Go'el avoids in Ruth 4. The Go'el gives up his shoe, but he does not hand over his seal, cord, or staff (cf. Gen 38:18).

Bothering Scriptures

Throughout history and across cultures, scriptures function as systems of beliefs and belongings, cellars for traditions and meanings, generators of memories and hope, but also as sources of pain and grief, destruction and despair (so Havea 2007). Some parts of scriptures are all of those for different people, at different places and times.

Thanks to the leadership of black, feminist, liberation, and postcolonial critics, especially, communities of readers are attentive to times when scriptures are songs of terror (cf. Trible 1984). Nonetheless, those readers also find comfort and healing in the same scriptures, and so there have been attempts to rescue the Bible from one-sided readings (see, e.g., Spong 1991 and Boer 2007, who have the same concern, but they come with different slants). The challenge herein is to engage scriptures in their complexities. Scriptures are, in this regard, as Sugirtharajah (2008) puts it, troublesome, bothersome, like thorns in the sides of readers; scriptures can be and are irritating. Scriptures are bothersome also because readers cannot be definitive about what those mean.

There is another challenge that comes from the spiraling of talanoa, which is to break out of limiting scriptures to the written and literary, and to textual cultures. Scriptures are "texts" that a community or religious movement considers important (sacred, standard, canon), and those "texts" are not limited to what writers and scribes produce. Egyptians, native Asians, and native Americans have sculptures, paintings, and dances that are canonical. In Oceania, first peoples and natives have songlines, dances, and legends (Havea, forthcoming). These scriptures "talk," that is, give meaning and signify, in ways similar to how written texts work and are equally dynamic and complex. In some circles, nonliterary scriptures talk better than books (Callahan 2006). The upshot of this deliberation is an invitation to reconsider the default association of scriptures with "the book." Echoing Bob Marley in "Redemption Song," why should we honor the book that has been used to justify aloofness? The problem for Marley has to do with those who want to "fulfill the book":

> How long shall they kill our prophets,
> While we stand aside and look? Ooh!
> Some say it's just a part of it:
> We've got to fulfill the book.

Resist, therefore, the fulfilling of the book. Talanoa readers can in this regard bother mainline (or "manline") scriptures through our readings and songs, and in the affirmation of nonliterary and nontraditional scriptures and cultures. We can bother nonliterary scriptures as well, and this obligation applies to local talanoa, legends, songlines, national anthems, and so forth.

In light of the talanoa challenge, one way to bother biblical scriptures is to engage those with scriptures that are foreign to the textual worlds of the Bible. One might thus counterpoint an oral legend and a biblical text (cf. Havea, forthcoming). I avoided doing that in this chapter because it is enough to hear the song of three biblical stories crossing, X-ing, at their feet. Another way is to read in a talanoa, oralizing, manner. The latter is what i attempt in this chapter, realizing that it is a form of reading that can burn without consuming and return without redeeming. On the other hand, this form of reading can help break the shackles of mental slavery and give service to the shoeless and barefoot.

Works Consulted

Amit, Yairah. 2001. *Reading Biblical Narratives*. Minneapolis: Fortress.
Boer, Roland. 2007. *Rescuing the Bible*. Oxford: Blackwell.
Boyarin, Daniel. 1990. *Intertextuality and the Reading of Midrash*. Bloomington: Indiana University Press.
Callahan, Allen Dwight. 2006. *The Talking Book: African Americans and the Bible*. New Haven: Yale University Press.
Chinitz, Jacob. 2007. The Role of the Shoe in the Bible. *Jewish Bible Quarterly* 35:41–46.
Fewell, Danna N., ed. 1992. *Reading between Texts: Intertextuality and the Hebrew Bible*. Louisville: Westminster John Knox.
Fewell, Danna N., and David M. Gunn. 1990. *Compromising Redemption: Relating Characters in the Book of Ruth*. Louisville: Westminster.
Figiel, Sia. 1999. *They Who Do Not Grieve*. Auckland: Vintage.
Freud, Sigmund. 1955. *Moses and Monotheism*. Translated by Katherine Jones. New York: Vintage.
Halvorson-Taylor, Martien A. 2011. *Enduring Exile: The Metaphorization of Exile in the Hebrew Bible*. Leiden: Brill.
Havea, Jione. 2007. Pleasure and Grief, in Violence. Pages 71–78 in *Religion and Violence*. Edited by Jonathan Inkpin. Adelaide: ATF.
———. 2010. Welcome to Talanoa. Pages 11–22 in *Talanoa Ripples: Across Borders, Cultures, Disciplines…*. Edited by Jione Havea. Auckland: Pasifika@Massey University.
———. 2012. Natives, in Transit. Paper presented at Story Weaving: Colo-

nial Contexts and Postcolonial Theology Conference. Whitley College, Melbourne. January 25.

———. 2013. Death Roots: Musings of Pacific Island Native. Pages 157–68 in *Pacific Identities and Wellbeing: Cross-Cultural Perspectives*. Edited by Margaret Agee, Tracey McIntosh, Philip Culbertson, and Cabrini 'Ofa Makasiale. New York: Routledge.

———. Forthcoming. Digging behind Songlines: Tonga's Prayer, Australia's Fair, David's House. In *Not behind Our Backs: Feminist Challenges to Public Theology*. Edited by Anita Monro and Stephen Burns. London: Equinox.

LaCocque, André. 2004. *Ruth: A Continental Commentary*. Translated by K. C. Hanson. Minneapolis: Fortress.

Linafelt, Tod, and Timothy K. Beal. 1999. *Ruth and Esther*. Berit Olam. Collegeville, Minn.: Liturgical Press.

McConville, J. G. 2006. *God and Earthly Power: An Old Testament Political Theology*. London: T&T Clark.

Spong, John Shelby. 1991. *Rescuing the Bible from Fundamentalism: A Bishop Rethinks the Meaning of Scripture*. San Francisco: Harper.

Sugirtharajah, R. S. 2008. *Troublesome Texts: The Bible in Colonial and Contemporary Culture*. Sheffield: Phoenix.

Sweeney, Marvin A. 2008. *Reading the Hebrew Bible after the Shoah: Engaging Holocaust Theology*. Minneapolis: Fortress.

Trible, Phyllis. 1984. *Texts of Terror: Literary-Feminist Readings of Biblical Narratives*. Minneapolis: Fortress.

The Sign of Jonah: Reading Jonah on the Boundaries and from the Boundaries

Gregory C. Jenks

In this essay I engage in an intertextual reading (cf. Fewell 1992; Hays et al. 2009) of Jonah. This particular reading will not focus exclusively on biblical intertexts, as for instance in the intertextual reading by Kim (2007). Rather, the starting point for this reading is the story of those edgy places where my life so far has been lived out.[1] I shall come to the canonical text soon enough, but first I begin with the personal. In particular, I start with the personal boundaries and those border spaces—physical and psychological—where my sense of belonging has been both affirmed and challenged. All three of the B-words (Bible, Borders, Belongings) converge in this story of personal marginality.

The Son of a Carpenter

My father was a carpenter, as were his father and both his brothers. My mother was a full-time wife and mother. I was born and raised in Lismore, a regional city in the rural Northern Rivers district of New South Wales (NSW), and a place with all the essentials for Western life in the 1950s and 1960s. While neither bushfire nor drought were much of a threat to our comfortable life, cyclones and floods could briefly disrupt our ordered existence. No supersized fish ever threatened to swallow us alive, but the waters would overwhelm us annually (and sometimes more often).

---

1. The impetus for attempting such an intertextual reading of Jonah was a seminar paper by my colleague Jione Havea, "Sitting Jonah with Job" (April 16, 2010). His contribution in this present collection of essays offers fresh encouragement to play with the possibilities as textual stories, oral stories, and lived stories interact.

As a New South Welshman, I inherited an ambiguous identity. New Wales, not the Wales to the west of England from whose border lands my Jenks forebears had derived. It was a "new" Wales, a place in which expectations and hopes from another place and time would be pursued. This is not only a new Wales, but also a "southern" Wales; Wales of the South—antipodean Wales, a topsy-turvy Wales. On the edges of "old northern" Wales, my ancestors had been tax collectors for the English kings, and one of them did well enough to build a stately home. Life was very different in the new Wales of the great south land in which I was born.

The essence of a "NSW" identity, it seemed at the time (and perhaps even now), was not being a "Victorian" (the state to the south) and certainly not being a "Queenslander" (the state very close to us on the north). The interstate rivalry was complicated by the considerable distance of the state capital in Sydney and the convenience of major city facilities in Brisbane. While over the border, and out of the state, Brisbane was much closer. We already had several relatives there with whom to stay during our summer holidays, and there were others along the roads in between with whom to share a "cuppa" when breaking the long journey on the narrow roads that predated the current multilane highways.

If the colonial power brokers had had their way in the mid-nineteenth century, our part of New South Wales would have been included within the borders of Queensland. The legacy of that colonial ambiguity was perhaps expressed in the sporadic efforts to create a new state, neither New South Wales nor Queensland. Perversely, the proposed name of this new state was "New England," another failure of antipodean imagination as we contemplated defining our identity as a new expression of someone else's place.

The provincial location of Lismore and its distance from Sydney complicated our public identity. However, the religious affiliation of my parents and a significant proportion of my extended family generated further complexities. We were active members of the Churches of Christ congregation in Lismore, and that created another kind of distance from our neighbors. So far as I can recall, at no stage during my ten years in school at Lismore was there ever another student of that same religious identity when it came time to arrange the religious education classes. I found myself in a very small group composed of those children whose families belonged to "other Protestant" communities: a handful of Baptists and the occasional Salvation Army student.

I envied the mixture of social acceptance and anonymity that the large-group—Church of England, Methodist, Presbyterian, and Roman

Catholic—religion classes provided. By the early years of high school I routinely "wagged" the small religion class to which I had been assigned and melted into the crowded "C of E" class.

The religious difference was reinforced by social practices. "Authentic Christians" (a term understood by my family and my church to exclude all Catholics and most Anglicans) did not dance, consume alcohol, smoke tobacco, or go to the beach on Sundays. In our self-imposed ghetto, we made earnest preparations for the second coming of Jesus, lived with a mixture of anticipation and dread at the imminence of the rapture, and felt vaguely superior to our "worldly" neighbors. At least in these respects there were clear borders and a very strong sense of belonging, or not.

When I was fifteen years of age, my family moved to Brisbane, and within three months my father died suddenly of an undiagnosed cardiac condition. We remained in Brisbane, and my widowed mother found strong support among networks of relatives and church members. We were now Brisbane people, but never Queenslanders—as the annual State of Origin rugby league series reminds us. In time I became an Anglican and, worse still, a liberal biblical scholar. This prodigal son had "left the church" and gone into a faraway country. Not a great distance in physical terms, but a considerable journey in the life of the soul.

As an Anglican I would find echoes of the English diaspora experience in this strange southern land, but also another kind of ambiguity. Anglicans are neither Roman Catholics nor Protestants. We have pretensions to being the state church in a society that has no fondness for such a thing. We resist pressures for new expressions of church in the antipodes. Like all Christian communities in the southern hemisphere, we persist in celebrating Easter in autumn, and we dream of a white Christmas as the summer heat hovers.

In time my work as a religion scholar was to take me to the biblical lands, where the seasons fit the liturgies but the borders are militarized and the sense of belonging is more than a cultural memory. While my dreams of pursuing doctoral studies at the Hebrew University were surrendered under threat of not being ordained, I was later to serve as a visiting professor and scholar-in-residence at St. George's College, Jerusalem, on a number of occasions.

Later I was to become very involved with the work of the Sabeel Ecumenical Liberation Theology Center in Jerusalem, and especially the Sabeel community in Nazareth. Both these institutions remain very special to me, and I have a deep attachment to the aspirations of the Palestinian people for their own identity, their homeland, and their desire for *just* borders within which to nurture a sense of belonging. Equally, I have many Israeli and Jewish friends, and an attachment to their aspirations for a Jewish future in the land they share with the Palestinians. Here Bible, borders, and belonging intersect in both heroic and tragic ways.

My journey in the borderlands of religious and secular communities increasingly generates that kind of ambiguity. After almost forty years as an Anglican I am comfortable in that identity and harbor no illusions about the grass being greener somewhere else. However, I also find myself in the no-man's land between a fading Anglo-Catholicism and a resurgent Evangelicalism. Looking around me from my own location as a religious progressive, I see the traditional boundaries shifting (again). Beliefs, practices, and structures that have shaped our sense of belonging—and served as secure borders that define who is "in" and who is "out"—are both irrelevant (at the global level) and yet once more highly contested (within the shrinking circle of Anglicanism).

The Son of Faithfulness

The character of Jonah is identified in 2 Kgs 14:25 and Jonah 1:1 as *ben-'ămittay*, "son of faithfulness." His father, who enjoyed this fascinating name (at least in the imagination of the biblical storytellers), is never mentioned elsewhere and plays no further part in our Jonah story. For the scion of such a reliable and solid patriarch, Jonah is something of a prodigal. Far from being an anchor for other members of the wider clan, this boy is a bit of a wanderer. He wanders across land and sea not only in the biblical narrative but in two very difficult canonical narratives as well as postbiblical traditions.

For those in the original audience with a flair for geography, the description of Jonah as coming from Gath-Hepher, a small village adjacent to the future site of Nazareth in the lower hill country of the Galilee, would have been significant. These days the village is known as Masshed, and the turnoff can be found on your right just as you reach the crest of the hill when driving into Nazareth from the southeast.

That seems like an innocent enough fact. But such an address locates Jonah on the northern margins of the biblical territories. This is some distance from the heartland of biblical Israel, and even farther from the southern tribes centered on Jerusalem with its claims to be the exclusive place for sacrifice and worship. Yet it is these faraway southerners who will claim Jonah ben-Amittai for themselves, celebrating his prediction of their northern rivals' destruction and repatriating him to Judah after a period of self-imposed exile in Lebanon. Some of those traditions are found only in the postbiblical texts, but already in Jonah 1:3 we find Jonah imagined as going "down to Joppa" to catch a ship that might take him as far away from God's call on his life as possible. The Joppa departure implies a southern location for Jonah, even if the phrase "went down" is not to be taken literally as a reflection of descent from the hill country of Judah to the coastal plains below.

The Galilee has long been marginal country, as it lies near the sources of the Jordan Valley and is something of a cul-de-sac with substantial mountains to the north and significant hill country to the east (today's Golan Heights) and west (the rugged terrain of upper Galilee). This was not a location from which to project power over neighbors near and far. Instead, and certainly during the biblical period, the Galilee was a territory variously controlled by Israel (to the south), Aram/Syria (to the east), and Tyre (to the west). The Galilee had little to attract the jealousy of its neighbors but periodically experienced the impact of their imperial ambitions. A key route linking Damascus to the Mediterranean crossed Galilee.

Jonah is remembered as coming from a very small village on the edge of the hills of lower Galilee overlooking the plain of Jezreel. Sitting on the hill and watching the passing parade of empire was to be a feature of Jonah's ministry in Nineveh. Mostly the armies were heading toward more lucrative targets on the coast, or else coming from Egypt to reassert its traditional hegemony over this region. Occasionally a local fortified city such as Hazor or the Geshurite capital of Tzer would be destroyed by these military incursions.

In the cultural imagination of the biblical authors and their earliest audiences, the Galilee was marginal country. In the Hellenistic and early Roman periods this was bandit country. Herod the Great earned his reputation by his success in controlling the bandits while serving as governor of the Galilee. He would later promote a policy of strategic Jewish settlement in the Galilee to reinforce its loyalty to Jerusalem, and the wide distribution of Herodian oil lamps in the region attests to the success of his program (Savage 2011).

Jonah's Galilean pedigree is a significant element of his characterization in the biblical and postbiblical traditions. Like a later and more famous prophet from the neighboring village of Nazareth, this Galilean seems to have found no honor in his own town. The story does not tell us whether he did not find the village worthy of his efforts, whether his neighbors did not appreciate his preaching, or whether Jonah only discovered his vocation as prophet as he left the familiar marginal lands of Galilee for even more exotic locations.

Heading to Joppa from Gath-Hepher to purchase a fare on a boat to no particular destination seems extreme. The harbor at Akko was much more convenient, and Tyre was an even busier port with many more options for finding a fast ship to anywhere. If we imagine Jonah leaving Gath-Hepher bound for Joppa, the movement from one margin to another is noteworthy. However, if we accept the implicit suggestion of the narrative that Jonah had already moved to Jerusalem, then his movement is from the margins (the border lands of the Galilee) to the center (where YHWH and the prophets "belonged"), before a desperate and doomed attempt to flee to the boundaries once more, to abrogate the call and the covenant by which he "belonged" to YHWH. Crossing borders can be an attempt to reconfigure our obligations to (and for) those with whom we belong.

Is Jonah Also among the Prophets?

No less than its central character, the book of Jonah functions at the intersection of certain biblical borders and invites us to rethink our sense of belonging to the spiritual traditions with their roots in the Bible. The three B's of this book are to be found here as well. To borrow the question once asked of Saul, "Is Jonah also among the prophets?" (cf. 1 Sam 10:12). This question has a literary dimension, as well as a larger cultural dimension.

As is well known, the canonical collection of the Twelve in the Tanak differs from the arrangement of the prophetic books in the Septuagint. The "Minor Prophets" of the Christian canon are gathered into a single scroll, "The Book of the Twelve," within the Jewish canon. This fourth and final prophetic scroll is no minor witness alongside the "major" prophets of Isaiah, Jeremiah, and Ezekiel. Rather, as a collected work—perhaps not unlike the disparate essays that constitute the current volume—these once isolated voices are brought together to create a canonical choir that delivers the final prophetic "book."

Unlike Daniel, the story of Jonah—that reluctant and too-successful preacher—finds a place among the Twelve. Jonah is indeed among the prophets. Once again, we find borders, and different ways of belonging— even within the Bible. The Jewish Bible honors the recalcitrant Jonah as a prophet, while the all-too-perfect Daniel is relegated to a place among the Writings. Among the Ketuvim, Daniel will find that the borders are less clear, the arguments over belonging are more shrill, and even its contents will change as further legends are attached to the document.

I like the idea that the Bible welcomes the marginal religious leader who is unsure of his calling, hesitant about the relevance of his message, and shocked by the eagerness of people to accept what he has to say. I also like the idea that Mr. Clean (a.k.a. Daniel), who has never put a foot wrong and always seems to know the correct theological position, now has an uncertain status among the Ketuvim, and even (in parts at least) among the dubious Deuterocanonicals.

Moving beyond the borders of the Bible, there is another sense in which the prophetic book of Jonah continues to challenge and confront. Yvonne Sherwood (2000) has explored these dimensions of Jonah in *A Biblical Text and Its Afterlives: The Survival of Jonah in Western Culture*. As she has so deftly demonstrated in her study of the reception history of this book over more than two thousand years, the book of Jonah has crossed many cultural boundaries over the centuries. Jonah has continued to enthrall generations of readers from very different cultural and religious contexts.

Sherwood (2000, 11–48) identifies and then discusses "four main clusters, meta-stories, or heaps" into which mainstream Christian and scholarly readings of Jonah can be organized.

1. *Jonah and the fathers*: Jonah and Jesus as typological twins (a study of the early Christian analogy between the exit from the fish and the resurrection—or the "belching" and the "grace," as Crane might put it)
2. *Jonah the Jew*: the evolution of a biblical character (tracing a Jonah stereotype from Augustine and Luther through to the Enlightenment)
3. *Divine disciplinary devices*: the book of Jonah as a tractate on producing docile disciple-bodies (a study of the dire red-letter warnings of the book of Jonah, as expounded in the sonorous Reformation sermons of John Calvin and John Hooper)
4. *Cataloguing the monstrous*: Jonah and the "cani cacharis" (an investigation of what happens when the book of Jonah begins to sense the *Origin of Species* creeping up behind it and threatening its credibility)

In our contemporary culture, the book of Jonah once more finds itself at the borders where religion and science often seem to confront one another, and where the Bible is a problematic and contested text. Indeed, this short text with fewer than a thousand words is something of a symbol for the fate of the Bible—as well as the religious traditions constructed around it—in the modern and postmodern world.

With its strange narrative of supernatural interventions into human affairs, both individual and political, this book encapsulates so much about religion that people find incredible. The central element of the story, as Jonah is ingested by a great fish and then safely spat out upon the shore to continue his interrupted preaching tour, is too much for most of us to swallow. Believers with a conservative disposition seize upon reports of other people said to have survived being swallowed by giant sea creatures, and in the process they demonstrate the resilience of religious faith in the face of critical scholarship, whether in history, religion, or the natural sciences.

Is Jonah among the prophets? Is this biblical book a relic of a premodern phase in our religious development? Is this unlikely prophetic text still able to be read as a source of wisdom for holy living? Can the Bible, to which Jonah belongs, still function as a sacred text with the power to speak to the human condition? Can Jonah be read afresh on the boundaries and from the boundaries—even, as Naim Ateek (2008) suggests, by Palestinians under Israeli occupation?

Telling Tales about Jonah

The character of Jonah features in numerous ancient Jewish texts. Several of these episodes are inscribed in the biblical book, and others are to be found in the subsequent history of the Jonah tradition. It may be helpful to survey some of them briefly.

Within the biblical text we have several vignettes that together constitute the canonical character of Jonah. Jonah is a prophet but seems not to function in the palace or the temple of ancient Israel. He comes from an obscure village on the northern edges of the biblical lands, but this land dweller runs away to sea in a doomed attempt to evade God's call on his life. Like a child who covers her eyes and thinks she is invisible to her parents, Jonah descends to the lowest point on the ship and falls asleep. Now YHWH will not know where he is!

This runaway Israelite finds himself the only Jew on a ship full of *goyim* and soon has to explain (identify) himself. Interestingly, and despite the probable Judean authorship of this text, Jonah describes himself not as Jewish but rather as a "Hebrew" (1:9) and a worshiper of YHWH. That is one way of expressing belonging. But it pays no attention to borders. Indeed, the Hebrews were characteristically nomadic people moving from place to place, occasionally causing political problems for the traditional land owners and refusing to be enslaved by what Crossan (2007) calls the "normalcy of civilization." Neither Pharaohs in Egypt nor local rulers in Canaan can domesticate the tribes of YHWH.

After Jonah's ejection from the ship, the crew now become devotees of Jonah's god, another inadvertent and unintentional evangelistic success. It will not be his last. For his part, Jonah discovers that he is indigestible food for a giant fish, specially prepared for him by the thoughtful YHWH. The mighty storm with its powerful winds and the heavy sea that was threatening the ship subsided as Jonah sank into the waves, and into the jaws of the great fish. Just when you thought it was safe to go back in the water…

In the dark oratory of the fish's belly, Jonah prays. He has succeeded in getting himself into a place where God truly seems distant, but Jonah prays. He had attempted to flee from YHWH, but now he invokes the presence of YHWH.

After his deliverance from the dark confines of the great fish, Jonah has rediscovered his vocation. He will go beyond the borders of Israel and preach to those who are far off. He will proclaim divine wrath upon those who do not belong to the covenant and whose unspecified "great wickedness" has come to the attention of YHWH. Jonah will act and speak out of the certainty derived from his secure sense of belonging. For him, the borders (boundaries) are clear. This is no Abraham negotiating with YHWH to spare the city if only a handful of righteous persons can be found there (Gen 18:22–33).

But Jonah is too successful for his own peace of mind. To his dismay the people of Nineveh embrace his message and repent. Everyone in the city repents. The king orders a collective act of penitence, with animals sharing in the fast and even being dressed in sackcloth! So Jonah finds himself a good vantage point outside Nineveh from which to watch and wait, to see what will become of the city.

Jonah's deepest fears are proved correct. Having prevented him from escaping the call to preach, and having gone to some amazing lengths to get Jonah back on task, God changes her mind. YHWH decides not to destroy the people of Nineveh after all. The boundaries between them and us are eradicated. It is no longer clear who belongs, or what belonging means. Like us, Jonah thinks he knows where the borders are, who is "in" and who is "out."

In deep despair at this loss of bearings, Jonah is angry. Jonah wants to die. Again! But once again YHWH does not allow Jonah to die. The preacher is exhausted. Burned out. "I knew you are a gracious God" (4:2). This is why I wanted out when this all started. Jonah is now a believer in exile. The borders that create a sense of belonging are being erased by the God who will not allow Jonah to escape into Sheol.

In the later Jewish traditions, Jonah would again seek in vain to die. This time Jonah is equated with the anonymous son of the widow of Zarephath with whom Elijah stays. The relevant passage from the *Lives of the Prophets* is worth citing in full:

> Jonah was from the district of Kariathmos, near the Greek city Azotus by the sea. And when he had been cast forth by the monster and had gone away to Nineveh and had returned, he did not remain in his district, but taking his mother along he sojourned in Sour, a territory (inhabited by) foreign nations; for he said, "So shall I remove my reproach, for I spoke falsely in prophesying against the great city of Nineveh." At that time Elijah was rebuking the house of Ahab, and when he had invoked famine upon the land he fled. And he went and found the widow with her son, for he would not stay with uncircumcised people; and he blessed her. And when her son died, God again raised him again from the dead through Elijah, for he wished to show to him that it is not possible to run away from God. And after the famine he arose and went into the land of Judah. And when his mother died along the way, he buried her near Deborah's Oak. And after sojourning in the land of Saraar, he died and was buried in the cave of Kenaz, who became judge of one tribe in the days of the anarchy. And he gave a portent concerning Jerusalem and the whole land, that whenever they should see a stone crying out piteously the end was at hand. And whenever they should see all the gentiles in Jerusalem, the entire city would be razed to the ground. (*Lives of the Prophets* 10.1–11)

Finally, even Jonah is allowed to die. As a doubly dead prophet Jonah even gets more than one grave! In the *Lives of the Prophets* we find a Judean burial in a "cave of Kenaz." In the time of Jesus it seems that there was also a tomb—an empty tomb for a legendary prophet?—at Gath-Hepher commemorating the prophet Jonah. Certainly, such a tomb was later known to Jerome. As a local Galilean prophet, was this Jonah—as Jonathan Reed (1996) suggests—a hero and a role model for Jesus? Was the "sign of Jonah" for Jesus the tomb of the prophet?

Even in death Jonah crosses borders and redefines religious affiliation. Today in the mosque of Mashhed, there is a tomb for the prophet Yunis. Jonah has become a Muslim saint, and his legacy as a Galilean holy man continues to be revered.

The Sign of Jonah

In the early Jesus traditions we find an enigmatic saying attributed to Jesus concerning the "sign of Jonah" (see Jenks 2011; Adam 1990; Chow 1995). To begin with, I cite just the simplest and least-developed version of that saying:

> An evil and adulterous generation asks for a sign, but no sign will be given to it except the sign of Jonah. (Matt 16:4)

So what is (was) the sign of Jonah? The Gospels of Matthew and Luke do not agree on this point, although their traditions seem clearly related. For Matthew the sign was connected with the three days and three nights during which Jonah was in the belly of the whale (*sic*).[2]

> For just as Jonah was three days and three nights in the belly of the sea monster, so for three days and three nights the Son of Man will be in the heart of the earth. The people of Nineveh will rise up at the judgment with this generation and condemn it, because they repented at the proclamation of Jonah, and see, something greater than Jonah is here! (Matt 12:40–41)

For Luke, on the other hand, the sign value of Jonah had nothing to do with his three-day sojourn in the belly of the fish/whale. Rather, there was something about Jonah himself that made him a prophetic sign to the people of Nineveh.

> For just as Jonah became a sign to the people of Nineveh, so the Son of Man will be to this generation. The queen of the South will rise at the judgment with the people of this generation and condemn them, because she came from the ends of the earth to listen to the wisdom of Solomon, and see, something greater than Solomon is here! The people

---

2. For Matthew the "great fish" (*dāg gādôl*) of Jonah 1:17 has become a "whale," or "sea monster" (*kētos*), following the Septuagint with its *kētei megaloi*.

of Nineveh will rise up at the judgment with this generation and condemn it, because they repented at the proclamation of Jonah, and see, something greater than Jonah is here! (Luke 11:30–32)

So how may this prophet from the borderlands of the Galilee have been a sign to the people of Nineveh, at least in the imagination of Jesus and the Gospel writers? To what reality (alternative? contested?) may Jonah-as-sign point? Can the character of Jonah be more than a three-day wonder? Can the book that keeps his story alive in the religious imagination of our secular age still function as a text of hope and liberation?

From his vantage point opposite the great city Jonah offers a different perspective on the "normalcy of civilization." Jonah invites us to see life in the contested borderlands as a natural location for people of faith, as well as those without faith (note the pagan sailors as well as the population—both human and herd—of Nineveh). This mirror image of reality reverses our usual assumptions, but it is perhaps what Jesus would later proclaim as God's empire of nobodies, the *basileia tou theou*, where the last comes first and the one who is greatest becomes the servant of all.

A prophet (or church) that offered such a message to our contemporary world would be crossing the borders of conventional wisdom and inviting us to rethink (repent) our assumptions about belonging, about judgment, and about blessing. I explored some of these themes in "Sign of Jonah" (Jenks 2013).

This may be a message that is especially needed in a global world. We no longer live in isolated villages and remote valleys. Rather, in our connected world the digital natives are never far from the frontier. The border loses some of its power to define our belonging as the World Wide Web creates multiple channels for communication that evade the control mechanisms of those in power. A prophet from the borderlands of Galilee might indeed be a "sign," and not just to those in nearby lands. Even in the Antipodes, the border-crossing prophet who challenges conventional wisdom about belonging to the covenant community might yet be a "sign" for our times.

As a prophet—even (and especially) as a reluctant prophet—Jonah might be a sign for us in other ways as well. One of those ways may be the question of "the call." What does it mean for the "word of YHWH" to penetrate our lives? Jonah invites us to reflect on how we discern and recognize such a divine call, and also to consider those many ways in which we embrace, reject, or stifle the call.

Allowing Jonah to serve as a sign for us in this way may also mean that we think more deeply about the one who calls. As Jonah discovers in this resilient tale, the one who calls is the border-dwelling, boundary-crossing God. From Abram of Ur to Mary of Nazareth—and in countless other places in between and ever since—people are surprised to find that no place is God-forsaken (beyond the borders of covenant belonging), even if the divine call takes us away from the familiar places where we belong to places of grace that were otherwise unimaginable. What else would we expect of the one who delights to be known as *'ehyeh 'ăšer 'ehyeh* ("I shall be what I shall be," Exod 3:14)?

Jonah can be "taken on board" as a sign of the inescapable ambiguity of life, perhaps even as a sign written in large letters for ease of reading by time-poor commuters (Hab 2:2). From the messiness of his own location on the borders of land and covenant, and from the ambiguities of his own belonging as a (sometimes prodigal) "son of faithfulness," Jonah is a sign of the God who calls. In such edgy places where messiness and lack of clarity are more likely to be the norm, we may yet discern the call to shape lives that are holy and true—even (and especially) on the borders.

For someone such as myself, Jonah may also be a sign that invites me to rethink my religion. Is our faith the tie that binds or a catalyst that releases the imagination, setting us free to dream dreams and see visions? As a religious professional does my religion harden the boundaries or open new vistas for exploration? Jonah the reluctant preacher serves as a sign alerting me to the capacity of my faith to liberate, but also to imprison me within traditional boundaries and familiar ways of belonging.

Jonah can be a sign—a demonstration—of the capacity to resist our best intuition that divine grace extends far wider than we have been told. For some ancient and Jewish commentators on this story, the reason for Jonah's flight was his realization that his mission would undermine the unique covenant relationship that Israel enjoyed with YHWH. For love of his own people, rather than hatred of the Gentiles, Jonah refused to preach to Nineveh (Jerome, *Commentary on Jonah* 1:3). The sign of Jonah points us to the father of the prodigal, who rejoices with heaven's angels at one sinner who repents, and maybe even with/for the sinners who do not.

By the story's end, Jonah is learning to live without the cucumber,[3] without the plant providentially provided for his comfort and just as sud-

---

3. The term *qîqāyôn* is usually translated as "bush" but perhaps refers to the caster

denly taken away from him. So I find myself wondering whether, in the end, the sign of Jonah is a call to live beyond religion, to embrace what Bonhoeffer described as "religionless Christianity." Can we cope without religion's traditional protection from the harsh realities of life on the borders? Will we rage at the loss of certainty, or share God's compassion for the multitude "who do not know their right hand from their left, and also many animals" (Jonah 4:11)?

Belonging to Country

When reading Jonah on the boundaries and from the boundaries, I find myself reflecting on how best to respond to the sign of Jonah. We share a diaspora experience. Jonah seems only to function as prophet somewhere other than the place where he belongs. Likewise, my entire adult life has been spent out of my own "country."[4]

Most of my life to this point has been located in Brisbane, just north of the border. But I belong just south of the border, as I realized in a new way recently when I drove back to Lismore for a speaking engagement. For the first time in many years (and perhaps for the first time ever), I made that trip alone. No one else was with me for that journey, and I was surprised by my interior reaction as I completed a turn in the highway and familiar features of the landscape came into view. The strong sense of homecoming (returning to country) took me by surprise, even though I am happily settled on the other side of the border.

No matter on which side of the border I happen to be(long), Jonah-as-sign continues to address me. In particular, I am drawn to Jonah as a parable of compassion and generosity—on God's part, at least. The final words addressed to Jonah go without an answer in the biblical text. Perhaps an answer is in responding with a fresh commitment to act always

---

oil plant. When Jerome was working on his translation of Jonah for the Latin Vulgate he opted for "cucumber" instead of the more traditional "gourd." Riots erupted in Carthage when the Christian crowds heard of this novelty.

4. "Country" is a term used by indigenous Australians for the particular lands where they were born and from which their identity derives. Where nonindigenous Australians will often ask what each other does for a living when they meet, indigenous Australians are more likely to ask about each other's country. I found this especially and unexpectedly powerful when meeting an indigenous person who (unknown to me) came from Lismore. We are from the same country and discovered an immediate depth of connection.

out of compassion, and to reflect (as best one can) the divine generosity in one's relationships with others?

Works Consulted

Adam, Andrew K. M. 1990. The Sign of Jonah: A Fish-Eye View. *Semeia* 51:177–91.
Ateek, Naim. 2008. Jonah, the First Palestinian Liberation Theologian. Pages 67–77 in *A Palestinian Christian Cry for Reconciliation*. Maryknoll, N.Y.: Orbis.
Chow, Simon. 1995. *The Sign of Jonah Reconsidered: A Study of Its Meaning in the Gospel Traditions*. Stockholm: Almqvist & Wiksell.
Crossan, John Dominic. 2007. *God and Empire: Jesus against Rome, Then and Now*. San Francisco: HarperSanFrancisco.
Fewell, Danna N., ed. 1992. *Reading between Texts: Intertextuality and the Hebrew Bible*. Louisville: Westminster John Knox.
Hare, Douglas R. A. 1984. The Lives of the Prophets: A New Translation and Introduction. Pages 379–99 in vol. 2 of *The Old Testament Pseudepigrapha*. Edited by J. H. Charlesworth. New York: Doubleday.
Hays, Richard B., et al., eds. 2009. *Reading the Bible Intertextually*. Waco, Tex.: Baylor University Press.
Hegedus, Timothy M. 1992. *Jerome's Commentary on Jonah: Translation with Introduction and Critical Notes*. Ottawa: National Library of Canada / Bibliothèque nationale du Canada.
Jenks, Gregory C. 2011. The Sign of the Prophet Jonah: Tracing the Tradition History of a Biblical Character in Ancient Judaism and Early Christianity. Pages 11–51 in *How Jonah Is Interpreted in Judaism, Christianity, and Islam: Essays on the Authenticity and Influence of the Biblical Prophet*. Edited by M. M. Caspi and J. T. Greene. North Richland Hills, Tex.: Mellen.
———. 2013. The Sign of Jonah: Rereading the Jonah Tradition for Signs of God's Generosity. Pages 72–84 in *Pieces of Ease and Grace*. Edited by A. Cadwallader. Adelaide: ATF.
Jerome. 1985. *Commentaire sur Jonas*. Edited and translated by Yves-Marie Duval. Sources Chrétiennes 323. Paris: Cerf.
Kim, H. C. Paul. 2007. Jonah Read Intertextually. *Journal of Biblical Literature* 126:497–528.
Reed, Jonathan L. 1996. The Sign of Jonah (Q 11:29–32) and Other Epic Traditions in Q. Pages 130–43 in *Reimagining Christian Origins: A*

Colloquium Honoring Burton L. Mack. Edited by E. A. Castelli and H. Taussig. Valley Forge, Penn.: Trinity Press International.

Savage, Carl. 2011. *Biblical Bethsaida: An Archaeological Study of the First Century*. Lanham, Md.: Lexington.

Scott, Robert B. Y. 1965. The Sign of Jonah: An Interpretation. *Interpretation* 19:16–25.

Sherwood, Yvonne. 2000. *A Biblical Text and Its Afterlives: The Survival of Jonah in Western Culture*. Cambridge: Cambridge University Press.

ENGAGING RESPONSES

Gospel Maps: Intersections of Life

Michele A. Connolly

In articles ranging across all four canonical Gospels, five authors read maps of human, divine, and cosmic interaction. Here, old exclusory borders are dissolved and new threads of belonging are spun.

Elaine M. Wainwright's "Save Us! We Are Perishing!" brings a poetic sensibility to scholarly reading of a biblical text. Wainwright works with the concepts of borders and belonging while reading Matt 8:23–27 from an ecological perspective. Wainwright is ultimately interested in an ethic for living with the cosmos as it unfolds, an ethic informed by the vision of *basileia* proclaimed by Jesus of Nazareth.

Driving her argument are two acts of poetry. The title of the essay, "Save Us! We Are Perishing!" sounds a plea that we hear repeated as a leitmotif through the essay. In the words of Matt 8:27, Wainwright evokes a raw human emotion that reaches from the ancient Sea of Galilee in storm to contemporary places of ecological stress and natural disasters. Second, Wainwright presents us with a visual image of earthquake as "the splitting open of Earth in Christchurch, New Zealand, February 22, 2011, in which 185 human lives were lost." This event gashing the planet occurs in a specific time and place and must be read on the human scale of death and grief from which we can only cry out, "Save us! We are perishing!"

Wainwright locates her approach within the work of both biblical and ecological scholars. Particularly important for her in this essay is the insight of Lorraine Code, who calls for a "new social imaginary" that brings what Wainwright calls a "hermeneutic of suspicion in relation to any form of mastery" to bear on analysis of any situation. Wainwright adapts categories from Vernon Robbins's sociorhetorical approach to provide the new category "habitat," by which she reads not only for social and cultural cues but also for what the interrelated actions of Earth reveal to us of G-d.

Wainwright's strategy is to read elliptically, from a Gospel passage up to contemporary experiences and understandings of the world, and then back to the Gospel again, always alert to the presence of the divine one. Driven by an ethical goal, she asks, "How might one read a Gospel story of a dangerous storm at sea out of and into engagement with Earth and its movements ... even our belonging in relationship with the divine one?" She seeks to know how the biblical text might open paths for its readers to live within the cosmos, revering its mysterious dynamisms as intended by G-d to unfold in its own authentic ways.

Reading Matt 8:23–27, Wainwright explores borders and belonging that are physical, political, and social to show that the revelation of G-d to us in Jesus exposes the limits of our human constructs of mastery over the Earth. In her reading, the Matthean "great storm," as also the "great calm," challenges us all, whether of little faith or not, to see that the G-d who acts in the unfolding of the whole Earth calls us to act with the ethic of the *basileia*.

Reading in some sympathy with Wainwright, David J. Neville turns to Luke 13 as a test text on which to determine whether the connection between natural calamity and the God of the Bible is "a dissociating borderline or a binding line of belonging."

To address this question, Neville focuses on Jerusalem in Luke–Acts, especially in Luke 13:1–5 and 31–35. The close reading of these two pericopes is made with attention to the concerns of the larger literary context of the Lukan journey of Jesus to Jerusalem, Luke 9:51–19:46. Neville explores Luke's theology of peace before he engages the category of prophecy to resolve the theological tensions that his exposition presents to us.

As Neville reveals, the Gospel of Luke emphasizes Jerusalem in a particular way. Jerusalem connects the two volumes, Luke and Acts; while the Gospel intensifies Jesus's journey to Jerusalem, it also warns four times that the city will be destroyed. Neville reads the first of these warnings, at Luke 13:34–35, as introducing a note of divine retribution against the city that stands in some tension with understandings of God's justice that Jesus has presented in the rest of Luke 13.

Neville notes that Luke 13 is placed halfway through Jesus's journey to Jerusalem. The chapter opens and closes with references to Jerusalem that highlight the theme of the urgent need for Jerusalem's people to change their ways. The two pericopes at verses 1–5 and 31–35 invite different readings. Neville shows that in 13:1–5 Jesus refuses to blame the victim of accidental violence, insisting instead that such events should call everybody to radical change. The threat to Jerusalem in 13:34–35 seems, however, to imply that Jerusalem will suffer for her treatment of the prophets—preeminently, in Christian eyes, of Jesus, who will die there.

For Neville, this internal tension raises the issue of the Gospel of Luke as a Gospel renowned for its focus on peace. Neville argues that as a man of his own time, the composer of Luke had not fully internalized the implications of his own Christology of peace. This argument is supported by a close reading of passages about peace in Luke 9:51–19:46, from which Neville concludes that there is very evident tension between the Gospel's promise of peace and its threat (19:41–44) that the children of Jerusalem will be violently destroyed because their city did not recognize the messiah when he came.

This tension that Neville makes us feel, he argues, can be resolved only if we accept the role and dynamism of Israelite prophecy. We can read Luke with hope, treading the boundary between disaster and the God of the Scriptures, if we bear in mind that "prophecies of divine judgment were sometimes conditional ... [because] prophets sometimes dared to hope for forgiveness and restoration." Neville finally points to an ecological perspective, arguing that in a world where natural calamities occur as an organic part of the process of unfolding, the Lukan Jesus portrays a world that is fundamentally good, resting in the hands of a God who can and will bring it to its final, intended fulfillment.

Like Wainwright and Neville, Rushton starts her reflection on the "Crossroads between Life and Death" with an earthquake, the one in the Otautahi Christchurch region in September 2010. She notes the boundaries or borders of meaning that the earthquake itself caused: the temporal border of "before" and "after" the series of earthquakes that forced new spatial borders on the city, color coded for degrees of danger; social borders as the citizens of a city torn apart relocated to new locations; theological boundaries as the loss of churches and their rituals, places of connection with God, raised intensely the question of God's role in the behavior of the natural environment. Rushton finds in the explorations of ecological theologians the understanding that all actions of the environment, even those that destroy human habitats, are part of an organism still forming, still coming to birth.

For Rushton, the metaphor of birth provides a way of seeing the Bible speak to the situation at Otautahi Christchurch. In conversation with Claudia Bergmann's work, Rushton sees a connection between earthquakes and birth, both as forms of crisis. While recognizing that earthquakes *per se* are not found in the Gospel of John, Rushton relates the birth imagery that she sees running throughout that Gospel to the dynamisms of the cosmos coming to birth, even in the form of earthquakes. Following Bergmann, Rushton identifies these two processes as similar, because once begun, each is unstoppable; each brings intense pain that must be endured; and each traverses the border between life and death.

In particular, Rushton reads the birth image of John 16:21, echoing the daughter of Zion of Isa 66, to refer to the death and resurrection of Jesus, an image of new life. Above all, what this biblical imagery offered to its original readers was the possibility of transformation, of the relationship between human beings and God, and of human understanding of how God works in the world.

Rushton dares to stand on the basis of this birth imagery of crisis and transformation to read the signs of life struggling into existence in Otautahi Christchurch. Shipping containers, suggesting the crossing of boundaries all around the planet, are providing new spaces for human life in Rushton's birth-marked city. Not only in New Zealand's broken city but all around the world people struggle to protect life and love in the midst of the coming to birth of this planet. Against a timeframe of 13.7 billion years, massively beyond the scale of human life, people in Otautahi Christchurch come to see that the new life they strive for in this context will come after their own times. Yet, for Rushton, for those who can receive the Johannine birth imagery, the "image of transformation … evoking death-resurrection offers the potential of re-creation, new priorities, and new ways of belonging in the borderlessness of God's emergent and evolutionary way."

The Gospel of John offers John Painter a completely different occasion to reflect on borders, belonging, and the biblical text. Painter sees borders in biblical texts and interpretations of those texts as points where meaning is negotiated and insight garnered. Painter focuses in his essay on the relationship of the prologue of the Gospel of John to the rest of the Gospel and, even more closely, on the places of division within the first eighteen verses of the Gospel.

As he does so, Painter locates himself within a community of scholars of the previous two centuries, whose interpretations of the Gospel of John constitute a territory of its own, mapped by borders that are constantly crossed and redrawn as new insights are integrated into understanding. Indeed, much of the shifting of the borders between interpretations occurs when scholars admit, or decline to admit, into their consideration material from outside the strict boundaries of the Gospel of John itself. The way in which Hebrew Bible Wisdom literature and the Hellenistic Logos theory of Philo of Alexandria are seen to influence—or not—the thought of the prologue determines how scholars read these eighteen verses and the rest of the Gospel.

Painter traces the history of scholarship from the Brooke Foss Westcott commentary on the Gospel of John ([1880] 1958) to a recently published Sheffield University Ph.D. dissertation on the Gospel of John by Peter M. Phillips (2006).[1] Painter categorizes major shifts within this scholarship on the basis of the way each new perspective sees the role of the prologue in relation to the rest of the Gospel. The prologue has been seen first, implicitly, as an entry point enabling ancient readers to bridge different historical-political and theological contexts (Westcott), as a buffer zone in which ancient "cultivated Hellenistic readers [could come to terms with] … a strange Hebraic Gospel" (Harnack), and as a more and more explicitly named entry point to the Gospel as a whole for ancient readers negotiating various religious, cultural, and philosophical barriers.

Painter's own sympathies lie in a trajectory leading from J. Rendel Harris (1917) to Rudolf Bultmann (1923), C. H. Dodd (1953), and C. K. Barrett (1955). Appreciating the contributions that all these scholars have made, Painter declares his own position, the borders that contain this Gospel for him: "The prologue is a bridge from the worldview of Genesis and Moses (John 1:17) to reveal that creation is not complete and that the Logos became flesh to make creation whole."

Painter's chapter is a wonderfully educative survey of the map of Johannine biblical scholarship since the late nineteenth century. On the basis of this survey, clearly identifying the borders that scholars have drawn and redrawn around texts, history, culture, and philosophical language, Painter makes it possible to read the Johannine prologue as a text drawing believers into the care of a "faithful God … [whose] purpose [is] to make creation whole." In this way, borders rich with human history make a space in which God and human beings can belong together.

Jeffrey W. Aernie takes us to the Gospel of Mark to read the story of the Syrophoenician woman, whose very identification combines forms

---

1. See the "Works Consulted" in Painter's essay, above, for full bibliographical information on the authors and works mentioned here.

of belonging and who crosses controversial boundaries as she interacts with Jesus. Aernie explores the way in which the Markan Jesus disallows destructive borders between people that class some fortunate few as "clean" to enjoy God's blessing while many others are said to be "unclean."

Aernie's reading sees Jesus—and the Syrophoenician woman—overcome limits imposed by ethnicity, geography, and politics. Historical research shows significant socioeconomic and political tension between the regions from which Jesus and the woman come, Galilee and Tyre, respectively. Evidence that the woman, as Hellenistic, may well be from a higher social stratum than Jesus emphasizes further the boundaries of conflict between Jesus and the Syrophoenician woman, before the issue of gender is considered. Aernie shows that in contrast to Jesus's readiness to heal others with needs similar to those of the Syrophoenician woman's daughter (see Mark 5), his apparent aloofness toward the Syrophoenician woman is all the more marked.

However, as Aernie shows by a close reading of Mark 7:27, Jesus offers a parabolic statement to the Syrophoenician woman, to which she also responds in parable. In this way, both Jesus and the woman skillfully negotiate difficult borders of demarcation that could deny to the woman's daughter the healing she so urgently needs. Given that Jesus has been depicted in Mark 7:1–23, immediately before this pericope, unambiguously and provocatively declaring that "neither food nor people are defiled by external factors," Jesus's encounter with the Syrophoenician woman serves as a dramatic test case for his assertion. On the authority of Jesus's "announcement" and the skillfull rhetoric of her speech of faith, cultural obstructions to faith in the God of Jesus are dismantled.

Aernie argues strongly that Jesus's statement in Mark 7:27 is meant to be understood ironically, conveying the sense that Jesus himself does not hold to the stereotypical view to which he gives voice. The woman, like the true hearer of parables that Mark's Jesus has already described as looking and perceiving, listening and understanding (4:11–12), does not merely comprehend Jesus's meaning. She already holds the same worldview that Jesus does. Indeed, as Aernie sums it up, "the Syrophoenician woman is the only person in the Markan narrative to manifest an immediate understanding of Jesus's parabolic framework." She is thus the true Markan disciple of Jesus.

Understood in this way, the interaction between Jesus and the Syrophoenician woman declares discipleship a borderless activity, where the divisive categories of Jew and Gentile no longer hold sway. If all that is required is faith-filled response to the word of Jesus, this woman has shown by her word that "the movement of the gospel ... cannot be hindered by the existence of the external borders of ethnicity, geography, or gender."

In their chapters reading various Gospel narratives, the five scholars I have discussed above have shown that the Bible enables us to read the issues with which borders and belonging confront us. Borders are made by the natural features of landforms and great bodies of water. But borders are also made by the human communities who live within the spaces that land and water define for us. Human communities shape themselves by their systems of meaning whether they are social, political, or religious.

We find that we cannot live without the boundaries that bring clarity and order to our sense of belonging. Nor can we exist without a sense of belonging to some form of human community. Today we yearn in a distinctly new way to live at peace with the Earth while we have always known that our deepest desire is to be in union with G-d. Yet we find that forces both within the dynamism of Earth, part only of an immense universe, and also within human beings can override the borders that make for peace and in their place bring destruction and grievous loss of life.

In their readings of the Gospels, Wainwright, Neville, Rushton, Painter, and Aernie each find that in the mysterious dynamism of the Earth and its human inhabitants, G-d is not remote but present to us in Jesus. The Gospels let us see that in the way G-d engages with the Earth as it continues to unfold, we can trust that G-d is bringing creation to an abundance in which we can all share.

Breaking Bible Boundaries

David M. Gunn

Invited to respond to the opening chapter, Jione Havea's "Engaging Scriptures from Oceania," and four other chapters, I would like, through them, to engage further with the topic of Scripture as a boundary.

Havea's charge is that the Bible is going stale in Oceania, that its freshness (or not) depends on its readers, and that he is one of those who believes that "the Bible is worth keeping fresh," even in a region that was colonized with the help of missionaries and their Bible. Clearly this volume is designed to encourage such a project by bringing into the interpretive process the lens of boundaries—those that bound the interpreters as much as those that may be expressed in the text—and the power relations that boundaries construct or support.

Borders, Havea observes, exclude and divide but are also necessary to maintain order and to condition people. "To break through borders does not necessarily dissolve order, or break people up, but transforms and redefines who people are," though the questions still need to be asked: "Whose order do borders maintain? Whose people do borders safeguard?" Borders may construct places—communities, identities—where people feel they belong, and this may be true of the Bible. Yet the Bible may make other people not belong, and so the Bible "invites and welcomes, opens and bridges ... but it also excludes and repels."

Borders and boundaries may be constitutive of belonging, and in Oceania, he argues, "Color is high on the scale of reasons for judging whether something belongs or does not belong." Color is linked to privileges. White people have more, and "fairer-skin people imagine that they are better and more privileged than darker-skin ones." In a region where people are of many shades of color, an underlying binary of white and black still exerts its power. That binary, Havea is arguing, needs to be undone; it needs "browning." So, for that matter, does biblical criticism.

One of the directions Havea takes this thought is toward the Bible as Scripture, where "scriptures" are understood as "texts honored by members of a community because those reveal something that helps them/others understand what the community is about and how it may endure and thrive." Such "texts" may come in a variety of forms, and not just literary forms. Scriptures understood thus are ongoing, subject to revision, correction, and supplementation. He appeals for a return to native scriptures in their own right, but also as supplements to biblical texts. By which I take it that we might also usefully think of biblical texts as potentially supplements to those native scriptures. In this way, biblical boundaries would be open to "browning."

To be sure, the Bible's boundaries (the canon of Scripture) have never quite been fixed but have been contested between Jews and Christians and in turn between one lot of Christians and another lot. In practice, however, the notion of Bible, for many Christians at least, has been a binary, like black and white—there is Bible and not-Bible—and the notion comes with powerful tags—Holy Scripture and Word of God, books given by divine inspiration to be the rule of faith and life.

With such exclusive claims built into notions of Bible it is no wonder that the business of crossing its boundaries can be beset with anxiety. In her essay, "Jewish Readings of the Fourth Gospel: Beyond the Pale?" Ruth Sheridan sensitively explores the experiences of two Jewish critics of the New Testament. She describes Daniel Boyarin as raising the topic of contemporary Jewish identity as it relates to a Jew reading John's Gospel "in all its exceedingly fraught dimensions." Sheridan quotes him where he "confesses" that he is a Jew drawn to Christianity. "He writes," she says, "from a 'conventional form of Jewish identification' [Boyarin's words], but his writing calls into question, historically, the terms of conventional, 'orthodox' identities." His compulsion to "come out" is expressed also, she notes, in metaphoric language, the geographic language of "borders," "place," "ground," "boundary," and their related verbs "exclude" and "belong."

When describing Adele Reinhartz's account of thinking through the relationship between the subject of her scholarly enterprise (again John's Gospel) and her Jewish identity, Sheridan observes that what bothered Reinhartz was not the Gospel's christological statements as much as the presentation, often hostile, of Jewish characters, laws, and practices. In particular Sheridan herself notes the unnuanced ("almost irreducibly negative") repetition of the term "the Jews," which, then as now, "tends to lump *all* Jews together, ignoring the variegated and diverse nature of

Jewish cultures and identities." As I see it, then, on the question of boundary drawing and identity construction, the New Testament here (John's Gospel) does a pretty lousy job (or does its job only too well), which would not matter so critically had not the text become bound into an exclusive Scripture so that its lousy job became privileged and doubly dangerous.

Sheridan concludes her discussion by revisiting "the perceived danger of boundary crossing (and the scandal it invokes) that inheres in a Jewish scholar's decision to investigate Christian sacred texts" and hoping that her essay has raised "further questions about the idea of canon as boundary, and of faith community as bounded by canon. In this light, what does it mean to make a scholarly inquiry into the canon of the Other? What message does it perhaps send to others? What fears might it raise?" In my view, she has successfully raised those further questions.

"Border or boundary crossings expose us to new lands and new cultures. ... The longer the stay across the border, the more likely one needs to wrestle with the issue of belonging." So begins Merilyn Clark's essay, "Mapping the Boundaries of Belonging: Another Look at Jacob's Story." Perhaps that is the problem some of Boyarin's fellow Jews are anticipating (see Sheridan's essay). Will he stay there, in New Testament Land, to the point of belonging and forgetting where he came from, his real home in Torah Land? Whose is the fear? The border-crosser's or those whose identity is challenged by the border-crosser?

But Clark's account of Jacob as resident alien also takes me (for the moment) from the question of reader as border-crosser to that of biblical character as border-crosser, Jacob as a model we might learn from today, a prism through which to view the issue of migration—"how identity, values, and lifestyle are challenged by border crossing; how belonging is shaped; and how difference can be negotiated and honored." In the scriptural story of Israel, she observes, "the motif of alienation is an important one. Israel remembered, in her sacred texts, being aliens and strangers in strange lands." Clark goes on to invoke James Sanders's view that by asking "Who are we?" and "What shall we do?" the canonical texts of sacred Scripture reveal the core relationship that binds the community of faith together, namely, its relationship with God: they were God's people and he was their God.

Jacob, Clark argues, exemplifies these aspects of Israel: Jacob is always an "alien" whose life is shaped by a special relationship with God.

> Although he is an alien in his birth land, his destiny, shaped by covenantal promises from God and numinous encounters, shapes a sense of

belonging to that land that he calls "home." Even in the promised land he differentiates himself from the host culture and his brother's community.

Despite his long years of work for his uncle and his marriage to his uncle's daughters, Jacob doesn't belong in Haran. He belongs back in Canaan. Clark sees the family of Abraham living in Canaan as an alien family having to deal with a foreign culture. While I doubt this reading, I'm interested in Clark's reading for alienation as a divine imperative, for Abraham, for Isaac, and for Jacob. If God's covenant promise is to be fulfilled, the family has to keep on being alien.

Yet Clark's conclusion oddly places alienation among the threats and dangers with which border crossings are fraught: "of provoking hostile responses, of loss of wealth, ... of alienation and isolation." And if the border-crossers can manage it, they may preserve and develop a distinctive identity and lifestyle from the dominant host culture; "separation can be negotiated without violence and alienation." What, then, does it mean to work at being alien without alienation? There's the challenge.

For Nāsili Vakaʻuta, in "Border Crossing/Body Whoring: Reading Rahab of Jericho with Native Women," the culmination of the promise of land as told in the book of Joshua is also a story of alienation, but this time of the forced alienation from their land of the people for whom the land was home. Jacob's blessing turns into Canaan's curse. Reading Rahab from a native woman's standpoint, Vakaʻuta (like Robert Alan Warrior) takes a Canaanite perspective. A reading that privileges Joshua, the spies, and the Israelites is, in his view, an imperialist reading.

In Deuteronomic rhetoric, harlotry pollutes both people and land—and foreign women are harlots, so Israelite men are not to marry them or have dealings with them. Foreign people must be cleansed to purify the land, for God "has chosen [Israel] out of all the peoples of the earth to be his people, his treasured possession" (Deut 7:6), a claim that "echoes throughout the Hebrew Bible and resonates with colonial border-crossing narratives." In short, Vakaʻuta is concerned to argue "that the depiction of 'native women' as harlots is a trope employed to justify the *invasion/occupation* of their lands and the *dispossession* of their people."

Having listed some of the ways colonizing rhetoric constructs indigenous women, he compares those with the biblical account of Rahab. To take but one of his examples, Rahab and the Canaanites are described as knowing Yhwh—and melting. "This is common imperial nonsense, that the colonizer's deity and belief system is superior to those of the natives.

The native inhabitants are therefore made to acknowledge the deity of the colonizers."

The reading problematizes the biblical narrative. At the same time, it raises further questions on its own account. Rahab and the Israelite spies make a covenant, to the detriment of Rahab's own people. So from a Canaanite perspective, is Rahab simply a self-serving traitor, a tool of the invaders? Then again, what would she, a native woman, say about herself and her actions? Or, from a quite different angle, why has this narrative, ostensibly in the service of an ideology that condemns foreign women as harlots to be avoided or expunged, focused upon this foreign woman, a harlot, who aids Israel and whose family lives in the midst of Israel "to this day"? Or, from yet another angle, what makes Israel in this story an imperial entity, or the agent of one? Does God play the part of empire in this account of conquest and colonization? Israel is hardly the agent of Egypt, though Israel's plight in Egypt might prompt us to ask another question: does the motivation of seeking security from servitude make a difference to the anti-imperialist/anticolonist reading?

The story of Rahab the wall-dwelling harlot is one of crossing boundaries and broken boundaries. As a story of alienation it is perhaps not so clear to me who is alienating whom within the story world, nor in whose interest Rahab's particular story lends itself to being read, even when taking a Canaanite or native woman's perspective.

Judith McKinlay is interested in interested parties. Her exploration of the conquest narrative, in "Slipping across Borders and Bordering on Conquest: A Contrapuntal Reading of Numbers 13," brilliantly teases out in dialogical style the diverse constituent parties (the early storyteller, the elitist Priestly scribe) whose interests have contributed, by spin and counterspin, to the construction of the final theological form of the text in Persian Yehud. The very diversity of their stories and strategies, she argues, highlights what they have in common—a political purpose aimed at dispossession and delegitimization. Woven into her reading of this story of common concern for justifying dispossession, McKinlay sets in counterpoint another story, of the Tuhoe people of Aotearoa New Zealand, "whose land was also entered, and their borders and boundaries crossed by an intrusive colonizing power who also planned and presumed to make it theirs." Introducing the Tuhoe fatally compromises the whole story of divine "promise." For the Tuhoe,

> it was not *promised* land, it *was* their land.... Of course, for the Amalekites, Hittites, Jebusites, Amorites, or Canaanites, it was also not

promised but their *inhabited* land. Promise, as in the divine gifting (Num 13:1), was simply the Israelite coded catchphrase.

And for the Israelites, it was necessary "to be distinct from these Other peoples, whose lands they will eventually seize, settle, and possess." And at the heart of their distinctiveness, their "identity," is their God, who, as McKinlay puts it, warrants the seizure and settlement.

Always one to seek nuance, McKinlay wonders whether there was perhaps another memory in the story, "a different view of the so-called conquest," a hint in the spies' report that some hesitated to enter land occupied by others. "Was it simply a matter of fear, or was there a sense of hesitation about taking what wasn't theirs?" What if, I wonder, they had encountered another woman, Gamiritj Gurruwiwi, under a frangipani tree, and heard her poem of land and seeds (see Havea, "Engaging Scriptures from Oceania," above). But if there was a memory of hesitation, McKinlay concludes, it is "overridden in the final version by the theology undergirding the dominant conquest theme."

McKinlay is meticulous in reflecting upon her own role as interpreter, attuned to her own location as reader/interpreter—including her circumstance as a descendent of Pakeha (European) colonists. I, too, am a descendent of Pakeha colonists.

In 1862 my paternal great-grandfather, Farquhar Gunn, came ashore in the South Island of the new British colony, New Zealand, after a more than three-month voyage from Scotland. In his possession was a new edition of John Brown's *Dictionary of the Holy Bible* (Brown 1859), a highly reputable compendium of Bible knowledge by the author of the famous *Self-Interpreting Bible* (Edinburgh, 1778). A shepherd, Farquhar was well educated, like many highland Scots, and loved to read. Whether he perused his dictionary on the voyage I don't know, but if he had chanced upon the entry concerning the Hebrews, this is (some of) what he would have read:

> In their entrance to Canaan, God, to give the Hebrews a horror of idolatry, ordered them to cut off every idolatrous Canaanite. They, however, through sinful pity or sloth, spared vast numbers of them, who enticed them to wickedness, and were sometimes God's rod to punish them. (Brown 1859)

And had he followed up with the entry on Canaan, there was more:

> When Ham sported with his father's nakedness, Noah pronounced a curse of the basest servitude, particularly against Canaan. ... What Noah did on his being made aware of his son's wickedness, flowed not from his paternal displeasure, but from the impulse of the Spirit of God, who is righteous in all his ways. ... And from the subsequent history it will appear, how the Canaanites were terribly enslaved by the posterity of Shem and of Japhet, according to the tenor of Noah's curse. (Brown 1859)

The descendants of Canaan were many, and some inhabited the land of Canaan. "They were generally very wicked, given to the vilest idolatry." In due course, "when Joshua succeeded Moses, and entered the promised land, the curse began to be inflicted in all its rigour," even following those Canaanites who escaped the servitude of Israel. The editor to this edition then adds a note explaining how the curse connects to the modern world:

> Noah's curse was not causeless, and therefore it came. And it has descended from generation to generation; as no distance from the seat of Canaan's original settlement, has hid the people of the curse from its operation, so no interval of time has weakened its power. The tribes of Africa appeared for ages to have escaped it. But when Japhet's posterity discovered and seized on the new world, they supplied themselves with servants from Africa, and the groans and oppression, the tears and the blood of Afric's sons, all proclaim that they own Ham for their father. To this day the slave trade is not suppressed, and the black population of both Americas, yet kept in degrading bondage, testifies the same truth. Christians justly labour for their freedom, but till the curse remove, the expectation of success is vain. The origin of the original tribes of America, now so nearly exterminated, hangs in great doubt, but if we could trace them to Canaan, their fate would at once be accounted for. (Brown 1859)

The 1860s saw fierce fighting between Maori and Pakeha (Europeans), what has come to be known for good reason as the Land Wars, though the immediate causes were many and varied. The armed conflicts took place in the North Island, a long way from the southern high country sheep station Farquhar found work on, but as, over the next decade or so, he heard the news of the wars, between his white folk and the brown indigenous people, I wonder what the biblical truth encapsulated in that dictionary might have had upon his understanding of the clash that was taking place. "Not very helpful" might be an understatement.

I come back to the question of border crossing. Clark sees Jacob as a model figure who preserves his God-given identity across borders through persistent self-sustained alienation. Alienation could have (and has historically) led to persecution and destruction. In the story of Jacob/Israel, however, the outcome is the promised land, and the destruction is inflicted by God on the indigenous inhabitants of the land. Sustained alienation is a great survival strategy—when God is on your side. Divine promise is very useful—when someone else, across the border, occupies the land you want.

As both Vaka'uta and McKinlay in their different ways make very clear, the story of Jacob/Israel as it issues in the conquest is a self-serving warrant for the dispossession of others. What better Bible could a colonist have in his traveling trunk? Blessings for some and curses for others, all divinely ordained. A world of chosen and rejected. And the takers of land—the chosen blessed. Not a story that the Tuhoe would warm to without some interpretive ingenuity, which is just what their close kinsman, Te Kooti, exercised when he claimed the role of Joshua and identified the colonists as Canaanites (Binney 1995; Gunn 1998).

If, as Sanders claims, our identity were to be somehow dependent on this story and our community constituted by our relationship with this God, what would that mean? Who are we? The people of a genocidal God. What shall we do? Wipe out others who are not our God's people and seize their land because it is what our God has promised us, and, anyway, they deserve destruction. Is this why we need to keep being alien in another land, lest our people and our God think we have become one of Them and seek our demise? There seems little room for browning in this Bible Land.

Of course, both Havea and McKinlay might well urge circumspection. The biblical story of conquest has its voices and countervoices; it is not a monologic narrative. Rahab's story alone makes that point, I would agree; Daniel Hawk nicely sets out the complications for "promise" in the book of Joshua (Hawk 1991); and I have often argued that the larger story, Genesis to Kings, tempers any triumphalist reading of the conquest story. But my point here is that this story remains, nevertheless, like John's story of "the Jews," a dangerous one, a prime candidate for enlisting in the cause of oppression and dispossession, a story that does not deserve a place of privilege in the identity formation of individuals or communities that have a commitment to respectful cohabitation with others.

The Bible's borders need browning, certainly. And bothering (see Havea, "Bare Feet Welcome," above). But how about simply breaking?

Works Consulted

Binney, Judith. 1995. *Redemption Songs: A Life of Te Kooti Arikirangi Te Turuku.* Auckland: Auckland University Press.

Brown, John. 1859. *Brown's Dictionary of the Holy Bible, Corrected and Improved According to the Advanced State of Information at the Present Day, by the Rev. James Smith.* Edinburgh: Blackie and Son.

Gunn, David M. 1998. Colonialism and the Vagaries of Scripture: Te Kooti in Canaan (A Story of Bible and Dispossession in Aotearoa/New Zealand). Pages 127–42 in *God in the Fray: A Tribute to Walter Brueggemann.* Edited by Tod Linafelt and Timothy K. Beal. Minneapolis: Fortress.

Hawk, L. Daniel. 1991. *Every Promise Fulfilled: Contesting Plots in Joshua.* Literary Currents in Biblical Interpretation. Louisville: Westminster John Knox.

Warrior, Robert Alan. 1989. Canaanites, Cowboys, and Indians: Deliverance, Conquest, and Liberation Theology Today. *Christianity and Crisis* 49:261–65.

Bordering on Redemption

Mark G. Brett

I was asked to respond in particular to the contributions from Jeanette Mathews, Monica Melanchthon, Jione Havea (his chapter on barefoot liminality), and Gregory Jenks. Reading through these papers provoked a very welcome sense not just of the authors' biographies, weaving in and out of the engagements with biblical texts, but of the wider political narratives that resonate through these readers' lives as they seek to engage with a classical literary canon.

The very idea of a canon, with its evocations of borders and belonging, illustrates the complexity of the issues at stake. Of course there are the familiar variations between Catholic, Protestant, and Orthodox canons, but Jeanette Mathews's paper raises questions about the borders of the Torah itself, that is, the limiting of the books of Moses and the social dimensions of that limiting. When Deut 34:10 asserts that Israel "never again" saw a prophet like Moses (contra Moses's own promise in Deut 18:15), we may be justified in finding here the work of an editor who is seeking to close a Pentateuch and to set this Torah at a higher level of authority than any compendium of prophetic claims subsequent to Moses's own claims (see, e.g., Römer and Brettler 2000; Dozeman et al. 2011). But why, we may ask, would an editorial intervention want to establish this particular border between the making of Mosaic law and its applications in the unfolding story of Israel? And why would Rabbinic Judaism reiterate this boundary in their traditional structuring of the Hebrew canon into Torah, Prophets, and Writings?

Mathews suggests that we should meditate on the significance of a "second law," a Deuteronomy, given in Moab and therefore still outside the promised land. This law was apparently handed down in the homeland of Ruth, the land of Moab, eastward across the Jordan. And we are told at the end of Deuteronomy that this is the very same country that hosts the body of Moses—in an unmarked grave in "the valley opposite Beth-Peor," a valley that is located in "the land of Moab" (Deut 34:6), or more specifically, in "the land of King Sihon of the Amorites, who reigned at Heshbon" (4:46). The scenario in which an Amorite king might be reigning over the northern part of Moab is clarified in Num 21:26 as an anomaly that arose through a history of conquest: "Now Heshbon was the city of Sihon king of the Amorites, who had fought against a *former* king of Moab and taken all the land from his hand, as far as the Arnon River." Thus when Moses took Sihon's land in a *ḥērem* war (Deut 2:26–35; 4:46), the Israelites were apparently exercising a right of conquest that Sihon had himself previously exercised in an intra-indigenous war. So this, apparently, is the story of the war-torn land of Moab, which Moses conquered, in which he gave his second law, and in which he died. But is there another way to tell this story?

There is a sense in which Moab was at some point claimed by Israel and, by implication, did *not* lie beyond its borders.[1] The specific kind of *ḥērem* conducted against Sihon the Amorite is virtually identical to what we find in the campaigns against Ai in Josh 8 and against the northern kings listed in Josh 11. In all these cases the *ḥērem* entailed the killing of men, women, and children and the sparing of animals, "according to the command of Moses" (Josh 11:12–15; 8:27; cf. Deut 2:34–35 for the same rules of engagement against Sihon). What these texts have in common, along with the Moabite traditions behind them, is arguably a conception of *ḥērem* that was shared across the local cultures of the region, within which such comprehensive ritual slaughter was thought to bind a people simultaneously to the land and to the divinity who provides it, excluding all the prior inhabitants from economic relations (Monroe 2007; Fleming 2012, 133–43). The early *ḥērem* was in this sense not simply a strategy for warfare; its ritual performance also served to secure a covenant relationship with the deity and consequent flourishing in the land.[2] In effect, it rendered a town "an empty vessel in which the conquering population and

---

1. For a comprehensive discussion of the ambivalence towards trans-Jordanian country, see Havrelock 2011. While some of Israel's social mapping is focused exclusively west of the Jordan, the "Euphrates maps" expand dramatically eastward, e.g., in Deut 1:7; 11:24; Josh 1:3–4; Gen 15:18.

2. A similar motivation lies behind the alternative model of *ḥērem* in Deut 13 and Josh 6:21 and 7:24–26, which assume that animals should also be killed. In 1 Sam 15, Saul is criticized on this very point.

its god set up residence" (Monroe 2007, 326). Adopting this angle of vision, Moses was buried in land that was claimed by conquest, and while he was prevented from crossing the Jordan (whether on account of collective or personal guilt[3]), the land nevertheless fell under Yhwh's jurisdiction.

Mathews understandably adopts the canonical view that Moab lies outside the promised land and infers that the laws of Moses are well suited, therefore, to those who live outside the land, whether in the distant diaspora or in the territories immediately adjacent to Judah/Yehud. The creators of the Pentateuch may also be attempting to balance the centrality of Jerusalem's place in Israel's social imagination (the single *māqôm* of Deut 12:5) with the lived experience of diaspora.[4] But these creators of the Pentateuch were apparently not the only editors of the Torah to have meditated on the question of borders and land possession.

Whether or not one is interested in the technical terminology of "Hexateuchal redaction," there is nonetheless a story stretching across the first six books of the Hebrew Bible, beginning with the divine promising of land in Genesis and finding fulfillment in the book of Joshua. The chapter that closes this Hexateuch story, Josh 24, is very peculiar indeed, since it manages to recount the entire story of creation, exodus, and conquest without mentioning the law of Moses. Instead, in this alternative rendering of how to close Israel's foundational narrative, Joshua makes a covenant in Shechem (northern Israelite country) with decrees and laws not housed in an ark but rather marked with "a great stone" erected "under the oak near the holy place of Yhwh" (Josh 24:25–26). In the story world that stretches from Genesis to Joshua, Abram might be forgiven for building his altar at Shechem beside an oak tree (Gen 12:6–7; contra Deut 16:21), but Joshua has no such license when he writes his own "law of God" beside the Shechemite oak in Josh 24:25–27. This is an example of narrative contestation of borders. The law belongs more to God than it does to Moses, we may infer, and this radical idea is attached particularly to the ancestors buried in the north—Joshua, Joseph, and Eleazer the son of Aaron (24:29–33).

---

3. Moses suffers Yhwh's anger against the people according to Deut 1:37; 3:26; 4:21, whereas Num 20:12 reduces Moses's exclusion from the land to a matter of personal unfaithfulness.

4. As Smith notes (1993, 51), "What is crucial for ethnicity is not the possession of the homeland, but the sense of mutual belonging, even from afar." Cf. Kennedy 2011, 67–72.

The implication of this alternative narrative arc is that northerners are free to choose Yhwh, to have their own sacred site of Yhwh, and to memorialize their own ancestors. In short, if there were a Hexateuch at some stage in the unfolding of Israelite tradition, with the promise of land in Genesis and the taking of land in Joshua *framing* the Moses story from Exodus to Deuteronomy, then this land would include Samaria. As is well known, this is the northern land that the Ezra-Nehemiah tradition regarded as beyond the pale, beyond the acceptable limits of holiness as defined by "the children of the exile" (see further Nihan 2007). In short, the northern borders of Israel were in some respects as contested as the eastern borders across the Jordan River. And pointing in each direction, the biblical *talanoa* has left its legacy of various narrative attempts to redeem the borders.

As Monica Melanchthon's chapter makes clear, the imperative for redemption is often expressed by women characters who exercise their agency against normal expectations (illustrated by Rahab, Rizpah, and Ruth, among others). An abstract summary of the notion of redemption would include the idea of "restoration to the family," but in the case of Rizpah, redemption has the more specific connotation of repatriation. As in the case of exiles who long for return to their native land (the Karen, Palestinians, traditional Aboriginal owners), no postmodern celebration of endlessly negotiable space is relevant here. A proper negotiation begins only when all the parties are accorded their due respect, beginning with their own account of ancestral belonging. The deafening silence of Rizpah ensures that the bones of her dead, her sons and nephews, are properly repatriated. Anyone who has attended a ceremony for the return of ancestral Aboriginal remains will sense the power of this kind of social process.

The slaughter of Rizpah's family by the Gibeonites is given a pretext in 2 Sam 21:1, where the reader is informed that Saul breached Joshua's covenant with the Gibeonites (Josh 9, a narrative that itself reveals a breach of the *ḥērem* law in Deut 20:10–18). But the books of Samuel provide no other record of this particular sin of Saul. Are we to take the "omniscient" narrator in 2 Sam 21:1 at face value, or is perhaps Yhwh's voice being turned by a storyteller to David's purposes? Considering the pattern of critical afterthoughts about David in 2 Sam 21–24, we might be justified in adopting the more suspicious view (cf. Brueggemann 1988, in contrast with Fokkelman 1990, 290).

Perhaps Rizpah's witness was seized on as an opportunity to display David's purity. In 2 Sam 21:12–14, it is David, not Rizpah, who takes the initiative to return the bones of Saul and Jonathan to their traditional land of Benjamin, along with Rizpah's sons and nephews. A public display of ethical purity often has political value, and no doubt David wants to claim that Yhwh *directed* him to negotiate the punishment that might fit Saul's evil intention—to leave the Gibeonites with "no place to stand in the border of Israel" (21:5). Yet this is apparently the same Yhwh who commands the genocide of Gibeonites in Deut 20 (cf. 2 Sam 21:2) and who informs Ezekiel that intergenerational punishment is unjust, and therefore children do not die for their father's sins (Ezek 18). If the narrator of 2 Sam 21:1 is omniscient and wants to lay claim to Yhwh's voice, then this omniscience is nothing more than a literary convention adopted for a particular narrative moment. The Yhwh of Ezek 18 would claim that the punishment visited on Rizpah's family did *not* fit the crime, and speaking as a theologian I would say that this Yhwh weeps with every mother like Rizpah and Priyatama who has lost family members to political violence. This Yhwh speaks not so much through a single verse but through the testimony and countertestimony of canonical argument, or perhaps *talanoa*.

Jione Havea's essay "Bare Feet Welcome" points us to some other dimensions of redemption. First, we encounter the example of the unnamed redeemer in Ruth 1:2, who finds the act of redemption too difficult to contemplate when his own estate is threatened (4:6). Boaz, on the other hand, does the right thing in respecting the name of the dead—securing the former husband's name and inheritance within "the gate of his place [*māqôm*]" in an apparently traditional manner (4:10). Kin and country are redeemed within their traditional borders in the most ironic way, through marriage with a Moabite woman. If this story were told in the face of the Ezra-Nehemiah tradition, the intention would be subversive of the exclusion of foreign women, explicitly including Moabite women in Ezra 9:1. The practice of redeeming traditional land, "the gate of his place," is effected by some ironic border crossing—perhaps doubly ironic when we consider that this land of Moab was taken by Moses in *ḥērem* war.

In the second of Havea's examples of barefoot liminality, Exod 3, we find that Moses meets God in a sacred tree on Mount Horeb (Abram and Joshua's Shechemite oak comes to mind). This divine encounter provides the future lawgiver with a lesson in what we might call nominalist philosophy: according to the omniscient narrator, or narrators, Moses learns here that the ancestral deities have another name, Yhwh, and that the meaning of this divine name is indeterminate: "I will be who I will be" (Exod 3:13–15). In an alternative version of Moses's call in Exod 6, the nominalism has a decidedly different twist: the names of the ancestral deities include not just "the *'ĕlōhê* of Abraham, the *'ĕlōhê* of Isaac, and the *'ĕlōhê* of Jacob" (3:6), but also "El," the name of the Creator and high god in the Canaanite pantheon (Exod 6:3; cf. Gen 14:18–22). In Exod 6, the "inclusive monotheism" of the omniscient narrator is probably reflecting a Priestly theology devised long after Deuteronomy's version of Yahwism (see de Pury 2000; Schmid 2011; Neemia 2012). The border-crossing Priestly God speaks a different dialect from the divine voice in Moses's barefoot encounter with the burning bush. The voice from the bush suggests that the promised land is not so much the land of El but rather "the place [*māqôm*] of Canaanites, Hittites, Amorities, Perizzites, Hivites, and Jebusites" (Exod 3:8).

Do these traditional groups need to be conquered in order to secure a sense of belonging? Or is the movement of Israel into Canaan a matter of redemption, of *returning* to a place that was already in the possession of Abraham, Isaac, and Jacob in a quite different way, the way of sojourners who could live alongside the natives, purchase their burial sites (Gen 23), and acknowledge other ways to understand God, land, and borders? While there is not the space here to discuss the alternative vision of the Priestly tradition, we can be assured that it provides a less nationalist view of belonging and borders (a view conditioned by exile) and, contrary to what Ezra 9 suggests, has no difficulty conceiving of foreign women joining the family and lineage of Jacob (cf. Brett 2012, 2013).[5]

Accordingly, regarding the issue of intermarriage, Yairah Amit has rightly distinguished between the exclusivist tendencies of Deuteronomic traditions and "the open option represented by the editing of the Holiness School," the successors to the Priestly writers (Amit 2010, 217). She suggests that the story of Judah and Tamar in Gen 38 should be seen as a composition of the Holiness School, which affirms divine blessing on a Canaanite woman on the grounds of her implied torah observance (specifically of levirate law) rather than her ethnicity (Amit 2009). On this view of holiness, the crucial roles given to Tamar (the mother of Perez in Gen 38:25–29) and Ruth (the mother of Obed in Ruth 4:13–17) in the genealogy of David are perfectly explicable, even when their names are occluded in the genealogies of Gen 46:12 and Ruth 4:18–22. The genealogies present an abstract picture of paternal lineage, while the preceding

---

5. This point about Ezra would hold true even if one accepts the arguments of Shectman 2011 that the pattern of endogamy exhibited by Abraham, Isaac, and Jacob is discontinued among the children of Jacob, once they are "at home" in the land (Gen 30:25; 31:3, 13–14; 32:10).

narratives make the agency of foreign women absolutely central to the life of the tradition.

This kind of lively biblical debate about the character of genealogies and redemption is left behind in Gregory Jenks's discussion, which tends to highlight an opposition between law and grace rather than an argument between competing legal traditions. He reads more deliberately as a white Australian Christian rather than vicariously through readers from other cultures. We postmodern Australians seem to possess what Charles Taylor has called a "buffered self," which is no longer vulnerable to the spiritual world "as immediate reality, like stones, rivers and mountains" (2007, 12). Unlike traditional Aboriginal owners, we are empowered to see religious construals precisely *as construals*, as contingent and constructed (2007, 3–39). Our social identities are therefore fabricated with all the contingencies, for example, of invented colonial borders, and accordingly a State of Origin football match between Queensland and New South Wales becomes a performance of identity unburdened by a thousand generations of metaphysical belongings.

Jenks begins his essay with the kind of anxious self-reflections that we white Australian intellectuals are much given to (cf. Potter 2003). Unlike the followers of our erstwhile prime minister John Howard, we progressives reject the very idea of borders and thereby reject the old biblical senses of redemption, so that we can be set free to celebrate "religionless Christianity" instead. Regrettably, this iconoclastic attack on Christendom inadvertently preserves a colonial logic: an indifference to "specifically coded territories" (cf. Hardt and Negri 2000, 186, 326–27). Divine grace can therefore be set over against traditional law and custom. It is perhaps not surprising, then, that the chosen biblical figure for Jenks's chapter is Jonah—the prophet whose message has no need for ancestral law.

Actually there are two biblical images of Jonah, the "true" prophet of 2 Kgs 14 and the "false" prophet of the book that takes his name (the oracle against Nineveh in Jonah 3:4 does not come true). The true prophet appears during the time of the northern king Jeroboam II, who enjoyed a long and distinguished reign, and who "restored the border of Israel according to the word of Yhwh, the God of Israel, which he spoke by his servant Jonah son of Amittai" (2 Kgs 14:23–29). When we read here that Jeroboam "lay down with his ancestors" after a long and successful reign, we might expect some praise for a job well done, redeeming the borders of Israel.

This version of success did not conform, however, to the expectations of Judean nationalism, and the Deuteronomists are compelled therefore to regard this northern king as evil. He is not guilty, it should be noted, of social injustices committed against widows, orphans, and aliens. Rather, he is charged with following the path of "Jeroboam son of Nebat," that is, the Jeroboam who led the northern kingdom in an exodus-shaped rebellion against the south, beginning with a political assembly in Shechem (1 Kgs 12:1; see Oblath 2000; Bodner 2012). For the Deuteronomist, who was looking at these events retrospectively, no conformity with the word of Yhwh delivered through Jonah the prophet could compensate for the northerners' failure to follow the law of centralization in Deut 12. Yet, as we have seen, even that very point was eventually contested in Josh 24 (cf. Josh 8:30–35; Deut 27:4–8).

From the point of view of Deuteronomy, the Jonah of 2 Kgs 14 presents something of a conundrum, since on the one hand, his Yahwist prophecy about restored borders comes true and thus satisfies the conditions of true prophecy in Deut 13:1–4 and 18:22. On the other hand, this prophet does not actually forecast the cultic reform of Israel and the demise of the house of Jeroboam, as 1 Kgs 13 does. The prophet of the book of Jonah is yet more of a maverick, however, since he is sent by Yhwh to provoke the repentance of the very Assyrians who were called on to punish the Israelite kings for their cultic impurity.

Moreover, a proposal for Assyrian repentance could not possibly require a return to covenantal law, since according to the logic of election, only one nation on earth could be shaped by this kind of divinely given law. Jonah's half of an oracle, "In forty days more, and Nineveh will be overthrown" (3:4), turns out to be a fantastically effective piece of evangelism, not because it was true, but because it provoked repentance. This provocative narrative was apparently designed not to show us that Jonah was an inspiring example for postmodern, lawless identities but to illustrate just how blinkered Deut 18's criteria for true prophecy actually are. This point is put with admirable simplicity in Jer 18:7–10, where we find that Yhwh has a rather more pragmatic view of truth than does Deut 18: "but if that nation, concerning which I have spoken, turns from its evil, I will *change my mind* about the disaster that I intended to bring on it" (Jer 18:8).

Beyond the borders of Judah, there may be no definitive list of divine statutes designed to govern the life of the Gentile nations, but nevertheless, Jeremiah seems to imply that there may be some natural knowledge of what the concept of justice might include. Otherwise, a deity capable of mind changes would be exercising a capricious power to evaluate human behavior according to standards that were unknowable. Not even the book of Job goes that far theologically: Job knows the Creator as El (or Eloah), derives his ethics from creation rather than from covenant law, and presents a fine example of ethical integrity beyond the borders of Israel. He does not find his way through the legal membranes of Israel's corporate body in the ways that Tamar, Rahab, and Ruth do. Ironically perhaps, like Moses the lawgiver, Job displays the paradoxical possibility of remaining both inside and outside the biblical arguments with God.

WORKS CONSULTED

Amit, Yairah. 2009. Narrative Analysis: Meaning, Context and Origins of Genesis 38. Pages 271–91 in *Method Matters: Essays on the Interpretation of the Hebrew Bible in Honor of David L. Petersen*. Edited by J. LeMon and K. H. Richards. Atlanta: Society of Biblical Literature.

———. 2010. The Case of Judah and Tamar in the Contemporary Israeli Context: A Relevant Interpolation. Pages 213–20 in *Genesis: Texts@ Contexts*. Edited by A. Brenner, A. C. C. Lee, and G. A. Yee. Minneapolis: Fortress.

Bodner, Keith. 2012. *Jeroboam's Royal Drama*. Oxford: Oxford University Press.

Brett, Mark G. 2012. The Politics of Marriage in Genesis. Pages 49–59 in *Making a Difference: Essays on the Bible and Judaism in Honor of Tamara Cohn Eskenazi*. Edited by D. J. A. Clines, K. H. Richards, and J. L. Wright. Sheffield: Sheffield Phoenix.

———. 2013. Permutations of Sovereignty in the Priestly Tradition. *Vetus Testamentum* 63:383–92.

Brueggemann, Walter. 1988. 2 Sam 21–24: An Appendix of Deconstruction? *Catholic Biblical Quarterly* 50:383–97.

Dozeman, Thomas B., Thomas Römer, and Konrad Schmid, eds. 2011. *Pentateuch, Hexateuch, or Enneateuch?* Atlanta: Society of Biblical Literature.

Fleming, Daniel E. 2012. *The Legacy of Israel in Judah's Bible: History, Politics and the Reinscribing of Tradition*. Cambridge: Cambridge University Press.

Fokkelman, Jan P. 1990. *Throne and City*. Vol. 3 of *Narrative Art and Poetry in the Books of Samuel*. Assen: Van Gorcum.

Hardt, Michael, and Antonio Negri. 2000. *Empire*. Cambridge: Harvard University Press.

Havrelock, Rachel S. 2011. *River Jordan: The Mythology of a Dividing Line*. Chicago: University of Chicago Press.

Kennedy, Elisabeth R. 2011. *Seeking a Homeland: Sojourn and Ethnic Identity in the Ancestral Narratives of Genesis*. Leiden: Brill.

Monroe, Lauren A. S. 2007. Israelite, Moabite and Sabaean War-ḥērem Traditions and the Forging of National Identity: Reconsidering the Sabaean Text RES 3945 in Light of Biblical and Moabite Evidence. *Vetus Testamentum* 57:318–41.

Neemia, Makesi. 2012. The Hebrew Bible and Postcolonial Samoan Hermeneutics. Paper presented at Story Weaving: Colonial Contexts and Postcolonial Theology Conference. Whitley College, Melbourne. January 25.

Nihan, Christophe. 2007. The Torah between Samaria and Judah: Shechem and Gerizim in Deuteronomy and Joshua. Pages 187–223 in *The Pentateuch as Torah*. Edited by G. N. Knoppers and B. M. Levinson. Winona Lake, Ind.: Eisenbrauns.

Oblath, Michael D. 2000. Of Pharaohs and Kings—Whence the Exodus? *Journal for the Study of the Old Testament* 87:23–42.

Potter, Emily. 2003. "Disconcerting Ecologies: Representations of Non-Indigenous Belonging in Contemporary Australian Literature and Cultural Discourse." Ph.D. diss., University of Adelaide.

Pury, Albert de. 2000. Abraham: The Priestly Writer's "Ecumenical" Ancestor. Pages 163–81 in *Rethinking the Foundations: Historiography in the Ancient World and in the Bible*. Edited by S. L. McKenzie and T. Römer. Berlin: de Gruyter.

Römer, Thomas, and Marc Brettler. 2000. Deuteronomy 34 and the Case for a Persian Hexateuch. *Journal of Biblical Literature* 119:401–19.

Schmid, Konrad. 2011. The Quest for "God": Monotheistic Arguments in the Priestly Texts of the Hebrew Bible. Pages 275–93 in *Reconsidering the Concept of Revolutionary Monotheism*. Edited by B. Pongratz-Leisten. Winona Lake, Ind.: Eisenbrauns.

Shectman, Sarah. 2011. Rachel, Leah, and the Composition of Genesis. Pages 207–22 in *The Pentateuch: International Perspectives on Current Research*. Edited by T. B. Dozeman, K. Schmid, and B. J. Schwartz. Tübingen: Mohr Siebeck.

Smith, Anthony D. 1993. The Ethnic Sources of Nationalism. *Survival: Global Politics and Strategy* 35:48–62.

Taylor, Charles. 2007. *A Secular Age*. Cambridge: Belknap.

Contributors

Jeffrey W. Aernie teaches in the area of New Testament studies at United Theological College and within the School of Theology of Charles Sturt University. His research interests revolve around the Gospel of Mark, the Pauline literature (especially 2 Corinthians), and Greek linguistics. He is particularly interested in the intersection between the study of the New Testament and the life of Christian discipleship.

Mark G. Brett grew up in Papua New Guinea, which formed the foundation for a lifelong exploration of the relationship between culture and theology. He studied philosophy and history at Queensland University (BA), but through studying at Princeton Seminary (MDiv) with many students from the Two-Thirds World, he discovered a passion for the Hebrew Bible. He is the author of *Biblical Criticism in Crisis?* (Cambridge, 1991), *Genesis: Procreation and the Politics of Identity* (Routledge, 2000), and *Decolonizing God: The Bible in the Tides of Empire* (Phoenix, 2008) and editor of *Ethnicity and the Bible* (Brill, 1996).

Merilyn Clark is an Academic Associate at Charles Sturt University, where she lectures in Hebrew and Old Testament studies. As a rhetorical critic, she delights in playing with the Hebrew texts from a literary perspective and in sharing these literary and hermeneutical insights with others. Given her environmental interests and concerns, she has particularly explored environmental insights in the Old Testament texts.

Michele A. Connolly teaches New Testament and is Academic Dean at the Catholic Institute of Sydney, Australia. Michele's academic interests are the Gospel of Mark, and literary and feminist criticisms. She could survive on a desert island with the music of J. S. Bach, a couple of cats, and, of course, food of every kind.

David M. Gunn grew up in New Zealand and Australia and then crossed the Pacific by ship bound (via Panama) for England and postgraduate study. He has taught Hebrew Bible at the University of Sheffield, Columbia Theological Seminary in Atlanta, and most recently Texas Christian University in Fort Worth. His writing includes literary-critical analyses of biblical narratives, feminist interpretation, and the cultural history (verbal and visual) of the Bible—its reception or use and influence. After a recent detour to look at Samson in children's Bibles, his current major undertaking is the professional and popular afterlife of the books of Samuel since late antiquity. For a whimsical take on one small part of the project, see: http://www.gunnzone.org/KingDavid/CoveringDavid.html.

Jione Havea is a native of Tonga who teaches biblical studies at United Theological College and School of Theology, Charles Sturt University. Jione is a Methodist minister who fishes for island hermeneutics and contexted readings with queer goggles and bare feet and enjoys grog, especially when the setting is informal.

Gregory C. Jenks is an Australian who teaches biblical studies in the School of Theology at Charles Sturt University. He was raised in the border districts of northern New South Wales and southeast Queensland and is now involved in archaeological research at *et-Tell* (Bethsaida) on the disputed boundaries of Israel, Palestine, and Syria. Although he is an Anglican Priest, his progressive religious practice locates him near the edges of acceptance in mainstream Australian church life.

Jeanette Mathews is an ordained Baptist minister who currently spends her time at St Mark's National Theological Centre as part of the teaching staff for the School of Theology of Charles Sturt University. She teaches Old Testament and researches in the area of biblical performance studies. She is committed to upholding, transmitting, and improvising the biblical traditions in all their wondrous diversity for new settings in our own times and places.

Judith E. McKinlay teaches biblical studies in the Department of Theology and Religion at the University of Otago and is the author of *Reframing Her: Biblical Women in Postcolonial Focus* (2004). Judith is the descendant of Presbyterian nineteenth-century settlers, and her interest lies in setting biblical texts alongside writings from Aotearoa New Zealand. It is the heady mix of Bible, history, and present context that allows her to consider the impact and effects of imperial and colonialist ideologies, both in the past and in the present.

Monica Jyotsna Melanchthon is native to India and teaches Old Testament/Hebrew Bible at the Uniting Church Theological College, United Faculty of Theology, within the University of Divinity, Melbourne. A Lutheran minister and contextual theologian, she has strong commitments to the marginalized, particularly women and Dalits, and reads the Bible drawing on insights from the social biographies of these communities.

David J. Neville teaches in the area of New Testament studies at St Mark's National Theological Centre and within the School of Theology of Charles Sturt University. His research interests include the Gospels, New Testament theology and ethics, and peace studies. He is a member of Charles Sturt University's Public and Contextual Theology Research Centre, within which he coordinates a focus group concerned with Scripture and public theology.

John Painter is research professor of theology at Charles Sturt University Canberra Campus. His research interests are in early Judaism, early Christianity, and contemporary Christian thought, especially hermeneutics. He loves sports (cricket, tennis, and rugby), the sea in a kayak, the mountains, the sculpture of Rodin, the paintings of Turner, Monet, Feininger, the Heidelberg School, Arthur Boyd, and Emily Kame Kngwarreye. He lives, works, and breathes to music from Monteverdi to Philip Glass.

Kathleen P. Rushton is a Sister of Mercy who is an independent researcher and part-time lecturer and tutor of Scripture and theology at the Catholic Education Office, Christchurch, Aotearoa New Zealand and the Ecumenical Institute of Distance Theological Studies.

Ruth Sheridan received her PhD from Australian Catholic University in 2011. Her work is published as *Retelling Scripture: The Jews and the Scriptural Citations in John 1:19–12:15* (Brill, 2012). She is currently a postdoctoral research fellow at Charles Sturt University (Australia).

Nāsili Vakaʻuta teaches Old Testament subjects at Trinity Methodist Theological College and School of Theology, University of Auckland, and is one of the founders of Oceania Biblical Studies Association. He also taught at Sia'atoutai Theological College, Tonga, and is committed to the cause of natives, especially the tu'a (commoners), as well as moana (sea) and fonua (land), as he reads and interprets biblical texts.

Elaine M. Wainwright is Head of the School of Theology at the University of Auckland, New Zealand. She is a New Testament scholar committed to exploring how ancient texts function within contexts of interpretation within the contemporary world to make meaning. Her current focus is ecological hermeneutics, and she is writing the Earth Bible Commentary on Matthew's Gospel.

Index of Primary Texts

Genesis
1:1	77, 79, 82, 85, 87, 98
1:1–2:4a	88
1:3–5	85
2–3	16
3:16–17	66, 71
4:10	13
6	131
6:1–4	132
12:6–7	261
14:13–22	264
15	114
15:18	260
17:16–21	113
18:22–33	211
19	148
23	264
25:29–34	214
27:4	113
27:7	113
27:10	113
27:11–12	116
27:13	113
27:13	116
27:18–19	3
27:19	114
27:20	114
27:33	116
27:34	116
27:34, 38	114
27:38	116
27:39–40	114
27:41	114
27:41	116
27:42–45	114
27:46	114
28	116–17
28:3–4	115
29	117
30	117
31	118
31:42, 53	114
32	118–120
32:26	177
34	18
36:24	179
38	211, 215, 218–19, 264, 267
38:11b	219
38:14	218
38:15–19	217
38:18	219
38: 24–26	217
38:26	215
42:9	127

Exodus
1:8–2:3	216
2:16–18	219
2:16–22	213
2:23–25	217
3	211, 263
3:8	264
3:12–15	98
3:14	235
6	263–264
6:3	264
22:31	196
34:15	144

Leviticus		Joshua	
19:29	144	1	152
		1:3–4	260
Numbers		2	16, 127, 143, 144, 148–54
1	129–30	6	152
13	125–39, 166, 253–54	8	260
14	133	8:30–35	266
14:29–30	130	9	175–76, 262
20:12	261	9–10	176
21:26	260	11	260
21:32	127	11:21–22	131
22–24	16	15:14	131
25:5	176	24	261, 266
34:1–15	126	24:30	186
Deuteronomy		Judges	
1:7	260	1:10, 20	131
1:22–25	125–26	2:9	186
1:37	261	18	127
2:11	131	19	149, 186
2:26–35	260		
3:26	261	Ruth	
4:21	261	1:2	212, 263
4:46	260	2–3	212–13
6:7	165	3	213–14
7	176	4	211–15, 219
7:1–6	144	4:6	263
7:6	252	4:10	263
8	158	4:13–17	264
11:24	260	4:18–22	264
12	266		
12:5	261	1 Samuel	
13:1–4	266	10:2	186
16:21	261	10:12	228
18	266	11:4	176
18:15	259	15	260
18:22	266	15:34	176
20	263	17:43	196
20:10–18	262	18:19	177
27:4–8	266	21:14	179
29	159, 164	22:1–2	219
30	157–69	31:3	179
34:6	260	31:8–13	179
34:10	259		

2 Samuel		Ezra	
2:5	179	9	264
3:6–11	178	9:1	263
3:7	178, 181		
4:1–3	176	Esther	
6:23	177	4:6	150
9	177	6:9, 11	150
10:3	127		
16:22	179	Job	
21:1	262, 263	1:9–10	8
21:1–2	175	2:23	8
21:1–14	175		
21:2	263	Psalms	
21:5–6	176	33:6	85
21:10–14	175–88	44:24–25	33
21:12	150	44:27	33
21:12–14	262	104:20–23	85
21–24	262	107:28–33	32
22:2	179		
22:3	179	Proverbs	
22:32	179	7:12	149
22:47	179	8:22–31	98
		26:11	196
1 Kings			
3:4	176	Isaiah	
12:1	266	6:9–10	200
13	266	6:9–13	200
21	16	6:13	200
21:23	196	26:17–18	64
22:38	196	30	179
		30:29	179
		40–66	65
2 Kings		42:1–7	66
8:13	196	49:1–7	66
9:36	196	49:14,21	66
14	265, 266	49:24	66
14:23–29	265	50:4–9	66
14:25	226	51:1–3a	179
21–25	51	51:17–52:2	66
25	160	51:9	30
		51:9–11	31, 33
1 Chronicles		52:13–53:12	66
1:40	178	54	179
		54:1–10	66
2 Chronicles		56:10–11	196
36:20	160		

Isaiah (cont.)		10:2, 4	52	
59:14	150	10:8	52	
66	65, 244			
66:7–14	66	Jonah		
		1:1	226	
Jeremiah		1:3	227, 235	
4:19	64	1:4–5	30	
4:31	64	1:9	231	
7:33	185	1:17	234	
8:1–2	185	3:4	265, 266	
9:21	185	4:2	232	
10	28	4:11	236	
10:22	28			
10:23	28	Habakkuk		
12:7	45	2:2	235	
12:7–13	51			
13:20–27	51	2 Baruch	47	
16:6	185			
18:7–10	266	4 Ezra	47	
18:8	266			
22:5	45	Matthew		
22:18–19	185	1:22	31	
25:1–14	51	1:23	31	
29	160	2:1–12	36	
29:1–9	165	3:15	31	
29:7	169	4:17	27, 32	
36:30	185	4:21,22	26	
		4:23	32	
Lamentations		4:25	27	
2	51	5:1	26	
		5:3	32	
Ezekiel		5:6	31	
3:12	28	5:9	46	
14:12–15:8	51	5:10	31, 32	
16:23–26	149–50	5:19	32	
18	263	5:20	31, 32	
38:18–23	28	6:1	31	
38:19	28	6:10	32	
		6:30	32	
Hosea		6:33	31, 32	
9–10	52	7:6	196	
9:7	42	7:21	32	
9:10	52	8:1	26	
9:13	52	8:1–15	26	
9:6	52	8:17	27	

8:21	26	5:22	195
8:23	26	5:23	195
8:23–9:8	26	5:24–29	195
8:24	29	5:25–34	195
8:23–27	21–35, 241–42	5:35–36	195
8:25	22	5:35–43	195
8:27	241	5:26	202
9:18–34	26	5:34	45
10:11–13	28	5:35	202
10:23	28	6:14–29	203
10:34	45	6:30–44	198, 203
12:16	33	6:42	198
12:40–41	233	6:52	203
13	37	7:1–5	198
13:15	201	7:1–23	198, 199, 246
13:52	37	7:14–15	198
15:21–28	191, 206, 207	7:17–23	199
16:4	233	7:17–31	198
17:18	33	7:18	201, 203
23:37–39	41	7:18–23	201
23:39	54	7:24	194
24:13–14	29	7:24–30	191–205
24:7	27, 29, 32, 61	7:25	195
24:8	64	7:26	194, 195
24:54	27, 29	7:27	196, 197, 198, 202, 246
27:51	61	7:28	197
27:54	61	7:31–37	192
28:2	27, 29, 61	7:31–8:10	198
		8:1–9	198
Mark		8:1–10	203
1:1	203, 204	8:14–21	203
2:1	192	8:34–35	204
2:1–5	195	8:8	198
3:20	192	9:11–12	197
3:27	197	9:14–27	195
3:7–12	197	9:35	204
4:9	201	10:52	195
4:23	201	11:27–28	202
4:11–12	200, 246	11:29	202
4:13	201	11:31–32	202
4:26–32	201	13:8	61, 64
4:28	197	13:10	197
5	246	15:21–28	191
5:1–20	107, 198		
5:21–24	195		

Luke

Reference	Page
1:5–23	40
1:68–79	50
1:79	45, 46
2:14,	45, 46, 50
2:22–52	40
2:25–26	40
2:38	40
2:29	45, 46
7:11–17	51
7:16	51
7:50	45
8:14–17	41
8:22–25	35
8:48	45
9:22	40
9:30–31	40
9:51	40
9:51–53	42, 47
9:51–56	48, 50
9:51–19:46	47, 51, 55, 242, 243
9:52	48
9:52–56	54
9:54–55	49
10	204
10:1	48
10:1–16	48
10:3	49
10:5–6	45, 46, 48
10:6	49
10:10–12	46
10:10–16	48
10:12–15	49
10:14–16	48
10:16	49
11:1–18	41
11:21	45
11:30–32	233–234
12:40–41	233
12:51	45, 46
13	39–54, 242
13:1–5	43, 44, 242
13:2–3	43
13:6–9	52
13:22	42, 47
13:31–33	41
13:31–35	43, 47, 52, 242
13:33	40
13:34–35	41, 42, 44, 50, 242, 243
13:35	44
14:32	45
15:1–33	41
17:25	40
19:21	41
19:28–44	48
19:38	45, 46, 49
19:41–44	42, 50, 52, 243
19: 42	45, 46, 49
19:43–44	45, 48
19:43–46	46
19:44	50
20:16–23:31	41
21:11	61
21:17–26	41
21:20–24	42, 45
21:22	52
22:37	40
23:26–31	42
23:28–31	52
23:31	42
24:1–41	40
24:7	40
24:13–25	51
24:26	40
24:36	45, 46
24:44–46	40
24:44–47	51
24:50–53	41

John

Reference	Page
1:1–5	73–89
1:1–14	74
1:1–18	73–89
1:6–8	73–89
1:6–18	73–89
1:10	98
1:10–11	62
1:10–13	79
1:11–12	80
1:12	67

1:12–13	62, 66, 70	12:31–32	67
1:13	67	12:32	66, 67
1:14	80	12:34	66, 67
1:14–18	80	12:35–36	79, 85
1:15–18	74–89	12: 46	79, 85
1:17	245	13:30	85
1:18	73	14:16	67
1:19	73	14:25–26	67
1:19–34	74, 79	14:26	67
1:19–20:31	73, 76, 81	16:12–13	67
1:35–36	80	16:21	62 ,63, 65, 66, 68, 70, 244
1:35–37	79	17:18	67
2:17	67	18:1	62, 66, 70
2:21–22	84, 88	19:17–19	66
2:22	67	19:25	66
3:2	85	19:30	67
3:3–8	66	19:31	66
3:14	66	19:34	67
3:19–21	79, 85	19:41	62, 66, 70
3:22–36	80	20:1	85
3:27–36	75, 79	20:1–18	62, 70
4:1	80	20:15	66
4:31–36	67, 75	20:18	67
4:39–42	67	20:31	67
5:32–36	79		
5:33–36	80	Acts of the Apostles	
6:35	94	8:1	41
7:37–38	66	8:14–17	41
8:12	79, 85	10:36	46, 51
8:28	66	11:1–18	41
3:31–59	101	15:1–33	41
9:3–5	79	19:21	41
9:4	85	21:17–26	41
9:5	85	20:16–23:31	41
9:39–41	79		
10:15–16	67	Romans	
10:40–42	79, 80	1:16	194,197
11:9–10	85		
11:50–52	67	1 Corinthians	
12:11	67	1:22–24	194
12:16	84, 88		
12:17	67	Philippians	
12:19	67	3:2	196
12:20	67		
12:24	67		

2 Peter
2:22 196

Revelation
11:13 61
11:19 61
16:18 61
22:15 196

Index of Modern Authors

Abel, Lee 14, 17
Abel, Sue 137, 139
Adam, Andrew K. M. 233, 237
Aernie, Jeffrey W. 7, 191, 245, 246, 247, 269
Akkara, Anto 172, 188
Alcock, Susan E. 132, 135, 141
Allison, Dale C., Jr. 49, 52, 54
Alter, Robert 110, 114, 115, 117, 119, 120, 122
Altheide, David L. 135, 139
Amit, Yairah 212, 221, 264, 267
Anderson, Benedict 128, 139, 172, 188
Andrew, M. E. 9, 17
Aquino, Frederick D. 198, 205
Assmann, Jan 132, 139
Ateek, Naim 230, 237
Aubin, Melissa 150, 154
Avrahami, Einat 96, 207
Bailey, Randall C. 7, 17,
Barrett, C. K. 73, 85, 86–88, 89, 95, 107, 245
Baskin, Judith Reesa 150, 154
Batto, Bernard F. 30, 35
Bauckham, Richard 154
Beal, Timothy K. 222
Beavis, Mary Ann 194, 205
Ben Zvi, Ehud 134, 139, 159, 169
Bengston, H., 194, 205
Bergmann, Claudia 61–65, 70, 243, 244
Berman, Joshua 120, 122
Bernard, J. H. 76, 78, 86, 89
Berquist, Jon L. 138, 139
Berryman, Kelvin 59, 71
Betsworth, Sharon 204, 205
Biddle, Mark 159, 160, 170
Bieringer, Reimund 81, 89
Binney, Judith 128, 129, 130, 131, 132, 136, 140, 256, 257
Bird, Phyllis 185, 188
Blenkinsopp, J. 175, 188
Bloch-Smith, Elizabeth M. 185, 188
Bodi, Daniel 182, 188
Boer, Roland 11, 17, 141, 220, 221
Boesak, Allan 184, 187, 188
Booth, Wayne 94, 104, 107
Boring, M. Eugene 197, 205
Bosch, Mineke 95, 107
Boyarin, Daniel 94, 96, 97–101, 106, 107, 210, 221, 250, 251
Brant, Jo-Ann 74, 89
Brenk, Frederick E. 83, 90
Brenner, Athalya 178, 188
Brett, Mark G. 9, 11, 17, 259, 264, 267, 269
Brettler, Marc Zvi 95, 108, 259, 268
Brueggemann, Walter 115, 116, 122, 160, 170, 262, 267
Buckman, Alyson R. 146, 154
Budden, Chris 167, 170
Bultmann, Rudolf 73, 77, 82–86, 89, 90, 245
Burgess, Ruth 61, 71
Byrne, Brendan 53, 54
Cadwallader, Alan H. 61, 71, 194, 197, 202, 205
Callahan, Allen Dwight 3, 17, 220, 221
Camery-Hoggatt, Jerry 199, 205
Campbell, Anthony F. 9, 17
Campbell, Jocelyn 59

-281-

Carden, Michael	11, 17	Fakasiʻiʻeiki, ʻIkani	4, 18
Carter, Warren	29, 31, 35	Feldman, Louis H.	150, 154
Cates, Lilian	138, 139, 141	Feldmeier, Reinhard	196, 205
Cazelles, H.	182, 188	Fensham, F. Charles	175, 177, 188
Chance, J. Bradley	41, 54	Fewell, Danna N.	176, 178, 179, 188, 210, 125, 221, 223, 237
Chinitz, Jacob	217, 221		
Chittister, Joan	121, 122	Figiel, Sia	5, 18, 210, 221
Chow, Simon	233, 237	Fisk, Bruce N.	52, 54
Clark, Merilyn	16, 109, 126, 160, 251, 252, 256, 269	Fogarty, David	24, 35
		Fox, Adam	76
Clinton, Hilary	6, 7	Fox, Derek	127, 140
Coats, George W.	126, 130, 140	France, R. T.	192, 201, 205
Code, Lorraine	25, 31, 35, 241	Fretheim, Terence E.	24, 35, 53, 54, 60, 71
Collins, Adela Yarbo	203, 205		
Cook, Michael	95, 107	Freud, Sigmund	215, 221
Connolly, Michele A.	241, 269	Garroway, Joshua	95, 107
Cotter, Wendy	31, 32, 35	Gauguin, Paul	145, 154,
Creed, Philip	58, 71	Gillmayr-Bucher, Susanne	150, 154
Crossan, John Dominic	231, 237	Glück, J. J.	177, 189
Crump, David	51, 55	Goldingay, John	122
Dalziel, Paul	68, 79, 70, 71	Good, Leslie	182, 189
Davies, Tim	59, 71	Gorman, Paul	58, 59, 71
Davis, Ellen F.	10, 17	Gottwald, Norman	176, 189
de Vaux, Roland	176, 188	Groody, Daniel G.	157, 170
Dershowitz, Alan M.	115, 116, 122	Guardiola-Saénz, Leticia A.	191, 206
Dodd, C. H.	77, 78, 80, 81–83, 85, 86, 87, 89, 90, 245	Guelich, Robert A.	197, 203, 206
		Gundry-Volf, Judith M.	111, 122
Donahue, John R.	193, 194, 195, 203, 205	Gunn, David M.	176, 178, 179, 188, 215, 221, 249, 256, 257, 270
Donaldson, Laura	136, 140	Gurruwiwi, Gamiritj	16, 254
Dube, Lucky	14, 17	Habel, Norman C.	10, 11, 18
Dube, Musa W.	127, 140	Hager, Nicky	6, 18
Dubovsky, Peter	127, 140	Halvorson-Taylor, Martien A.	210, 212, 214, 221
Eakin, Paul John	96, 107		
Edwards, Bryce	137, 140	Hare, Douglas R. A.	237
Edwards, Denis	24, 30, 31, 32, 34, 35, 60, 71	Harnack, Adolf von	73, 78–81, 90, 245
		Harper, Sheila	186, 189
Edwards, James R.	196, 200, 201, 203, 205	Harrington, Daniel J.	193, 194, 195, 203, 205
Ellis, Marc H.	158, 170	Harris, Elizabeth	75, 91
Elsakker, M.	62, 71	Harris, J. Rendel	77, 85, 91, 245
Elvey, Anne	21, 26, 27, 35	Hauʻofa, ʻEpeli	7, 18
Everson, A. Joseph	65, 70, 71	Havea, Jione	3, 18, 127, 209, 221, 223, 249, 259, 263, 270
Exum, J. Cheryl	175, 177, 178, 180, 183, 185, 188		
		Hawkins, Peter S.	154

Hays, Richard B.	223, 237
Heather, Ben	69, 71
Hegedus, Timothy M.	237
Horrell, David G.	10, 18, 25, 35
Hubbard, Anthony	6, 18
Hunt, Cherryl	18, 35
Hurtado, Larry W.	194, 206
Iverson, Kelly R.	195, 196, 197, 187, 200, 201, 206
Jackson, Moana	137, 140
Jenks, Gregory C.	7, 126, 223, 233, 234, 237, 265, 270
Johnston, J. S.	78, 79, 80, 83, 91
Kannabiran, Kalpana	173, 189
Kaplanovsky, A.	36
Kass, Leon	113, 119, 122
Kearney, P. J.	175, 189
Keenan, Danny	129, 137, 140
Kelso, Julie	11, 18
Kendra, Vikas Adhyayan	172, 174, 175, 189
Kim, H. C. Paul	223, 237
Kluge, Alexander	171, 189
Knierim, Rolf P.	126, 140
Koch, Klaus	53, 54
Kraus, Michael	95, 104, 108
Kristeva, Julia	143, 147, 154
LaCocque, Andre	222
Law, Tina	68, 71
Lawson, Veronica	21
Lee, Won W.	140
Leota, Peniamina	11, 19
Levenson, Jon D.	179, 189
Levine, Amy-Jill	95, 108
Levine, Baruch A.	126, 131, 135, 140
Liew, Tat-Siong Benny	7, 17, 138, 140
Linafelt, Tod	222
Liverani, Mario	133, 141
Lorde, Audre	4, 19
Lowenthal, David	132, 141
Macgregor, G. H. C.	67, 71
Maddison, Sarah	12, 19
Māhina, 'Okusitino	14, 19
Mahoney, Jack	60, 71
Malamat, A.	175, 189
Malamud, Bernard	93, 107, 108
Malbon, Elizabeth Struthers	195, 203, 204, 206
Malina, Bruce J.	29, 36
Manoa, Pio	7, 19
Mansfield, Ken	150, 154
Marcus, Joel	193, 195, 197, 206
Marley, Bob	14, 209, 211, 220
Marshall, Christopher D.	52, 55, 195, 206
Martin, Luther H.	33, 36
Matera, Frank J.	42, 55
Mathews, Jeanette	5, 70, 128, 157, 165, 170, 210, 259, 261, 270
Mauser, Ulrich	50, 55
McCarter Jr., P. Kyle	132, 141, 176, 178, 189
McClintock, Anne	147, 148, 154
McConville, J. G.	216, 222
McKinlay, Judith E.	10, 11, 16, 19, 125, 151, 154, 166, 210, 253, 254, 256, 270
McLemore, A. Brian	198, 205
McNamara, Martin	77, 91, 98
Mead, Margaret	145, 155
Melanchthon, Monica J.	5, 171, 259, 262, 271
Milgrom, Jacob	126, 141
Miller, Susan	194, 198, 201, 202, 204, 206
Mohanty, Chandra Talpade	173, 189
Montefiore, Claude	94, 103, 107, 108
Moore, Stephen D.	138, 141
Moyers, William	122
Muecke, D. C.	200, 206
Muricken, Ajit	174, 175, 189
Nanos, Mark D.	196, 206
Negt, Oskar	171, 189
Neumark, Heidi	184, 189
Neville, David J.	3, 9, 11, 39, 60, 209, 242, 243, 247, 271
Noble, Paul R.	148, 155
Noh, Eun-Ju	199, 206
Nun, Mendel	28, 29, 36
O'Brien, Mark A.	9, 17
Okure, Teresa	67, 72

Olson, Dennis T.   130, 131, 133, 141
Olyan, Saul M.   180, 185, 189
Ortega, Ofelia   176, 180, 181, 185, 189
Pagels, Elaine   74, 91
Painter, John   8, 62, 72, 73, 77, 81, 82, 83, 85, 88, 89, 91, 244, 245, 247, 271
Palu, Ma'afu   4, 19
Pardes, Ilana   150, 155
Patte, Daniel   139, 141
Pattel-Gray, Anne   12, 19
Pearce, Liz   61, 72
Penner, Todd   138, 139, 141
Phelan, James   94, 108
Phillips, Peter M.   83–86, 92, 245
Pigott, Susan M.   175, 178, 189
Plumwood, Val   25, 31, 36
Polhill, C.   61, 71
Prior, John Mansford   155
Puskas, Charles B.   51, 55
Radford Ruether, Rosemary   179, 190
Redman, Peter   96, 108
Reed, Jonathan L.   232, 237
Reinhartz, Adele   94, 96, 97, 101–6, 107, 108, 250
Reiser, Marius   43, 55
Rhoads, David   194, 198, 202, 203, 206
Ringe, Sharon H.   194, 206
Roach, John   24, 36
Robbins, Vernon   25, 36, 241
Robert, Hannah   146, 155
Robin, Corey   134, 141
Robinson, Bernard P.   151, 155
Rofé, Alexander   165, 170
Ronning, John   77, 92
Rountree, Kathryn   145, 155
Runions, Erin   151, 155
Rushton, Kathleen P.   11, 139, 57, 62, 65, 66, 72, 163, 210, 243, 244, 247, 271
Said, Edward W.   157, 158, 165, 166, 167, 168, 169, 170
Sakenfeld, Katharine Doob   141
Salote, Kuini   14
Sanday, William   76, 78, 29, 80, 83. 92
Sanders, James A.   110, 122, 160, 170, 251, 256

Sandmel, Samuel   95, 103, 108
Sarna, Nahum M.   120, 122
Saulwick, Jacob   23, 36
Savage, Carl   227, 238
Sayer, Duncan   190
Schlabach, Gerald W.   158, 159, 167, 170
Schneiders, Sandra M.   72, 94, 108
Schottroff, Luise   43, 55
Scott, Robert B. Y.   238
Seeman, Don   150, 155
Segovia, Fernando F.   7, 17, 138, 141
Serruya, S.   36
Shah, Riddhi   12, 19
Sharp, Carolyn J.   129, 141, 150, 155
Sheridan, Ruth   4, 93, 95, 104, 108, 250, 251, 271
Sherwood, Yvonne   138, 141, 229, 238
Sim, Margaret G.   200, 201, 206
Singh, Ajay Kumar   172, 190
Smith, Anthony D.   261, 268
Smith, Bridie   24, 36
Smith-Christopher, Daniel   158, 170
Soskice, Janet Martin   62, 72
Southgate, Christopher   18, 35
Spivak, Gayatri Chakravorty   6, 10, 19
Spong, John Shelby   220, 222
Stander, H. F.   151, 155
Stavrakopoulou, Francesca   18, 35, 190
Stein, Robert H.   193, 197, 206
Stevick, Daniel B.   67, 72
Stewart, Eric C.   27, 36
Stone, Ken   172, 181, 190
Styers, Randall   129, 141
Subrahmaniam, Vidya   172, 190
Sugirtharajah, R. S.   7, 19, 127, 128, 137, 141, 220, 222
Sunder Rajan, Rajeswari   184, 190
Swartley, Willard M.   45, 46, 48, 49, 55
Sweeney, Marvin A.   215, 222
Swetnam, James   67, 72
Tannehill, Robert C.   53, 55
Tatlock, Jason   176, 182, 190
Teeger, Chana   183, 190
Theissen, Gerd   193, 194, 204, 207
Thelle, Rannfrid I.   150, 155

Thompson, Greg	167, 170
Tiede, David L.	41, 53, 55
Toorn, Karel van der	179, 190
Travis, Stephen H.	45, 55
Trible, Phyllis	220, 222
Tromp, K. J.	111, 112, 122
Trudinger, Peter	11, 18
Vaka'uta, Nāsili	3, 5, 9, 19, 143, 150, 155, 252, 256, 271
Van Dyke, Ruth M.	132, 141
Vete, Henelī	14, 19
Via, Dan O.	53, 54, 55
Vinitzsky-Seroussi, Vered	183, 190
Volf, Miroslav	111, 122, 123
Volohonsky, H.	28, 36
Wachsmann, Shelley	26, 36
Wainwright, Elaine M.	11, 19, 21, 25, 26, 36, 39, 61, 191, 207, 241, 242, 243, 247, 272
Walker, Peter W. L.	41, 55
Walters, Stanley D.	177, 179, 190
Weaver, Alain Epp	158, 170
Welch, Sharon D.	161, 162, 165, 167, 170
Welch, Twilla R.	181, 190
West, Gerald O.	139, 142, 176, 190
Westcott, Brooke Foss	73, 76–78, 79–81, 86, 87, 88, 92, 245
Whybray, R. N.	190
Williams, Joel F.	199, 200, 201, 207
Williams, P. J.	73, 74, 92
Wiseman, D. J.	151, 155
Witherington, Ben, III	193, 207
Wu, Rose	150, 155
Yee, Gale A.	134, 142
Yoder, J. H.	158, 170
Zhang, Zhixing	6

Index of Subjects

Aboriginal people, 15, 145, 146, 262, 265
aftershocks, 24, 57, 60, 58
alien(s), 110–22, 251, 252, 256, 266
alienation, 109, 110, 112, 121, 149, 210, 251, 252, 253, 256
antipodes, 225, 234
Aotearoa, 9, 13, 17, 21, 39, 58, 68, 127, 137, 139, 140, 253, 257, 270
Asia-Pacific, 6, 10
Bhagavad Gita, 13
Blackbirds, 3
border crossing, 17, 109, 111, 121, 122, 129, 143–54, 234, 251, 252, 256, 263, 264
boundary crossing, 106, 109, 111, 120, 235, 251
Burmese, 161, 163, 164
calamity, 39–54, 66, 175, 242
Canaan, 115, 116, 126, 132, 135, 150, 152, 159, 160, 215, 231, 252, 254, 255, 264
Christchurch, 24, 39, 57–70, 241, 243, 244, 271
color, 11–13, 58, 243, 249
conquest, 125, 131, 133, 135, 136, 146, 147, 151, 152, 253, 254, 256, 260, 261
contextual, ix, 8, 9, 11, 193, 195, 196, 197, 198, 199, 200, 201, 203, 271
contrapuntal, 17, 125, 127, 128, 137, 166, 168, 169, 210, 253
cosmology, 31, 35, 62
crisis, 46, 60, 61, 63–70, 115, 139, 148, 152, 178, 244, 157, 169
critical theory, 8, 11, 18, 141
cultural memory, 132, 139, 225
cyclone, 23, 39, 223

darkness, 5, 62, 79, 85, 86, 88, 89
daughter of Zion, 63, 65, 67, 68, 244
dead bodies, 175, 184, 185–87, 215
detachment, 137, 158
diaspora, 113, 211, 225, 236, 261
discipleship, 27, 46, 47, 191–205, 246, 269
divine action, 53, 54
divine judgment, 39, 40, 41, 44, 45, 47, 51, 52, 53, 54, 243
dysfunctional relationships, 112
earthquake, x, 24, 27, 28, 29, 32, 34, 35, 39, 44, 57–70, 241, 243, 244
ecojustice, 10
ecology/ecological, x, 8, 9, 10, 11, 15, 16, 18, 22, 25, 28, 29, 34, 35, 53, 69, 241, 243
evolutionary universe, 60, 70
exile, 28, 30, 113, 116, 157, 158, 159, 160, 161, 165–69, 210, 212, 215, 227, 232, 262, 264
faithfulness, 80, 88, 157, 166, 168, 169, 226, 235, 261
fear, 8, 27, 31, 64, 100, 106, 114, 118, 119, 134, 135, 136, 137, 146, 148, 152, 186, 231, 251, 254
feminist, 4, 11, 102, 173, 183, 220, 269, 270
FOB, 3, 6
Galilee, 26, 27, 28, 29, 40, 43, 193, 226, 227, 228, 234, 241, 246
Gath-Hepher, 226, 228, 232
gender, 12, 100, 172, 173, 174, 181, 191, 194, 195, 203, 204, 212, 246, 247
Gentile(s), 42, 76, 192–204, 232, 235, 246, 266

Greek (culture), 194, 195, 197, 203
Hellenistic, 31, 33, 62, 78, 79, 81, 87, 227, 245, 246
hermeneutics/hermeneutical, 9, 10, 11, 25, 51, 83, 101, 106, 166, 203, 241, 169, 270, 271, 272
homeland, x, 109, 110, 158, 163, 165, 166, 226, 259, 261
Indigenous Australia, 15, 16, 166, 167, 236
interanimative, theory of, 62, 63
intertextual/intertextuality, 28, 29, 30, 31, 63, 64, 83, 85, 88, 210, 221, 223
intratextual references, 83, 84
intratextual tension, 39–54
irony, 22, 75, 129, 130, 141, 157, 199, 200, 201, 205, 206
Jerome, 75, 232, 235, 236, 237
Jerusalem, 22, 40-42, 43, 44, 45, 47-53, 225, 226, 227, 228, 232, 242, 243, 261
justice, 47, 100, 116, 138, 150, 173, 176, 181, 182, 187, 242, 266
kingdom, 32, 46, 64, 196, 197, 198, 200, 201, 202, 203, 204, 266
Kiribati, 15, 16
lament, 30, 40, 41, 42, 44, 49, 50, 52, 53, 165, 187
lifestyle, 109, 110, 111, 112, 121, 251, 252
Lismore, 223, 224, 236
logos, 62, 81, 82, 97, 98, 99, 202, 203, 204, 205, 245
Māori, 21, 128, 129, 136, 137, 145, 146, 153, 255
Melanesia, 6
metaphor, 4, 61, 62, 63, 64, 65, 66, 68, 100, 146, 179, 190, 243
Micronesia, 6
migration, 5, 68, 97, 109, 111, 170, 210, 251
Moab, 157, 159, 160, 164, 170, 212, 215, 259, 260, 261, 263
moana, 3, 272
mothers, 178, 180, 187,
mystery, 54, 75, 76, 78, 116, 162, 196,
nationalism, 158, 265

native(s), 5, 11, 15, 16, 21, 70, 128, 143–148, 151–54, 211, 213, 218, 220, 221, 234, 250, 252, 253, 262, 264, 270–72
natural disasters, 39, 54, 60, 69, 241
Nazareth, 225, 226, 227, 235, 241
Nephilim, 131, 132, 133
network (of association), 12, 62, 66, 110, 225
New South Wales, 23, 223, 224, 265, 270
Nineveh, 227, 231, 232, 233, 234, 235, 265, 266
Oceania, ix, x, 5–17, 22, 24, 68, 109, 122, 143, 145, 147, 153, 204, 210, 211, 213, 220, 249, 254, 272
Palestine/Palestinian, 76, 77, 79, 80, 97, 98, 165, 166, 187, 225, 226, 230, 262, 270
parable, 37, 55, 66, 72, 196, 197, 198, 200, 201, 202, 204, 236, 247
parable of woman in childbirth (John 16:21), 62, 65, 70, 75
paradox/paradoxical(ly), 70, 87, 95, 138, 267
peace, 45–54, 118, 120, 121, 122, 231, 242, 243, 247, 271
Philo, 31, 36, 77, 79, 80, 81, 97
pogrom, 174, 175
Polynesia, 3, 6
postcolonial, 8, 9, 11, 128, 129, 137, 138, 139, 157, 220, 270
postexilic, 159
Promised Land, 110, 113, 126, 128, 130, 132, 143, 159, 163, 167, 168, 169, 252, 253, 255, 256, 259, 261, 264
prophetic tradition, 51
Qumran, 73
Qur'ān, 13
reconciliation, 15, 111, 171
Redemption Song, 14, 209, 211, 213, 215, 218, 219, 220, 257
refugee(s), x, 70, 109, 110, 111, 157–69
relationships, 31, 33, 35, 110, 112, 237
relevance theory, 199
rhetoric(al), 43, 75, 94, 103, 104, 105, 106, 111, 165, 191, 192, 246, 252,

ring of fire, 3, 58, 59
rock, 179, 185, 190
sacrifice, 43, 114, 118, 144, 173, 177, 182, 183, 226,
seeds, 16, 212, 254
silence, 111, 136, 173, 179, 180, 183, 184, 262
sleep, 30, 31, 32, 34, 58, 184, 213, 218, 219
spies, 125–31, 133, 135, 136, 143, 148, 150–53, 252, 253, 254
stranger(s), 109, 110, 111, 112, 120, 121, 122, 145, 148, 149, 153, 164, 213
talanoa, 18, 209, 210–21, 262, 263
Te Urewera, 127, 140
tectonic plates, 28, 59, 60, 70
transformation, 63, 66, 67, 68, 70, 78, 88, 91, 186, 188, 244
tsunami(s), x, 24, 27, 28, 34, 35, 39, 44, 60, 69
Tuhoe, 127–29, 132, 136, 137, 139, 253, 256
Tuvalu, 15
victim(s), 12, 14, 23, 44, 54, 145, 173, 183, 187, 242
Yolngu, 16
Yothu Yindi, 16
Zionism, 168

www.ingramcontent.com/pod-product-compliance
Lightning Source LLC
Chambersburg PA
CBHW031707230426
43668CB00006B/139